P9-DOB-292

DOM Scripting

Web Design with JavaScript and the Document Object Model

Second Edition

Jeremy Keith
with Jeffrey Sambells

DOM Scripting: Web Design with JavaScript and the Document Object Model: Second Edition

Copyright © 2010 by Jeremy Keith with Jeffrey Sambells

All rights reserved. No part of this work may be reproduced or transmitted in any form or by any means, electronic or mechanical, including photocopying, recording, or by any information storage or retrieval system, without the prior written permission of the copyright owner and the publisher.

ISBN 978-1-4302-3389-3

ISBN 978-1-4302-3390-9 (eBook)

Trademarked names, logos, and images may appear in this book. Rather than use a trademark symbol with every occurrence of a trademarked name, logo, or image we use the names, logos, and images only in an editorial fashion and to the benefit of the trademark owner, with no intention of infringement of the trademark.

The use in this publication of trade names, trademarks, service marks, and similar terms, even if they are not identified as such, is not to be taken as an expression of opinion as to whether or not they are subject to proprietary rights.

Publisher and President: Paul Manning
Lead Editor: Ben Renow-Clarke
Technical Reviewer: Rob Drimmie
Editorial Board: Steve Anglin, Mark Beckner, Ewan Buckingham, Gary Cornell, Jonathan Gennick, Jonathan Hassell, Michelle Lowman, Matthew Moodie, Duncan Parkes, Jeffrey Pepper, Frank Pohlmann, Douglas Pundick, Ben Renow-Clarke, Dominic Shakeshaft, Matt Wade, Tom Welsh
Coordinating Editors: Candace English
Copy Editor: Jim Compton and Marilyn Smith
Compositor: MacPS, LLC
Indexer: Toma Mulligan
Artist: April Milne
Cover Designer: Anna Ishchenko

Distributed to the book trade worldwide by Springer Science+Business Media, LLC., 233 Spring Street, 6th Floor, New York, NY 10013. Phone 1-800-SPRINGER, fax (201) 348-4505, e-mail orders-ny@springer-sbm.com, or visit www.springeronline.com.

For information on translations, please e-mail rights@apress.com, or visit www.apress.com.

Apress and friends of ED books may be purchased in bulk for academic, corporate, or promotional use. eBook versions and licenses are also available for most titles. For more information, reference our Special Bulk Sales–eBook Licensing web page at www.apress.com/info/bulksales.

The information in this book is distributed on an "as is" basis, without warranty. Although every precaution has been taken in the preparation of this work, neither the author(s) nor Apress shall have any liability to any person or entity with respect to any loss or damage caused or alleged to be caused directly or indirectly by the information contained in this work.

For Jessica, my wordridden wife
—Jeremy

For Stephanie, Addison, and Hayden, always by my side
—Jeffrey

Contents at a Glance

Contents

About the Authors

■ **Jeremy Keith** is a web developer living and working in Brighton, England. Working with the web consultancy firm Clearleft (`www.clearleft.com`), Jeremy enjoys building accessible, elegant websites using the troika of web standards: XHTML, CSS, and the DOM. His online home is `http://adactio.com`. Jeremy is also a member of the Web Standards Project (`www.webstandards.org`), where he serves as joint leader of the DOM Scripting Task Force. When he is not building websites, Jeremy plays bouzouki in the alt.country band Salter Cane (`www.saltercane.com`). He is also the creator and curator of one of the Web's largest online communities dedicated to Irish traditional music, The Session (`www.thesession.org`).

■ **Jeffrey Sambells** is a Canadian designer of pristine pixel layouts and a developer of squeaky clean code. Back in the good-old days of the Internet, he started a little company called We-Create. Today, he is still there as Director of Research and Development / Mobile. The title "Director of R&D" may sound flashy, but really, that just means he is in charge of learning and cramming as much goodness into products as possible—ensuring they're all just awesome. He is currently having fun exploring mobile design and development techniques. Jeffrey loves to learn. He has as much enthusiasm for digging in the dirt or climbing a cliff as he does for precisely aligning pixels or forcing that page to load just a little faster. What really pushes him forward is taking the bits of knowledge he has collected and piecing them together into something new and unique—something other people can be excited about, too. Along the way, Jeffrey has managed to graduate university, start a few businesses, write some books, and raise a wonderful family.

About the Technical Reviewer

■ **Rob Drimmie** is lucky. He has an amazing wife, two awesome kids, and a brand-new keyboard. Rob's creative urges tend to manifest in the form of web applications, and he prefers they be fueled by pho and hamburgers (the creative urges, that is).

Acknowledgments

This book owes its existence to my friends and colleagues, Andy Budd (http://andybudd.com) and Richard Rutter (http://clagnut.com). Andy runs a (free) training event in our hometown of Brighton called Skillswap (http://www.skillswap.org). Way back in July 2004, Richard and I gave a joint presentation on JavaScript and the Document Object Model. Afterward, we adjourned to the cozy confines of a nearby pub, where Andy put the idea in my head of expanding the talk into the first edition of this book.

I would never have learned to write a single line of JavaScript if it weren't for two things. The first is the view source option built in to almost every web browser. Thank you, view source. The second is the existence of JavaScript giants who have been creating amazing code and explaining important ideas over the years. Scott Andrew, Aaron Boodman, Steve Champeon, Peter-Paul Koch, Stuart Langridge, and Simon Willison are just some of the names that spring to mind. Thank you all for sharing.

Thanks to Molly Holzschlag for sharing her experience and advice with me, and for giving me feedback on early drafts. Thanks to Derek Featherstone for many a pleasurable JavaScriptladen chat; I like the way your mind works.

Extra-special thanks to Aaron Gustafson who provided invaluable feedback and inspiration during the writing of this book.

While I was writing the first edition of this book, I had the pleasure of speaking at two wonderful events: South by Southwest in Austin, Texas, and @media in London. Thanks to Hugh Forrest and Patrick Griffiths, respectively, for orchestrating these festivals of geekery that allowed me to meet and befriend the nicest, friendliest bunch of people I could ever hope to call my peers.

Finally, I'd like to thank my wife, Jessica Spengler, not only for her constant support, but also for her professional help in proofreading my first drafts. *Go raibh míle maith agat, a stór mo chroí.*

Jeremy Keith

Introduction

This book deals with a programming language, but it isn't intended for programmers. This is a book for web designers. Specifically, this book is intended for standards-aware designers who are comfortable using CSS and HTML. If that sounds like you, read on.

This book is made up of equal parts code and concepts. Don't be frightened by the code. I know it might look intimidating at first, but once you've grasped the concepts behind the code, you'll find yourself reading and writing in a new language.

Learning a programming language might seem like a scary prospect, but it needn't be. Document Object Model (DOM) scripting might appear to be more verbose than, say, CSS. But once you have the hang of the syntax, you'll find yourself armed with a powerful web development tool. In any case, the code is there simply to illustrate the concepts.

I'll let you in on a secret: no one memorizes all the syntax and keywords that are part and parcel of any programming language. That's what reference books are for. This isn't a reference book. I'm going to cover the bare minimum of syntax required to get up and running with JavaScript.

In this book, I focus on the ideas behind DOM scripting. A lot of these ideas might already be familiar to you. Graceful degradation, progressive enhancement, and user-centered design are important concepts in any aspect of front-end web development. These ideas inform all the code examples given in this book.

You'll find scripts for creating image galleries, animating slideshows, and enhancing the look and feel of page elements. If you want, you can simply cut and paste these examples, but it's more important to understand the hows and whys that lie behind the code.

If you're already using CSS and HTML to turn your designs into working web pages, then you already know how powerful web standards can be. Remember when you discovered that you could change the design throughout an entire site just by changing one CSS file? The DOM offers an equal level of power. But with great power comes great responsibility. That's why I'm not just going to show you cool DOM scripting effects. I'm also going to show you how to use DOM scripting to enhance your web pages in a usable, accessible way.

To get all the code examples discussed in the book, pay a visit to www.friendsofed.com and find this book's page. At the friends of ED site, you can also find out about all the other great books the publisher has to offer on web standards, Flash, Dreamweaver, and much more besides.

Your exploration of DOM scripting needn't end when you close this book. I've set up a website at http://domscripting.com/, where I continue the discussion of modern, standards-based JavaScript. I hope you'll pay the site a visit. In the meantime, enjoy the book.

CHAPTER 1

A Brief History of JavaScript

What this chapter covers:

- The origins of JavaScript

- The browser wars

- The evolution of the DOM

When the first edition of this book was published in 2005, it was an exciting time to be a web designer. Thankfully, five years later, it still is. This is especially true for JavaScript, which has been pulled from the shadows and into the spotlight. Web development has evolved from its chaotic, haphazard roots into a mature discipline. Designers and developers are adopting a standards-based approach to building websites, and the term *web standards* has been coined to describe the technologies that enable this approach.

Whenever designers discuss the subject of web standards, Hypertext Markup Language (HTML) and Cascading Style Sheets (CSS) usually take center stage. However, a third technology has been approved by the World Wide Web Consortium (W3C) and is supported by all standards-compliant web browsers. This is the Document Object Model (DOM), which allows us to add interactivity to our documents in much the same way that CSS allow us to add styles.

Before looking at the DOM, let's examine the language that you'll be using to make your web pages interactive. The language is JavaScript, and it has been around for quite some time.

The origins of JavaScript

JavaScript was developed by Netscape, in collaboration with Sun Microsystems. Before JavaScript, web browsers were fairly basic pieces of software capable of displaying hypertext documents. JavaScript was later introduced to add some extra spice to web pages and to make them more interactive. The first version, JavaScript 1.0, debuted in Netscape Navigator 2 in 1995.

At the time of JavaScript 1.0's release, Netscape Navigator dominated the browser market. Microsoft was struggling to catch up with its own browser, Internet Explorer, and was quick to follow Netscape's lead by releasing its own VBScript language, along with a version of JavaScript called JScript, with the delivery of Internet Explorer 3. As a response to this, Netscape and Sun, together with the European Computer Manufacturers Association (ECMA), set about standardizing the language. The result was ECMAScript, yet another name for the same language. Though the name never really stuck, we should really be referring to JavaScript as ECMAScript.

JavaScript, ECMAScript, JScript—whatever you want to call it—was gaining ground by 1996. Version 3 browsers from Netscape and Microsoft both supported the JavaScript 1.1 language to varying degrees.

This was clearly a ridiculous situation. Developers needed to double their code to accomplish any sort of DOM scripting. In effect, many scripts were written twice: once for Netscape Navigator and once for Internet Explorer. Convoluted browser sniffing was often required to serve up the correct script.

DHTML promised a world of possibilities, but anyone who actually attempted to use it discovered a world of pain instead. It wasn't long before DHTML became a dirty (buzz)word. The technology quickly garnered a reputation for being both overhyped and overly difficult to implement.

Raising the standard

While the browser manufacturers were busy engaging in their battle for supremacy, and using competing DOMs as weapons in their war, the W3C was quietly putting together a standardized DOM. Fortunately, the browser vendors were able to set aside their mutual animosity. Netscape, Microsoft, and other browser manufacturers worked together with the W3C on the new standard, and DOM Level 1 was completed in October 1998.

Consider the example in the previous section. We have a <div> with the ID myelement, and we're trying to ascertain the value that has been applied to its left position so that we can store that value as the variable xpos. Here's the syntax we would use with the new standardized DOM:

```
var xpos = document.getElementById('myelement').style.left
```

At first glance, that might not appear to be an improvement over the nonstandard, proprietary DOMs. However, the standardized DOM is far more ambitious in its scope.

While the browser manufacturers simply wanted some way to manipulate web pages with JavaScript, the W3C proposed a model that could be used by *any* programming language to manipulate *any* document written in *any* markup language.

Thinking outside the browser

The DOM is what's known as an application programming interface (API). APIs are essentially conventions that have been agreed upon by mutual consent. Real-world equivalents would be things like Morse code, international time zones, and the periodic table of the elements. All of these are standards, and they make it easier for people to communicate and cooperate. In situations where a single convention hasn't been agreed upon, the result is often disastrous. For example, competition between metric and imperial measurements has resulted in at least one failed Mars mission.

In the world of programming, there are many different languages, but there are many similar tasks. That's why APIs are so handy. Once you know the standard, you can apply it in many different environments. The syntax may change depending on the language you're using, but the convention remains the same.

So, while we focus specifically on using the DOM with JavaScript in this book, your new knowledge of the DOM will also be useful if you ever need to parse an XML document using a programming language like PHP or Python.

The W3C defines the DOM as "A platform- and language-neutral interface that will allow programs and scripts to dynamically access and update the content, structure, and style of documents." The independence of the standardized DOM, together with its powerful scope, places it head and shoulders above the proprietary DOMs created by the bickering browser manufacturers.

The end of the browser wars

Microsoft won the battle against Netscape for browser market-share supremacy. Ironically, the clash of competing DOMs and proprietary markup had little effect on the final outcome. Internet Explorer was destined to win simply by virtue of the fact that it came preinstalled on all PCs running the Windows operating system.

The people who were hit hardest by the browser wars were web designers. Cross-browser development had become a nightmare. As well as the discrepancies in JavaScript implementations mentioned earlier, the two browsers also had very different levels of support for CSS. Creating style sheets and scripts that worked on both browsers became a kind of black art.

A backlash began against the proprietary stance of the browser manufacturers. A group was formed, calling itself the Web Standards Project, or the WaSP for short (http://webstandards.org/). The first task that the WaSP undertook was to encourage browser makers to adopt W3C recommendations—the very same recommendations that the browser manufacturers had helped draft.

Whether it was due to pressure from the WaSP or the result of internal company decisions, there was far greater support for web standards in the next generation of web browsers.

A new beginning

A lot has changed since the early days of the browser wars, and things are still changing almost daily. Some browsers, such as Netscape Navigator, have all but vanished, and new ones have appeared on the scene. When Apple debuted its Safari web browser in 2003 (based on WebKit), there was no question that it would follow the DOM standards. Today, Firefox, Chrome, Opera, Internet Explorer, and a number of different WebKit-based browsers all have excellent support for the DOM. Many of the latest smartphone browsers are using the WebKit rendering engine, pushing browser development forward and making the browser-in-your-pocket superior to some desktop browsers.

■ **Note** WebKit (http://webkit.org) is the open source web browser engine use in Safari and Chrome. Open source engines such as WebKit and Gecko (used in Firefox, https://developer.mozilla.org/en/Gecko) have played a big role in pushing proprietary browser engines such as Microsoft's Trident (in Internet Explorer) to adopt more progressive web standards.

Today, pretty much all browsers have built-in support for the DOM. The browser wars of the late 1990s appear to be truly behind us. Now it's a race to implement the latest specification first. We've already seen an explosion of DOM scripting with the advent of asynchronous data transfers (Ajax), and the advancements in the HTML5 DOM are adding many new possibilities. HTML5 gives us vastly improved semantics, control over rich media with the <audio> and <video> elements, the capability of drawing with the <canvas> element, local browser storage for more than just cookies, built-in drag-and-drop support, and a lot more.

Life has improved greatly for web designers. Although no single browser has implemented the W3C DOM perfectly, all modern browsers cover about 95% of the specification, and they are each implementing the latest features almost as fast as we can adopt them. This means there's a huge amount that we can accomplish without needing to worry about branching code. Instead of writing scripts with forked code served up with complicated browser sniffing, we are now in a position to write something once and publish it everywhere. As long as we follow the DOM standards, we can be sure that our scripts will work almost universally.

What's next?

As you learned in this brief history lesson, different browsers used to accomplish the same tasks in different ways. This inescapable fact dominated not just the writing of JavaScript scripts, but also how books about JavaScript were written.

You can even kill two birds with one stone by declaring a variable and assigning it a value at the same time:

```
var mood = "happy";
var age = 33;
```

You could even do this:

```
var mood = "happy", age = 33;
```

That's the most efficient way to declare and assign variables. It has exactly the same meaning as doing this:

```
var mood, age;
mood = "happy";
age = 33;
```

The names of variables, along with just about everything else in JavaScript, are case-sensitive. The variable mood is not the same variable as Mood, MOOD or mOOd. These statements would assign values to two different variables:

```
var mood = "happy";
MOOD = "sad";
```

The syntax of JavaScript does not allow variable names to contain spaces or punctuation characters (except for the dollar symbol, $). The next line would produce a syntax error:

```
var my mood = "happy";
```

Variable names can contain letters, numbers, dollar symbols, and underscores. In order to avoid long variables looking all squashed together, and to improve readability, you can use underscores in variable names:

```
var my_mood = "happy";
```

Another stylistic alternative is to use the *camel case* format, where the space is removed and each new word begins with a capital letter:
var myMood = "happy";

Traditionally the camel case format is preferred for function and method names as well as object properties.

The text "happy" in that line is an example of a *literal*. A literal is something that is literally written out in the JavaScript code. Whereas the word var is a keyword and my_mood is the name of a variable, the text "happy" doesn't represent anything other than itself. To paraphrase Popeye, "It is what it is!"

Data types

The value of mood is a *string literal*, whereas the value of age is a *number literal*. These are two different types of data, but JavaScript makes no distinction in how they are declared or assigned. Some other languages demand that when a variable is declared, its data type is also declared. This is called *typing*.

Programming languages that require explicit typing are called *strongly typed* languages. Because typing is not required in JavaScript, it is a *weakly typed* language. This means that you can change the data type of a variable at any stage.

The following statements would be illegal in a strongly typed language but are perfectly fine in JavaScript:

```
var age = "thirty three";
age = 33;
```

JavaScript doesn't care whether age is a *string* or a *number*.

Now let's review the most important data types that exist within JavaScript.

Strings

Strings consist of zero or more characters. Characters include letters, numbers, punctuation marks, and spaces. Strings must be enclosed in quotes. You can use either single quotes or double quotes. Both of these statements have the same result:

```
var mood = 'happy';
var mood = "happy";
```

Use whichever one you like, but it's worth thinking about what characters are going to be contained in your string. If your string contains the double-quote character, then it makes sense to use single quotes to enclose the string. If the single-quote character is part of the string, you should probably use double quotes to enclose the string:

```
var mood = "don't ask";
```

If you wanted to write that statement with single quotes, you would need to ensure that the apostrophe (or single quote) between the n and the t is treated as part of the string. In this case, the single quote needs to be treated the same as any other character, rather than as a signal for marking the end of the string. This is called *escaping*. In JavaScript, escaping is done using the backslash character:

```
var mood = 'don\'t ask';
```

Similarly, if you enclose a string with double quotes, but that string also contains a double-quote character, you can use the backslash to escape the double-quote character within the string:

```
var height = "about 5'10\" tall";
```

These backslashes don't actually form part of the string. You can test this for yourself by adding the following to your example.js file and reloading test.html:

```
var height = "about 5'10\" tall";
alert(height);
```

Here's an example of the output of a variable using backslashes to escape characters:

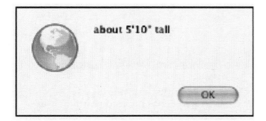

Personally, I like to use double quotes. Whether you decide to use double or single quotes, it's best to be consistent. If you switch between using double and single quotes all the time, your code could quickly become hard to read.

Numbers

If you want a variable to contain a numeric value, you don't have to limit yourself to whole numbers. JavaScript also allows you to specify numbers to as many decimal places as you want. These are called *floating-point numbers*:

```
var age = 33.25;
```

You can also use negative numbers. A minus sign at the beginning of a number indicates that it's negative:

```
var temperature = -20;
```

Negative values aren't limited to whole numbers either:

```
var temperature = -20.33333333
```

These are all examples of the *number* data type.

Boolean values

Another data type is *Boolean*.

Boolean data has just two possible values: true or false. Let's say you wanted a variable to store one value for when you're sleeping and another value for when you're no. You could use the string data type and assign it values like "sleeping" or "not sleeping," but it makes much more sense to use the Boolean data type:

```
var sleeping = true;
```

Boolean values lie at the heart of all computer programming. At a fundamental level, all electrical circuits use only Boolean data: either the current is flowing or it isn't. Whether you think of it in terms of "true and false," "yes and no," or "one and zero," the important thing is that there can only ever be one of two values.

Boolean values, unlike string values, are not enclosed in quotes. There is a difference between the Boolean value false and "false" as a string.

This will set the variable married to the Boolean value true:

```
var married = true;
```

In this case, married is a string containing the word "true":

```
var married = "true";
```

Arrays

Strings, numbers, and Boolean values are all examples of *scalars*. If a variable is a scalar, then it can only ever have one value at any one time. If you want to use a variable to store a whole set of values, then you need an *array*.

An array is a grouping of multiple values under the same name. Each one of these values is an *element* of the array. For instance, you might want to have a variable called beatles that contains the names of all four members of the band at once.

In JavaScript, you declare an array by using the Array keyword. You can also specify the number of elements that you want the array to contain. This number is the *length* of the array:

```
var beatles = Array(4);
```

Sometimes you won't know in advance how many elements an array is eventually going to hold. That's OK. Specifying the number of elements is optional. You can just declare an array with an unspecified number of elements:

```
var beatles = Array();
```

Adding elements to an array is called *populating* it. When you populate an array, you specify not just the value of the element, but also where the element comes in the array. This is the *index* of the element. Each element has a corresponding index. The index is contained in square brackets:

```
array[index] = element;
```

Let's start populating our array of Beatles. We'll go in the traditional order of John, Paul, George, and Ringo. Here's the first index and element:

```
beatles[0] = "John";
```

It might seem counterintuitive to start with an index of zero instead of one, but that's just the way JavaScript works. It's easy to forget this. Many novice programmers have fallen into this common pitfall when first using arrays.

Here's how we'd declare and populate our entire beatles array:

```
var beatles = Array(4);
beatles[0] = "John";
beatles[1] = "Paul";
beatles[2] = "George";
beatles[3] = "Ringo";
```

You can now retrieve the element "George" in your script by referencing the index 2 (beatles[2]). It might take a while to get used to the fact that the length of the array is four when the last element has an index of three. That's an unfortunate result of arrays beginning with the index number zero.

That was a fairly long-winded way of populating an array. You can take a shortcut by populating your array at the same time that you declare it. When you are populating an array in a declaration, separate the values with commas:

```
var beatles = Array( "John", "Paul", "George", "Ringo" );
```

An index will automatically be assigned for each element. The first index will be zero, the next will be one, etc. So referencing beatles[2] will still give us "George."

You don't even have to specify that you are creating an array. Instead, you can use square brackets to group the initial values together:

```
var beatles = [ "John", "Paul", "George", "Ringo" ];
```

The elements of an array don't have to be strings. You can store Boolean values in an array. You can also use an array to store a series of numbers:

```
var years = [ 1940, 1941, 1942, 1943 ];
```

You can even use a mixture of all three:

```
var lennon = [ "John", 1940, false ];
```

An element can be a variable:

```
var name = "John";
beatles[0] = name;
```

This would assign the value "John" to the first element of the beatles array.

The value of an element in one array can be an element from another array. This will assign the value "Paul" to the second element of the beatles array:

```
var names = [ "Ringo", "John", "George", "Paul" ];
beatles[1] = names[3];
```

In fact, arrays can hold other arrays! Any element of an array can contain an array as its value:

```
var lennon = [ "John", 1940, false ];
var beatles = [];
beatles[0] = lennon;
```

Now the value of the first element of the beatles array is itself an array. To get the values of each element of this array, we need to use some more square brackets. The value of beatles[0][0] is "John," the value of beatles[0][1] is 1940 and the value of beatles[0][2] is false.

This is a powerful way of storing and retrieving information, but it's going to be a frustrating experience if we have to remember the numbers for each index (especially when we have to start counting from zero). Luckily, there are a couple more ways of storing data. First, we'll look at a more readable way of populating arrays, and then move on to the preferred method, storing data as an object.

Associative arrays

The beatles array is an example of a *numeric array*. The index for each element is a number that increments with each addition to the array. The index of the first element is zero, the index of the second element is one, and so on.

If you only specify the values of an array, then that array will be numeric. The index for each element is created and updated automatically.

It is possible to override this behavior by specifying the index of each element. When you specify the index, you don't have to limit yourself to numbers. The index can be a string instead:

```
var lennon = Array();
lennon["name"] = "John";
lennon["year"] = 1940;
lennon["living"] = false;
```

This is called an *associative array*. It's much more readable than a numeric array because you can use strings instead of numbers, but they're actually considered bad form and we recommend that you don't use them. The reason for this is that when you create an associative array, you're actually creating properties on the Array object. In JavaScript, all variables are really objects of some type. A boolean is a Boolean object. An array is an Array object, and so on. In this example you are giving the lennon array new name, year and living properties. Ideally you don't want to be modifying the properties of the Array object. Instead, you should be using a generic Object.

Objects

Like an array, an *object* is a grouping of multiple values under the same name. Each one of these values is a *property* of the object. For instance, the lennon array in the previous section could be created as an object instead:

```
var lennon = Object();
lennon.name = "John";
lennon.year = 1940;
lennon.living = false;
```

Again, like the Array, an object is declared by using the Object keyword, but instead of using square brackets with an index to specify elements, you use dot notation and specify the property name the same way you would on any JavaScript object. For more about Objects, see the section "Objects" at the end of this chapter.

Alternatively you can use the more compact curly-brace {} syntax:

```
{ propertyName:value, propertyName:value }
```

For example, the lennon object could also be created like this:

```
var lennon = { name:"John", year:1940, living:false };
```

Property names follow the same naming rules as JavaScript variable names and the value can be any JavaScript value, including other objects.

Using objects instead of numeric arrays means you can reference elements by name instead of relying on numbers. It also makes for more readable scripts.

Let's create a new array named beatles and populate one of its elements with the lennon object that we created previously:

```
var beatles = Array();
beatles[0] = lennon;
```

Now we can get at the elements we want without using as many numbers. Instead of using beatles[0][0], under our new structure now beatles[0].name is "John"

That's an improvement, but we can go one further. What if beatles itself was an object instead of a numerical array? Then, instead of using numbers to reference each element of the array, we could use descriptive properties like "drummer" or "bassist":

```
var beatles = {};
beatles.vocalist = lennon;
```

Now the value of beatles.vocalist.name is "John", beatles.vocalist.year is 1940, and beatles.vocalist.living is false.

Operations

All the statements we've shown you have been very simple. All we've done is create different types of variables. In order to do anything useful with JavaScript, we need to be able to do calculations and manipulate data. We want to perform *operations*.

Arithmetic operators

Addition is an operation. So are subtraction, division, and multiplication. Every one of these *arithmetic operations* requires an *operator*. Operators are symbols that JavaScript has reserved for performing operations. You've already seen one operator in action. We've been using the equal sign (=) to perform assignment. The operator for addition is the plus sign (+), the operator for subtraction is the minus sign (-), division uses the backslash (/), and the asterisk (*) is the symbol for multiplication operations.

Here's a simple addition operation:

```
1 + 4
```

You can also combine operations:

```
1 + 4 * 5
```

```
  alert("The number is in the right range.");
}
```

This code uses the AND operator, represented by two ampersands (&&). This is an example of a *logical operator*.

Logical operators work on Boolean values. Each operand returns a Boolean value of either true or false. The AND operation will be true only if both operands are true.

The logical operator for OR is two vertical pipe symbols (||). The OR operation will be true if one of its operands is true. It will also be true if both of its operands are true. It will be false only if both operands are false.

```
if ( num > 10 || num < 5 ) {
  alert("The number is not in the right range.");
}
```

There is one other logical operator. It is represented by a single exclamation point (!). This is the NOT operator, which works on just a single operand. Whatever Boolean value is returned by that operand gets reversed. If the operand is true, the NOT operator switches it to false:

```
if ( !(1 > 2) ) {
  alert("All is well with the world");
}
```

Notice that we've placed the operand in parentheses to avoid any ambiguities. We want the NOT operator to act on everything between the parentheses.

You can use the NOT operator on the result of a complete conditional statement to reverse its value. The following statement uses another set of parentheses so that the NOT operator works on both operands combined:

```
if ( !(num > 10 || num < 5) ) {
  alert("The number IS in the right range.");
}
```

Looping statements

The if statement is probably the most important and useful conditional statement. Its only drawback is that it can't be used for repetitive tasks. The block of code contained within the curly braces is executed once. If you want to execute the same code a number of times, you'll need to use a *looping statement*.

Looping statements allow you to keep executing the same piece of code over and over. There are a number of different types of looping statements, but they all work in much the same way. The code within a looping statement continues to be executed as long as the condition is met. When the condition is no longer true, the loop stops.

The while loop

The while loop is very similar to the if statement. The syntax is the same:

```
while (condition) {
  statements;
}
```

The only difference is that the code contained within the curly braces will be executed over and over as long as the condition is true. Here's an example of a while loop:

```
var count = 1;
while (count < 11) {
  alert (count);
  count++;
}
```

Let's take a closer look at this code. We began by creating a numeric variable, count, containing the value one. Then we created a while loop with the condition that the loop should repeat as long as the value of count is less than eleven. Inside the loop itself, the value of count is incremented by one using the ++ operator. The loop will execute ten times. In your web browser, you will see an annoying alert dialog box flash up ten times. After the loop has been executed, the value of count will be eleven.

It's important that something happens within the while loop that will affect the test condition. In this case, we increase the value of count within the while loop. This results in the condition evaluating to false after ten loops. If we didn't increase the value of the count variable, the while loop would execute forever.

The do...while loop

As with the if statement, it is possible that the statements contained within the curly braces of a while loop may never be executed. If the condition evaluates as false on the first loop, then the code won't be executed even once.

There are times when you will want the code contained within a loop to be executed at least once. In this case, it's best to use a do loop. This is the syntax for a do loop:

```
do {
  statements;
} while (condition);
```

This is very similar to the syntax for a regular while loop, but with a subtle difference. Even if the condition evaluates as false on the very first loop, the statements contained within the curly braces will still be executed once.

Let's look at our previous example, reformatted as a do...while loop:

```
var count = 1;
do {
  alert (count);
  count++;
} while (count < 11);
```

The result is exactly the same as the result from our while loop. The alert message appears ten times. After the loop is finished, the value of the variable count is eleven.

Now consider this variation:

```
var count = 1;
do {
  alert (count);
  count++;
} while (count < 1);
```

In this case, the condition never evaluates as true. The value of count is one to begin with so it is never less than one. Yet the do loop is still executed once because the condition comes after the curly braces. You will still see one alert message. After these statements are executed, the value of count is two even though the condition is false.

The for loop

The for loop is a convenient way of executing some code a specific number of times. In that sense, it's similar to the while loop. In a way, the for loop is just a reformulation of the while loop we've already used. If we look at our while loop example, we can formulate it in full like this:

```
initialize;
while (condition) {
  statements;
  increment;
}
```

The for loop simply reformulates that as follows:

```
for (initial condition; test condition; alter condition) {
  statements;
}
```

This is generally a cleaner way of executing loops. Everything relevant to the loop is contained within the parentheses of the for statement.

If we reformulate our while loop example, this is how it looks:

```
for (var count = 1; count < 11; count++ ) {
  alert (count);
}
```

Everything related to the loop is contained within the parentheses. Now we can put code between the curly braces, secure in the knowledge that the code will be executed exactly ten times.

One of the most common uses of the for loop is to act on every element of an array. This is achieved using array.length, which provides the number of elements. It's important to remember that the index of the array begins at 0, not 1. In the following example, the array has four elements. The count variable increases from 0 once for every element in the array. When count reaches 4, the test condition fails and the loop ends, leaving 3 as the last index that was retrieved from the array:

```
var beatles = Array("John","Paul","George","Ringo");
for (var count = 0 ; count < beatles.length; count++ ) {
  alert(beatles[count]);
}
```

If you run this code, you will see four alert messages, one for each Beatle.

Functions

If you want to reuse the same piece of code more than once, you can wrap the statements up inside a *function*. A function is a group of statements that can be invoked from anywhere in your code. Functions are, in effect, miniature scripts.

It's good practice to define your functions before you invoke them.

A simple function might look like this:

```
function shout() {
  var beatles = Array("John","Paul","George","Ringo");
  for (var count = 0 ; count < beatles.length; count++ ) {
    alert(beatles[count]);
  }
}
```

This function performs the loop that pops up the names of each Beatle. Now, whenever you want that action to occur later in your script, you can invoke the function by simply writing

```
shout();
```

That's a useful way of avoiding lots of typing whenever you want to carry out the same action more than once. The real power of functions is that you can pass data to them and then have them act on that data. When data is passed to a function, it is known as an *argument*.

Here's the syntax for defining a function:

```
function name(arguments) {
  statements;
}
```

JavaScript comes with a number of built-in functions. You've seen one of them already: the alert function takes a single argument and then pops up a dialog box with the value of the argument.

You can define a function to take as many arguments as you want by separating them with commas. Any arguments that are passed to a function can be used just like regular variables within the function.

Here's a function that takes two arguments. If you pass this function two numbers, the function will multiply them:

```
function multiply(num1,num2) {
  var total = num1 * num2;
  alert(total);
}
```

You can invoke the function from anywhere in your script, like this:

```
multiply(10,2);
```

The result of passing the values 10 and 2 to the multiply() function is as follows:

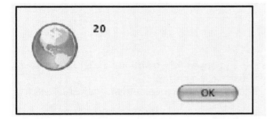

This will have the effect of immediately popping up an alert dialog with the answer (20). It would be much more useful if the function could send the answer back to the statement that invoked the function. This is quite easily done. As well as accepting data (in the form of arguments), functions can also return data.

You can create a function that returns a number, a string, an array, or a Boolean value. Use the return statement to do this:

```
function multiply(num1,num2) {
  var total = num1 * num2;
  return total;
}
```

Here's a function that takes one argument (a temperature in degrees Fahrenheit) and returns a number (the same temperature in degrees Celsius):

```
function convertToCelsius(temp) {
```

```
    var result = temp - 32;
    result = result / 1.8;
    return result;
}
```

The really useful thing about functions is that they can be used as a data type. You can assign the result of a function to a variable:

```
var temp_fahrenheit = 95;
var temp_celsius = convertToCelsius(temp_fahrenheit);
alert(temp_celsius);
```

The result of converting 95 degrees Fahrenheit into Celsius is as follows:

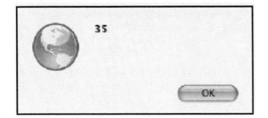

In this example, the variable temp_celsius now has a value of 35, which was returned by the convertToCelsius function.

You might be wondering about the way we've named my variables and functions. For variables, we've used underscores to separate words. For my functions, we've used capital letters after the first word (following the camel case naming style mentioned earlier). We've done this purely for that we can easily distinguish between variables and functions. As with variables, function names cannot contain spaces. Camel casing is simply a convenient way to work within that restriction.

Variable scope

We've mentioned already that it's good programming practice to use var when you are assigning a value to a variable for the first time. This is especially true when you are using variables in functions.

A variable can be either global or local. When we differentiate between local and global variables, we are discussing the *scope* of variables.

A *global variable* can be referenced from anywhere in the script. Once a global variable has been declared in a script, that variable can be accessed from anywhere in that script, even within functions. Its scope is global.

A *local variable* exists only within the function in which it is declared. You can't access the variable outside the function. It has a local scope.

So, you can use both global and local variables within functions. This can be useful, but it can also cause a lot of problems. If you unintentionally use the name of a global variable within a function, JavaScript will assume that you are referring to the global variable, even if you actually intended the variable to be local.

Fortunately, you can use the var keyword to explicitly set the scope of a variable within a function.

If you use var within a function, the variable will be treated as a local variable. It only exists within the context of the function. If you don't use var, the variable will be treated as a global variable. If there is already a variable with that name, the function will overwrite its value.

Take a look at this example:

```
function square(num) {
```

```
  total = num * num;
  return total;
}
var total = 50;
var number = square(20);
alert(total);
```

The value of the variable has been inadvertently changed:

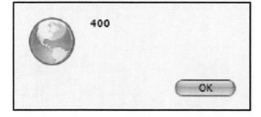

The value of the variable total is now 400. All we wanted from the square() function was for it to return the value of number squared. But because we didn't explicitly declare that the variable called total within the function should be local, the function has changed the value of the global variable called total.

This is how we should have written the function:

```
function square(num) {
  var total = num * num;
  return total;
}
```

Now we can safely have a global variable named total, secure in the knowledge that it won't be affected whenever the square() function is invoked.

Remember, functions should behave like self-contained scripts. That's why you should always declare variables within functions as being local in scope. If you always use var within functions, you can avoid any potential ambiguities.

Objects

There is one very important data type that we haven't looked at yet: *objects*. An object is a self-contained collection of data. This data comes in two forms: *properties* and *methods*:

- A property is a variable belonging to an object.

- A method is a function that the object can invoke.

These properties and methods are all combined in one single entity, which is the object.
Properties and methods are both accessed in the same way using JavaScript's dot syntax:

```
Object.property
Object.method()
```

You've already seen how variables can be used to hold values for things like mood and age. If there were an object called, say, Person, then these would be properties of the object:

```
Person.mood
```

```
Person.age
```

If there were functions associated with the Person object—say, walk() or sleep()—then these would be methods of the object:

```
Person.walk()
Person.sleep()
```

Now all these properties and methods are grouped together under one term: Person.

To use the Person object to describe a specific person, you would create an *instance* of Person. An instance is an individual example of a generic object. For instance, you and I are both people, but we are also both individuals. We probably have different properties (our ages may differ, for instance), yet we are both examples of an object called Person.

A new instance is created using the new keyword:

```
var jeremy = new Person;
```

This would create a new instance of the object Person, called jeremy. We could use the properties of the Person object to retrieve information about jeremy:

```
jeremy.age
jeremy.mood
```

We've used the imaginary example of a Person object just to demonstrate objects, properties, methods, and instances. In JavaScript, there is no Person object. It is possible for you to create your own objects in JavaScript. These are called *user-defined objects*. But that's quite an advanced subject that we don't need to deal with for now.

Fortunately, JavaScript is like one of those TV chefs who produce perfectly formed creations from the oven, declaring, "Here's one I made earlier." JavaScript comes with a range of premade objects that you can use in your scripts. These are called *native objects*.

Native objects

You've already seen objects in action. Array is an object. Whenever you initialize an array using the new keyword, you are creating a new instance of the Array object:

```
var beatles = new Array();
```

When you want to find out how many elements are in an array, you do so by using the length property:

```
beatles.length;
```

The Array object is an example of a native object supplied by JavaScript. Other examples include Math and Date, both of which have very useful methods for dealing with numbers and dates respectively. For instance, the Math object has a method called round which can be used to round up a decimal number:

```
var num = 7.561;
var num = Math.round(num);
alert(num);
```

The Date object can be used to store and retrieve information about a specific date and time. If you create a new instance of the Date object, it will be automatically be prefilled with the current date and time:

```
var current_date = new Date();
```

The date object has a whole range of methods like `getDay()`, `getHours()`, and `getMonth()` that can be used to retrieve information about the specified date. `getDay()`, for instance, will return the day of the week of the specified date:

```
var today = current_date.getDay();
```

Native objects like this provide invaluable shortcuts when you're writing JavaScript.

Host objects

Native objects aren't the only kind of premade objects that you can use in your scripts. Another kind of object is supplied not by the JavaScript language itself, but by the environment in which it's running. In the case of the Web, that environment is the web browser. Objects that are supplied by the web browser are called *host objects*.

Host objects include `Form`, `Image`, and `Element`. These objects can be used to get information about forms, images, and form elements within a web page.

We're not going to show you any examples of how to use those host objects. There is another object that can be used to get information about any element in a web page that you might be interested in: the document object. For the rest of this book, we are going to be looking at lots of properties and methods belonging to the document object.

What's next?

In this chapter, we've shown you the basics of the JavaScript language. Throughout the rest of the book, we'll be using terms that have been introduced here: statements, variables, arrays, functions, and so on. These concepts will become clearer once you see them in action in a working script. You can always refer back to this chapter whenever you need a reminder of what these terms mean.

We've just introduced the concept of objects. Don't worry if it isn't completely clear to you just yet. The next chapter will take an in-depth look at one particular object, the document object. We want to start by showing you some properties and methods associated with this object. These properties and methods are provided courtesy of the Document Object Model.

In the next chapter, we will introduce you to the idea of the DOM and show you how to use some of its very powerful methods.

CHAPTER 3

The Document Object Model

What this chapter covers:

- The concept of nodes
- Five very handy DOM methods: `getElementById`, `getElementsByTagName`, `getElementsByClassName`, `getAttribute`, and `setAttribute`

It's time to meet the DOM. This chapter introduces you to the DOM and shows you the world through its eyes.

D is for document

The DOM can't work without a document. When you create a web page and load it in a web browser, the DOM comes to life. It takes the document that you have written and turns it into an object.

In normal everyday English, the word *object* isn't very descriptive. It simply means *thing*. In programming languages, on the other hand, *object* has a very specific meaning.

Objects of desire

At the end of the previous chapter, you saw some examples of objects in JavaScript. You'll remember that objects are self-contained bundles of data. Variables associated with an object are called *properties* of the object. Functions that can be executed by an object are called *methods* of the object.

There are three kinds of objects in JavaScript:

- User-defined objects created from scratch by the programmer. We won't be dealing with these in this book.
- Native objects like `Array`, `Math`, and `Date`, which are built in to JavaScript.
- Host objects that are provided by the browser.

From the earliest days of JavaScript, some very important host objects have been made available for scripting. The most fundamental of these is the `window` object.

The `window` object is nothing less than a representation of the browser window itself. The properties and methods of the `window` object are often referred to as the Browser Object Model (although perhaps Window Object Model would be more semantically correct). The Browser Object Model has methods like `window.open` and `window.blur`. These methods, incidentally, are responsible for all those annoying pop-up and pop-under windows that have plagued the Web. No wonder JavaScript has a bad reputation!

When you're applying styles to a document, there are times when you will want to target specific elements. You might want to make one paragraph a certain size and color, but leave other paragraphs unaffected. To get this level of precision, you need to insert something into the document itself to mark the paragraph as a special case. To mark elements for special treatment, you can use one of two attributes: class or id.

The class attribute

The class attribute can be applied as often as you like to as many different elements as you like:

```
<p class="special">This paragraph has the special class</p>
<h2 class="special">So does this headline</h2>
```

In a style sheet, styles can then be applied to all the elements of this class:

```
.special {
  font-style: italic;
}
```

You can also target specific types of elements with this class:

```
h2.special {
  text-transform: uppercase;
}
```

The id attribute

The id attribute can be used once in a web page to uniquely identify an element:

```
<ul id="purchases">
```

In a style sheet, styles can then be applied specifically to this element:

```
#purchases {
  border: 1px solid white;
  background-color: #333;
  color: #ccc;
  padding: 1em;
}
```

Although the id itself can be applied only once, a style sheet can use the id to apply styles to elements nested within the uniquely identified element:

```
#purchases li {
  font-weight: bold;
}
```

Here is an example of styles applied to a list with a unique `id`:

The `id` attribute acts as a kind of "hook" that can be targeted by CSS. The DOM can use the same hook.

Getting Elements

Three hn 306.210dy DOM methods allow you to access element nodes by ID, tag name, and class name.

getElementById

The DOM has a method called `getElementById`, which does exactly what it sounds like: it allows you to get straight to the element node with the specified `id`. Remember that JavaScript is case-sensitive, so `getElementById` must always be written with case preserved. If you write `GetElementById` or `getElementbyid`, you won't get the results you expect.

`getElementById` is a function associated with the `document` object. Functions are always followed by parentheses that contain the function's arguments. `getElementById` takes just one argument: the `id` of the element you want to get to, contained in either single or double quotes.

```
document.getElementById(id)
```

Here's an example:

```
document.getElementById("purchases")
```

This is referencing the unique element that has been assigned the HTML `id` attribute `"purchases"` in the `document` object. This element also corresponds to an object. You can test this for yourself by using the `typeof` operator. This will tell you whether something is a string, a number, a function, a Boolean value, or an object.

I don't recommend mixing a lot of inline JavaScript into a document, but purely for testing purposes, insert this `<script>` with JavaScript into the shopping list document. Put it directly before the closing `</body>` tag:

```
<!DOCTYPE html>
<html lang="en">
  <head>
```

```
        <meta charset="utf-8" />
        <title>Shopping list</title>
    </head>
    <body>
        <h1>What to buy</h1>
        <p title="a gentle reminder">Don't forget to buy this stuff.</p>
        <ul id="purchases">
            <li>A tin of beans</li>
            <li class="sale">Cheese</li>
            <li class="sale important">Milk</li>
        </ul>
        <script>
            alert(typeof document.getElementById("purchases"));
        </script>
    </body>
</html>
```

When you load the XHTML file in a web browser, you will be greeted with an annoying pop-up box stating the nature of `document.getElementById("purchases")`. It is an object.

In fact, each element in a document is an object. Using the DOM, you can "get" at all of these elements. Obviously you shouldn't give a unique id to every single element in a document. That would be overkill. Fortunately, the document object provides another method for getting at elements that don't have unique identifiers.

getElementsByTagName

If you use the method `getElementsByTagName`, you have instant access to an array populated with every occurrence of a specified tag. Like `getElementById`, `getElementsByTagName` is a function that takes one argument. In this case, the argument is the name of a tag:

element`.getElementsByTagName(`*tag*`)`

It looks very similar to `getElementById`, but notice that this time you can get element*s*—plural. Be careful when you are writing your scripts that you don't inadvertently write `getElementsById` or `getElementByTagName`.

Here it is in action:

`document.getElementsByTagName("li")`

This is an array populated with all the list items in the document object. Just as with any other array, you can use the length property to get the total number of elements.

Delete the alert statement you placed between <script> tags earlier and replace it with this:

```
alert(document.getElementsByTagName("li").length);
```

This will tell you the total number of list items in the document, which in this case is three. Every value in the array is an object. You can test this yourself by looping through the array and using typeof on each value. For example, try this with a for loop:

```
for (var i=0; i < document.getElementsByTagName("li").length; i++) {
  alert(typeof document.getElementsByTagName("li")[i]);
}
```

Even if there is only one element with the specified tag name, getElementsByTagName still returns an array. The length of the array will simply be 1.

Now you will begin to notice that typing out document.getElementsByTagName("li") every time is tedious, and that the code is getting harder to read. You can reduce the amount of unnecessary typing and improve readability by assigning a variable to contain document.getElementsByTagName("li"). Replace the alert statement between the <script> tags with these statements:

```
var items = document.getElementsByTagName("li");
for (var i=0; i < items.length; i++) {
  alert(typeof items[i]);
}
```

Now you'll get three annoying alert boxes, each saying the same thing: **object**.

You can also use a wildcard with getElementsByTagName, which means you can make an array with every single element. The wildcard symbol (the asterisk) must be contained in quotes to distinguish it from the multiplication operator. The wildcard will give you the total number of element nodes in a document:

```
alert(document.getElementsByTagName("*").length);
```

You can also combine getElementsByTagName with getElementById. So far, we've applied getElementsByTagName to only the document object. But if you're interested in finding out how many list items are inside the element with the id "purchases", you could apply getElementsByTagName to that specific object:

```
var shopping = document.getElementById("purchases");
var items = shopping.getElementsByTagName("*");
```

Now the items array holds just the elements contained by the "purchases" list. In this case, that happens to be the same as the total number of the list items in the document:

```
alert (items.length);
```

And, if any further proof is needed, you can test that each one is an object:

```
for (var i=0; i < items.length; i++) {
  alert(typeof items[i]);
}
```

getElementsByClassName

A welcome addition to the HTML5 DOM (http://www.whatwg.org/specs/web-apps/current-work/) is the getElementsByClassName method. This method adds a way of accessing elements by their class names in the class attribute. That said, it is still a relatively new addition to the DOM, so you need to be cautious when you choose to use it. First, let's see what it does, and then we'll discuss how we can make it work reliably.

Like getElementsByTagName, the getElementsByClassName method takes one argument. In this case, the argument is the name of a class:

```
getElementsByClassName(class)
```

It also behaves in the same way as getElementsByTagName by returning an array of elements with a common class name. Here's an example that will return all the elements that have "sale" in their class attribute:

```
document.getElementsByClassName("sale")
```

You can also include multiple class names to locate elements that have more than one class. To include more than one class, simply separate the class names with a space. For example, add the following alert statement between the <script> tags:

```
alert(document.getElementsByClassName("important sale").length);
```

Notice that you'll get a 1 in the alert box. Only one element matched, because only one has both the "important" and "sale" class. Also notice that the function still matches, even though the class attribute in the document is "sale important" not "important sale". The order of the class names doesn't matter, and it would match if the element had additional class names as well.

As with getElementsByTagName, you can also combine getElementsByClassName with getElementById. If you want to find out how many list items have the "sale" class inside the element with the id "purchases", you can apply getElementsByClassName to that specific object:

```
var shopping = document.getElementById("purchases");
var sales = shopping.getElementsByClassName("sale");
```

Now the sales array contains just the elements with the "sale" class that are also contained by the "purchases" list. If you try the following alert, you'll see that happens to be two items:

```
alert (sales.length);
```

The getElementsByClassName method is quite useful, but it's supported by only modern browsers. To make up for this lack of support, DOM scripters have needed to roll their own getElementsByClassName function using existing DOM methods, sort of like a rite of passage. In most cases, these functions look similar to the following getElementsByClassName function, and are written to work in both older and newer browsers:

```
function getElementsByClassName(node, classname) {
  if (node.getElementsByClassName) {
    // Use the existing method
    return node.getElementsByClassName(classname);
  } else {
    var results = new Array();
    var elems = node.getElementsByTagName("*");
    for (var i=0; i<elems.length; i++) {
      if (elems[i].className.indexOf(classname) != -1) {
        results[results.length] = elems[i];
      }
    }
    return results;
  }
}
```

This getElementsByClassName function takes two arguments. The first is node, which represents the point in the tree where the search will start, and the second is classname, which is the class to search for. If the proper getElementsByClassName function already exists as a method on the node, then the new function will return the list of nodes as expected. If the getElementsByClassName doesn't exist, the new function loops through all the tags and crudely looks for the elements with the appropriate class name. (This example doesn't work as well for multiple class names). Using this function to mimic what we did earlier with the shopping list, we might do something like this:

```
var shopping = document.getElementById("purchases");
var sales = getElementsByClassName(shopping, "sale");
```

How you choose to search for the matching DOM elements can vary widely, however, there are a few excellent examples, such as "The Ultimate getElementsByClassName" by Robert Nyman (http://robertnyman.com/2008/05/27/the-ultimate-getelementsbyclassname-anno-2008/).

In Chapter 5, we'll discuss these support issues and how to best deal with them. In Chapter 7, we'll look at the DOM manipulation methods in more detail.

Taking stock

By now, you are probably truly fed up with seeing alert boxes containing the word **object**. I think you get the point: every element node in a document is an object. Not only that, but every single one of these objects comes with an arsenal of methods, courtesy of the DOM. Using these supplied methods, you can retrieve information about any element in a document. You can even alter the properties of an element.

Here's a quick summary of what you've seen so far:

- A document is a tree of nodes.

- There are different types of nodes: elements, attributes, text, and so on.

- You can go straight to a specific element node using getElementById.

- You can go directly to a collection of element nodes using getElementsByTagName or getElementsByClassName.

- Every one of these nodes is an object.

Now let's look at some of the properties and methods associated with these objects.

Getting and Setting Attributes

So far, you've seen three different ways of getting to element nodes: using getElementById, getElementsByTagName, or getElementsByClassName. Once you have the element, you can find out the values of any of its attributes. You can do this with the getAttribute method. And using the setAttribute method, you can change the value of an attribute node.

getAttribute

getAttribute is a function. It takes only one argument, which is the attribute that you want to get:

object.getAttribute(*attribute*)

```
var body_element = document.getElementsByTagName("body")[0];
```

Now the variable body_element refers to the body element in our document. To access the children of the body element, you just need to use

```
body_element.childNodes
```

That's a lot easier than writing this:

```
document.getElementsByTagName("body")[0].childNodes
```

Now that you can get at all the children of the body element, let's take a look at what you can do with that information.

First, you can find out exactly how many children the body element has. Because childNodes returns an array, you can use the length property to find out how many elements it contains:

```
body_element.childNodes.length;
```

Try adding this little function to the showPic.js file:

```
function countBodyChildren() {
  var body_element = document.getElementsByTagName("body")[0];
  alert (body_element.childNodes.length);
}
```

This simple function will pop up an alert dialog with the total number of the body element's children.

You'll want this function to be executed when the page loads, and you can use the onload event handler to do this. Add this line to the end of the code:

```
window.onload = countBodyChildren;
```

When the document loads, the countBodyChildren function will be invoked.

Refresh the gallery.html file in your web browser. You will be greeted with an alert dialog containing the total number of children of the body element. The result may surprise you.

Introducing the nodeType property

Looking at the structure of the gallery.html file, it would appear that the body element has just three children: the h1 element, the ul element, and the img element. Yet, when we invoke the countBodyChildren function, we get a much higher figure. This is because elements are just one type of node.

The childNodes property returns an array containing all types of nodes, not just element nodes. It will bring back all the attribute nodes and text nodes as well. In fact, just about everything in a document is some kind of node. Even spaces and line breaks are interpreted as nodes and are included in the childNodes array.

That explains why the result produced by countBodyChildren is so high.

Fortunately, we can use the nodeType property on any node in a document. This will tell us exactly what kind of node we're dealing with. Unfortunately, it won't tell us in plain English.

The nodeType property is called with the following syntax:

node.nodeType

However, instead of returning a string like "element" or "attribute," it returns a number.

Change the alert statement in the countBodyChildren function so that it now gives us the nodeType of body_element:

```
alert(body_element.nodeType);
```

Refresh the browser window that's displaying gallery.html. Now you'll see an alert dialog containing the number 1. Element nodes have a nodeType value of 1.

There are twelve possible values for nodeType, but only three of them are going to be of much practical use:

- Element nodes have a nodeType value of 1.

- Attribute nodes have a nodeType value of 2.

- Text nodes have a nodeType value of 3.

This means that you can target specific types of nodes in your functions. For instance, you could create a function that only affects element nodes.

Adding a description in the markup

To improve the image gallery function, I want to manipulate a text node. I want to replace its value with a value taken from an attribute node (the title attribute in a link).

First, I need to have somewhere to put the text. I'm going to add a new paragraph to gallery.html. I'll place it right after the img tag. I'm going to give it a unique id so that I can reference it easily from the JavaScript function:

```
<p id="description">Choose an image.</p>
```

I've given the id attribute the value "description", which describes its role fairly accurately. For now, it contains the text "Choose an image." Here, you can see that a new paragraph has been added.

I plan to replace this text with text taken from a link's title attribute. I want this to happen at the same time as the placeholder image is replaced with the image taken from the link's href attribute. To achieve this, I need to update the showPic function.

53

Changing the description with JavaScript

I'm going to update the showPic function so that the text in the description paragraph is replaced with the text from a title attribute in a link.

This is how the showPic function looks right now:

```
function showPic(whichpic) {
  var source = whichpic.getAttribute("href");
  var placeholder = document.getElementById("placeholder");
  placeholder.setAttribute("src",source);
}
```

I'm going to begin my improvements by getting the value of the title attribute of whichpic. I'll store this value in a variable called text. This is easily done using getAttribute:

```
var text = whichpic.getAttribute("title");
```

Now I want to create a new variable so that I have an easy way of referencing the paragraph with the id "description". I'll call this variable description also:

```
var description = document.getElementById("description");
```

I have my variables:

```
function showPic(whichpic) {
  var source = whichpic.getAttribute("href");
  var placeholder = document.getElementById("placeholder");
  placeholder.setAttribute("src",source);
  var text = whichpic.getAttribute("title");
  var description = document.getElementById("description");
}
```

Now it's time to do the text swapping.

Introducing the nodeValue property

If you want to change the value of a text node, there is a DOM property called nodeValue that can be used to get (and set) the value of a node:

```
node.nodeValue
```

Here's a tricky little point. If you retrieve the nodeValue for description, you *won't* get the text within the paragraph. You can test this with an alert statement:

```
alert (description.nodeValue);
```

This will return a value of null. The nodeValue of the paragraph element itself is empty. What you actually want is the value of the text within the paragraph.

The text within the paragraph is a different node. This text is the first child node of the paragraph. Therefore, you want to retrieve the nodeValue of this child node.

This alert statement will give you the value you're looking for:

```
alert(description.childNodes[0].nodeValue);
```

This will return a value of "Choose an image." This means that you're accessing the childNodes array and getting the value of the first element (index number zero).

Introducing firstChild and lastChild

There is a shorthand way of writing `childNodes[0]`. Whenever you want to get the value of the first node in the `childNodes` array, you can use `firstChild`:

node`.firstChild`

>   This is equivalent to

node`.childNodes[0]`

>   This is a handy shortcut and it's also a lot easier to read.
>   The DOM also provides a corresponding `lastChild` property:

*nod*e`.lastChild`

>   This refers to the last node in the `childNodes` array. If you wanted to access this node without using the `lastChild` property, you would have to write

node`.childNodes[`*node*`.childNodes.length-1]`

>   That's clearly very unwieldy. It's a lot easier to simply use `lastChild`.

Using nodeValue to update the description

Now we'll go back to the `showPic` function. I'm going to update the `nodeValue` of the text node within the description paragraph.
>   In the case of the `description` paragraph, only one child node exists. I can use either `description.firstChild` or `description.lastChild`. I'm going to use `firstChild` in this case.
>   I can rewrite my alert statement so that it now reads

```
alert(description.firstChild.nodeValue);
```

>   The value is the same ("Choose an image"), but now the code is more readable.
>   The `nodeValue` method is very versatile. It can be used to retrieve the value of a node, but it can also be used to set the value of a node. That's exactly what I want to do in this case.
>   If you recall, I've already set aside a string in the variable `text`, which I retrieved from the `title` attribute of the link that has been clicked. I'm now going to update the value of the first child node of the description paragraph:

```
description.firstChild.nodeValue = text;
```

>   These are the three new lines that I've added to `showPic` function:

```
var text = whichpic.getAttribute("title");
var description = document.getElementById("description");
description.firstChild.nodeValue = text;
```

>   In plain English, I'm saying:

- Get the value of the `title` attribute of the link that has just been clicked and store this value in a variable called `text`.

- Get the element with the `id` "description" and store this object as the variable `description`.

- Update the value of the first child node of the `description` object with the value of `text`.

This is how the final function looks:

```
function showPic(whichpic) {
  var source = whichpic.getAttribute("href");
  var placeholder = document.getElementById("placeholder");
  placeholder.setAttribute("src",source);
  var text = whichpic.getAttribute("title");
  var description = document.getElementById("description");
  description.firstChild.nodeValue = text;
}
```

If you update the showPic.js file with these new lines and then refresh gallery.html in your browser, you can test the expanded functionality. Clicking a link to an image now produces two results. The placeholder image is replaced with the new image, and the description text is replaced with the title text from the link.

You can find my image gallery script and markup at http://friendsofed.com/. All of my images are there, too, but if you want to have some fun with this script, try using your own pictures.

If you want to liven up the image gallery, you can add a style sheet like this one:

```
body {
  font-family: "Helvetica","Arial",serif;
  color: #333;
  background-color: #ccc;
  margin: 1em 10%;
}
h1 {
  color: #333;
  background-color: transparent;
}
a {
  color: #c60;
```

```
    background-color: transparent;
    font-weight: bold;
    text-decoration: none;
}
ul {
    padding: 0;
}
li {
    float: left;
    padding: 1em;
    list-style: none;
}
img {
    display:block;
    clear:both;
}
```

You can save that CSS in a file called layout.css in a directory called styles. You can then reference this file from a <link> tag in the <head> of gallery.html:

```
<!DOCTYPE html>
<html lang="en">
<head>
    <meta charset="utf-8" />
    <title>Image Gallery</title>
    <link rel="stylesheet" href="styles/layout.css" media="screen" />
</head>
<body>
    <h1>Snapshots</h1>
    <ul>
        <li>
            <a href="images/fireworks.jpg" title="A fireworks display"
➥ onclick="showPic(this); return false;">Fireworks</a>
        </li>
        <li>
            <a href="images/coffee.jpg" title="A cup of black coffee"
➥ onclick="showPic(this); return false;">Coffee</a>
        </li>
        <li>
            <a href="images/rose.jpg" title="A red, red rose"
➥ onclick="showPic(this); return false;">Rose</a>
        </li>
        <li>
            <a href="images/bigben.jpg" title="The famous clock"
➥ onclick="showPic(this); return false;">Big Ben</a>
        </li>
    </ul>
    <img id="placeholder" src="images/placeholder.gif" alt="my image gallery" />
    <p id="description">Choose an image.</p>
    <script src="scripts/showPic.js"></script>
</body>
</html>
```

Following is an example of the image gallery with a simple style sheet attached.

What's next?

In this chapter, you've seen some applied JavaScript. You've also been introduced to some new DOM properties, such as

- `childNodes`
- `nodeType`
- `nodeValue`
- `firstChild`
- `lastChild`

You've learned how to put together an image gallery script using some of the methods offered by the Document Object Model. You've also learned how to integrate JavaScript into your web pages using event handlers.

On the surface, this JavaScript image gallery probably appears to be a complete success. However, there's actually quite a lot of room for improvement, which I'll be covering shortly.

The next chapter covers the best practices that should be used when writing JavaScript. You'll see that how you achieve a final result is as important as the result itself.

Then, in Chapter 6, you'll see how to apply those best practices to the image gallery script.

CHAPTER 5

Best Practices

What this chapter covers:

- Graceful degradation: ensuring that your web pages still work without JavaScript
- Unobtrusive JavaScript: separating structure from behavior
- Backward compatibility: ensuring that older browsers don't choke on your scripts
- Performance considerations: making sure that your script is performing at its best

Together, JavaScript and the DOM form a powerful combination. It's important that you use this power wisely. This chapter describes some best practices that you can use to ensure that your scripts don't do more harm than good.

Mistakes of the past

Before we get to the specifics of best practices for having web pages work correctly, let's take a quick look at some reasons that things can go wrong.

Don't blame the messenger

Technologies with a low barrier to entry can be a double-edged sword. A technology that people can use speedily and easily will probably be adopted very quickly. However, there is likely to be a correspondingly low level of quality control.

HTML's ease of use is one of the reasons behind the explosive growth of the World Wide Web. Anyone can learn the basics of HTML in a short space of time and create a web page very quickly. It's even possible to use What You See Is What You Get (WYSIWYG) editors to make web pages without ever seeing a line of markup.

The downside to this is that most pages on the Web are badly formed and don't validate. Browser manufacturers have chosen to accept this state of affairs by making their software very forgiving and unfussy. Instead of requiring clean, valid markup, browsers desperately try to render any code they are given. As a result, much of the code in browser software is dedicated to handling ambiguous use of HTML and trying to second-guess how authors want their web pages to be rendered.

In theory, there are billions of HTML documents on the Web. In practice, only a small fraction of those documents are made of well-formed, valid markup. This legacy makes the process of advancing web technologies like HTML and CSS much more difficult. HTML's low barrier to entry has been a mixed blessing for the World Wide Web.

The situation with JavaScript isn't quite as drastic. If JavaScript code isn't written with the correct syntax, the coder will be alerted because it will cause an error (as opposed to HTML, which, in most cases, will render anyway). Nonetheless, a lot of very bad JavaScript is out there on the Web.

Many web designers wanted to reap the benefits of using JavaScript for adding spice to their web pages without spending the time to learn the language. It wasn't long before WYSIWYG editors began offering snippets of code that could be attached to documents.

Even without a WYSIWYG editor, it was still quite easy to find snippets of JavaScript. Many websites and books offered self-contained functions that could be added to web pages easily. Cutting and pasting was the order of the day.

Unfortunately, many of these functions weren't very well thought out. On the surface, they accomplished their tasks and added extra interactivity to web pages. In most cases, however, little thought was given to how these pages behaved when JavaScript was disabled. Poorly implemented scripts sometimes had the effect of inadvertently making JavaScript a requirement for navigating a website. From an accessibility viewpoint, this was clearly a problem. It wasn't long before the words *JavaScript* and *inaccessible* became linked in many people's minds.

In fact, there's nothing inherently inaccessible about JavaScript. It all depends on how it's used. In the words of the old song, "It ain't what you do, it's the way that you do it."

The Flash mob

In truth, there are no bad technologies. There are just bad uses of a technology. The cruel hand that fate had dealt JavaScript reminds me of another much maligned technology: Adobe's Flash.

Many people once associated Flash with annoying splash pages, overlong download times, and unintuitive navigation. None of these things are intrinsic to Flash. They're simply by-products of poorly implemented Flash.

It's ironic that Flash became associated with overlong download times. One of the great strengths of Flash is its ability to create light, compressed vector images and movies. But once it became the norm for Flash sites to have bloated splash intro movies, it took a long time to reverse the trend.

Similarly, JavaScript can and should be used to make web pages more usable. Yet it has had a reputation for decreasing the usability and accessibility of websites.

The problem was one of both inertia and momentum. If a technology is used in a thoughtless way from very early on, and that technology is then quickly adopted, it becomes very hard to change those initial bad habits.

I'm sure that all the pointless Flash intro movies on splash pages didn't spring up simultaneously. Instead, it was a case of "monkey see, monkey do." People wanted splash pages because other people had splash pages. No one stopped to ask why it was necessary.

JavaScript suffered a similar fate. Badly written functions, particularly those written by WYSIWYG editors, have shown a remarkable tenacity. The code has been copied and pasted. The functions have spread far and wide across the Web, but no one has ever questioned whether they could have been better.

Question everything

Whenever you use JavaScript to alter the behavior of your web pages, you should question your decisions. First and foremost, you should question whether the extra behavior is really necessary.

JavaScript has been misused in the past to add all sorts of pointless bells and whistles to websites. You can use scripts that move the position of the browser window or even cause the browser window to shake.

Most notorious of all, some scripts cause ad-containing content overlays or pop-up windows to appear when a page loads. Unfortunately for JavaScript and DOM scripters, some people deal with these invasive advertising tactics by disabling JavaScript entirely. The browser manufacturers themselves took steps to deal with the problem by offering built-in pop-up blockers, but advertisers continued to find ways around these.

Advertising pop-under windows and content overlays are the epitome of JavaScript abuse. Ostensibly, they are supposed to solve a problem: how to deliver advertising to users. In practice, they only increase user frustration. The onus was on the user to close these overlays and windows—something that often turned into an unhappy game of whack-a-mole.

If only someone had asked, "How will this benefit the user?"

Fortunately, this question is being asked more often these days. Any approach besides user-centric web design is, in the long term, doomed to failure.

Whenever you are using JavaScript, you should ask yourself how it will affect the user's experience. There's another very important question you should also ask yourself: what if the user doesn't have JavaScript?

Graceful degradation

It's always worth remembering that a visitor to your site might be using a browser that doesn't support JavaScript. Or maybe the user has disabled JavaScript (perhaps after being exposed to one too many pop-under windows). If you don't consider this possibility, you could inadvertently stop visitors from using your site.

If you use JavaScript correctly, your site will still be navigable by users who don't have JavaScript. This is called *graceful degradation*. When a technology degrades gracefully, the functionality may be reduced, but it doesn't fail completely.

Take the example of opening a link in a new window. Don't worry—I'm not talking about spawning a new window when the page loads. I'm talking about creating a pop-up window when the user clicks a link. This can be quite a useful feature. Many e-commerce websites will have links to terms of service or delivery rates from within the checkout process. Rather than having the user leave the current screen, a pop-up window can display the relevant information without interrupting the shopping experience.

Note Popping up a new window should be used only when it's absolutely required. There are accessibility issues involved, For example, some screen-reading software doesn't indicate that a new window has been opened. It's a good idea to make it clear in the link text that a new browser window will be opened.

JavaScript uses the open() method of the window object to create new browser windows. This method takes three arguments:

```
window.open(url,name,features)
```

All of the arguments are optional:

- The first argument is the URL for the document you want to open in a new window. If this is missing, an empty browser window will be created.

- The second argument is the name that you can give this newly created window. You can use this name in your code to communicate with your new window.

- The final argument is a comma-separated list of features that you want your new window to have. These include the size of the window (width and height) and aspects of the browser chrome that you want to enable or disable (including toolbars, menu bar, location, and so on). You don't need to list all of the features (and anyway, it's a good idea not to disable too many features).

This method is a good example of using the Browser Object Model. Nothing about the functionality affects the contents of the document (that's what the DOM is for). The method is purely concerned with the browsing environment (in this case, the `window` object).

Here's an example of a typical function that uses `window.open()`:

```
function popUp(winURL) {
  window.open(winURL,"popup","width=320,height=480");
}
```

This will open up a new window (called `"popup"`) that's 320 pixels wide by 480 pixels tall. Because we're setting the name of the window in the function, any time a new URL is passed to the function, the function will replace the existing spawned window rather than creating a second one.

You can save this function in an external file and link to it from a `<script>` tag within the `<head>` of a web page. By itself, this function doesn't have any usability implications. What matters is how you use it.

One way of calling the `popUp` function is to use what's known as a *pseudo-protocol*.

The javascript: pseudo-protocol

Real protocols are used to send packets of information between computers on the Internet. Examples are HTTP (`http://`), FTP (`ftp://`), and so on. A pseudo-protocol is a nonstandard take on this idea. The `javascript:` pseudo-protocol is supposed to be used to invoke JavaScript from within a link.

Here's how the `javascript:` pseudo-protocol would be used to call the `popUp` function:

```
<a href="javascript:popUp('http://www.example.com/');">Example</a>
```

This will work just fine in browsers that understand the `javascript:` pseudo-protocol. Older browsers, however, will attempt to follow the link and fail. Even in browsers that understand the pseudo-protocol, the link becomes useless if JavaScript has been disabled.

In short, using the `javascript:` pseudo-protocol is usually a very bad way of referencing JavaScript from within your markup.

Inline event handlers

You've already seen event handlers in action with the image gallery script in the previous chapter. The image-swapping function was invoked from within an `<a>` tag by adding the `onclick` event handler as an attribute of the same tag.

The same technique will work for the `popUp` function. If you use an `onclick` event handler from within a link to spawn a new window, then the `href` attribute might seem irrelevant. After all, the important information about where the link leads is now contained in the `onclick` attribute. That's why you'll often see links like this:

```
<a href="#" onclick="popUp('http://www.example.com/');
➥ return false;">Example<a>
```

The `return false` has been included so that the link isn't actually followed. The `"#"` symbol is used for internal links within documents. (In this case, it's an internal link to nowhere.) In some browsers, this will simply lead to the top of the current document. Using a value of `"#"` for the `href` attribute is an attempt to create a blank link. The real work is done by the `onclick` attribute.

This technique is just as bad as using the `javascript:` pseudo-protocol. It doesn't degrade gracefully. If JavaScript is disabled, the link is useless.

Who cares?

You might be wondering about this theoretical situation of users using a browser without JavaScript enabled. Is it really worth making sure that your site works for this kind of user?

Imagine a visitor to your website who browses the Web with both images and JavaScript disabled. You might think that this visitor is very much in the minority, and you would be right. But this visitor is important.

The visitor that you've just imagined is a *searchbot*. A searchbot is an automated program that spiders the web in order to add pages to a search engine's index. All the major search engines have programs like this. Right now, very few searchbots understand JavaScript. So, if your JavaScript does not degrade gracefully, your search engine rankings might be seriously damaged.

In the case of the popUp function, it's relatively easy to ensure that the JavaScript degrades gracefully. As long as there is a real URL in the href attribute, the link can be followed.

```
<a href="http://www.example.com/"
➥ onclick="popUp('http://www.example.com'; return false;">Example</a>
```

That's quite long-winded bit of code because the URL appears twice. Fortunately, there's a shortcut that can be used within the JavaScript. The word this can be used to refer to the current element. Using a combination of this and getAttribute, you can extract the value of the href attribute:

```
<a href="http://www.example.com/"
➥ onclick="popUp(this.getAttribute('href'); return false;">Example</a>
```

Actually, that doesn't save all that much space. There's an even shorter way of referencing the href of the current link by using the standardized DOM property, this.href:

```
<a href="http://www.example.com/"
➥ onclick="popUp(this.href; return false;">Example</a>
```

In either case, the important point is that the value of the href attribute is now a valid one. This is far better than using either href="javascript:..." or href="#".

So you see, if JavaScript isn't enabled (or if the visitor is a searchbot), the link can still be followed if you've used a real URL in the href attribute. The functionality is reduced (because the link doesn't open in a new window), but it doesn't fail completely. This is a classic example of graceful degradation.

This technique is certainly the best one covered so far, but it is not without its problems. The most obvious problem is the need to insert JavaScript into the markup whenever you want to open a window. It would be far better if all the JavaScript, including the event handlers, were contained in an external file.

The lessons of CSS

Earlier, I referred to both JavaScript and Flash as examples of technologies that were often implemented badly in the wild, anarchic days when they were first unleashed. We can learn a lot from the mistakes of the past.

There are other technologies that were implemented in a thoughtful, considered manner right from their inception. We can learn even more from these.

Separation of structure and style

CSS is a wonderful technology. Style sheets allow for great control over every aspect of a site's design. Ostensibly, there's nothing new about this. It has always been possible to dictate a design using <table>

and `<font>` tags. The great advantage of CSS is that you can separate the structure of a web document (the markup) from the design (the styles).

It's entirely possible to use CSS in an inefficient manner. You could just add `style` attributes in almost every element of your web document, for example. But the real benefits of CSS become apparent when all your styles are contained in external files.

CSS arrived on the scene much later than Flash and JavaScript. Web designers were able to learn from their experience with Flash and JavaScript, and immediately use CSS in a thoughtful, constructive way from day one.

The separation of structure and style makes life easier for everyone. If your job is writing content, you no longer need to worry about messing up the design. Instead of swimming through a tag soup of `<table>` and `<font>` tags, you can now concentrate on marking up your content correctly. If your job is creating the design for a site, you can now concentrate on controlling colors, fonts, and positioning using external style sheets, without touching the content. At most, you'll need to add the occasional `class` or `id` attribute.

A great advantage of this separation of structure and style is that it guarantees graceful degradation. Browsers that are capable of interpreting CSS will display the web pages in all their styled glory. Older browsers, or browsers with CSS disabled, will still be able to view the content of the pages in a correctly structured way.

When it comes to applying JavaScript, we can learn a lot from CSS.

Progressive enhancement

"Content is king" is an oft-used adage in web design. It's true. Without any content, there's little point in trying to create a website.

That said, you can't simply put your content online without first describing what it is. The content needs to be wrapped up in a markup language like HTML or XHTML. Marking up content correctly is the first and perhaps the most important step in creating a website. A revised version of the web design adage might be "well-marked-up content is king."

When a markup language is used correctly, it describes the content semantically. The markup provides information such as "this is an item in a list" or "this is a paragraph." They are all pieces of content, but tags like `<li>` and `<p>` distinguish them.

Once the content has been marked up, you can dictate how the content should look by using CSS. The instructions in the CSS form a presentation layer. This layer can then be draped over the structure of the markup. If the presentation layer is removed, the content is still accessible (although now it's a king with no clothes).

Applying layers of extra information like this is called *progressive enhancement*. Web pages that are built using progressive enhancement will almost certainly degrade gracefully.

Like CSS, all the functionality provided by JavaScript and the DOM should be treated as an extra layer of instructions. Where CSS contains information about presentation, JavaScript code contains information about behavior. Ideally, this behavior layer should be applied in the same way as the presentation layer.

CSS style sheets work best when they are contained in external files, separate from the markup. It's entirely possible to use CSS in an inefficient manner and mix styles in with the markup, like this:

```
<p style="font-weight: bold; color: red;">
Be careful!
</p>
```

It makes more sense to keep the style information in an external file that can be called via a `<link>` tag in the head of the document:

```
.warning {
  font-weight: bold;
```

```
  color: red;
}
```

The class attribute can then be used as a hook to tie the style to the markup:

```
<p class="warning">
Be careful!
</p>
```

This is far more readable. It's also a lot easier to change the styles. Imagine you have 100 documents with the warning class peppered throughout. Now suppose you want to change how warnings are displayed. Maybe you prefer them to be blue instead of red. As long as your presentation is separated from your structure, you can change the style easily:

```
.warning {
  font-weight: bold;
  color: blue;
}
```

If your style declarations were intermingled with your markup, you would need to do a lot of searching and replacing.

It's clear that style sheets work best when they are unobtrusive. What works for the presentation layer will also work for the behavior layer.

Unobtrusive JavaScript

The JavaScript you've seen so far has already been separated from the markup to a certain degree. The functions that do all the work are contained in external files. The problem lies with inline event handlers.

Using an attribute like onclick in the markup is just as inefficient as using the style attribute. It would be much better if we could use a hook, like class or id, to tether the behavior to the markup without intermingling it. This is how the markup could indicate that a link should have the popUp function performed when it is clicked:

```
<a href="http://www.example.com/" class="popup">Example</a>
```

Fortunately, this is entirely possible. Events don't need to be handled in the markup. You can attach an event to an element in an external JavaScript file:

```
element.event = action...
```

The tricky part is figuring out which elements should have the event attached. That's where hooks like class and id come in handy.

If you want to attach an event to an element with a unique ID, you can simply use getElementById:

```
getElementById(id).event = action
```

With multiple elements, you can use a combination of getElementsByTagName and getAttribute to attach events to elements with specific attributes.

Here's the plan in plain English:

- Make an array of all the links in the document.

- Loop through this array.

- If a link has the class "popup", execute this behavior when the link is clicked:

  - Pass the value of the link's href attribute to the popUp function.

- Cancel the default behavior so that the link isn't followed in the original window.

This is how it looks in JavaScript:

```
var links = document.getElementsByTagName("a");
for (var i=0; i<links.length; i++) {
  if (links[i].getAttribute("class") == "popup") {
    links[i].onclick = function() {
      popUp(this.getAttribute("href"));
      return false;
    }
  }
}
```

Now the connection between the links and the behavior that should occur when the links are clicked has been moved out of the markup and into the external JavaScript. This is unobtrusive JavaScript.

There's just one problem. If you put that code in your external JavaScript file, it won't work. The first line reads:

```
var links = document.getElementsByTagName("a");
```

This code will be executed as soon as the JavaScript file loads. If the JavaScript file is called from a `<script>` tag in the `<head>` of your document, the JavaScript file will load before the document. Likewise, if the `<script>` tag is at the bottom of the document before the `</body>` there's still no guarantee which files will finish loading first (the browser may download more than one at a time). Because the document may be incomplete when the script loads, the model of the document is also incomplete, and methods like `getElementsByTagName` simply won't work.

You need to execute the code once you're sure the document has finished loading. Fortunately, the complete loading of a document is an event with a corresponding event handler.

The document loads within the browser window. The document object is a property of the `window` object. When the `onload` event is triggered by the `window` object, the document object then exists.

Let's wrap up the JavaScript inside a function called `prepareLinks`, and attach this function to the `onload` event of the `window` object. This way, you know that the DOM will be ready and working.

```
window.onload = prepareLinks;
function prepareLinks() {
  var links = document.getElementsByTagName("a");
  for (var i=0; i<links.length; i++) {
    if (links[i].getAttribute("class") == "popup") {
      links[i].onclick = function() {
        popUp(this.getAttribute("href"));
        return false;
      }
    }
  }
}
```

Don't forget to include the `popUp` function as well:

```
function popUp(winURL) {
  window.open(winURL,"popup","width=320,height=480");
}
```

This is a very simple example, but it demonstrates how behavior can be successfully separated from structure. In Chapter 6, you'll see more elegant ways to attach events when the document loads.

Backward compatibility

Along with considering that visitors to your website might not have JavaScript enabled, you also need to be aware that there are degrees of JavaScript support. Most browsers support JavaScript to some degree, and modern browsers have excellent support for the DOM. Very old browsers, however, might not be able to understand DOM methods and properties. So even if a user visits your site with a browser that supports some JavaScript, some of your scripts may not work.

Object detection

The simplest solution to this problem is to quiz the browser on its level of JavaScript support. This is a bit like those signs at amusement parks that read, "You must be this tall to ride." The DOM scripting equivalent would be, "You must understand this much JavaScript to execute these statements."

This is quite easy to accomplish. If you wrap a method in an `if` statement, the statement will evaluate to either true or false, depending on whether the method exists. This is called *object detection*. As you saw in Chapter 2, methods are objects, just like almost everything else in JavaScript. This makes it quite easy to exclude browsers that don't support a specific DOM method.

```
if (method) {
statements
}
```

If you have a function that uses `getElementById`, you can test whether that method is supported before attempting to use it. When using object detection, it's important to leave off the usual parenthesis at the end of the method. If the parenthesis were present, you would be testing the result of the method, not whether or not the method itself exists.

```
function myFunction() {
  if (document.getElementById) {
    statements using getElementById
  }
}
```

If a browser doesn't understand `getElementById`, it will never even get to the statements using that method.

The only disadvantage in the way this function is written is that it adds another set of curly braces. If you do that every time you want to test for a particular method or property, then you'll end up with the most important statements being wrapped in layers and layers of curly braces. That won't be much fun to read.

It would be much more convenient to say, "If you don't understand this method, leave now."

To turn "if you do understand" into "if you don't understand," all that's needed is the NOT operator, represented by an exclamation point:

```
if (!method)
```

You can use `return` to achieve the "leave now" part. Seeing as the function is ending prematurely, it makes sense that the Boolean value being returned is false. This is how it would look in a test for `getElementById`:

```
if (!getElementById) {
  return false;
}
```

Because just one statement needs to be executed (`return false`), you can shorten the test even further by putting it on one line:

```
if (!getElementById) return false;
```

If you need to test for the existence of more than one method or property, you can join them together using the OR logical operator, represented by two vertical pipe symbols:

```
if (!getElementById || !getElementsByTagName) return false;
```

If this were a sign in an amusement park, it would read, "If you don't understand getElementById or getElementsByTagName, you can't ride."

You can put this into practice with your page-load script that attaches the onclick event to certain links. It uses getElementsByTagName, so you want to be sure that the browser understands that method.

```
window.onload = function() {
  if (!document.getElementsByTagName) return false;
  var lnks = document.getElementsByTagName("a");
  for (var i=0; i<lnks.length; i++) {
    if (lnks[i].getAttribute("class") == "popup") {
      lnks[i].onclick = function() {
        popUp(this.getAttribute("href"));
        return false;
      }
    }
  }
}
```

By just adding this one line, you can be sure that older browsers won't choke on your code. This is ensuring backward compatibility. Because you've used progressive enhancement to add behavior to your web page, you can be sure that the functionality will degrade gracefully in older browsers. Browsers that understand some JavaScript, but not the DOM, can still access your content.

Browser sniffing

Testing for the existence of a specific property or method that you're about to use in your code is the safest and surest way of ensuring backward compatibility. There is another technique that was very popular during the dark days of the browser wars.

Browser sniffing involves extracting information provided by the browser vendor. In theory, browsers supply information (readable by JavaScript) about their make and model. You can attempt to achieve backward compatibility by parsing this information, but it's a very risky technique.

For one thing, browsers sometimes lie. For historical reasons, some browsers report themselves as being a different user agent. Other browsers allow the user to change this information at will.

As the number of different browsers being used increases, browser-sniffing scripts become more and more complex. They need to test for all possible combinations of vendor and version number in order to ensure that they work cross-platform. This is a Sisyphean task that can result in extremely convoluted and messy code.

Many browser-sniffing scripts test for an exact match on a browser's version number. If a new version is released, these scripts will need to be updated.

Thankfully, the practice of browser sniffing is being replaced with the simpler and more robust technique of object detection.

Performance considerations

One thing that many new DOM scripters overlook is the impact scripts have on the overall performance of a web application. To keep things running along smoothly, there are a number of things you should consider when both writing and applying scripts to your document.

Minimizing DOM access and markup

The way you choose to manipulate the DOM can have a big impact on the overall performance of your script. Consider the following bit of code:

```
if (document.getElementsByTagName("a").length > 0) {
  var links = document.getElementsByTagName("a");
  for (var i=0; i<links.length; i++) {
    // do something to each link.
  }
}
```

The problem here is quite obvious if you think about what the code is doing. First, it retrieves all the <a> elements and checks to see if there are more than 0:

```
if (document.getElementsByTagName("a").length > 0) {
```

Then if there are more than 0, it retrieves all the <a> elements *again* and loops through them applying some sort of logic:

```
var links = document.getElementsByTagName("a");
for (var i=0; i<links.length; i++) {
```

The example works as expected, but it's not very well optimized. Whenever you query the DOM to find elements, the browser must search the entire DOM tree for any matching elements. This poorly coded example uses the getElementsByTagName method twice to do the same thing, doubling the work necessary. A better solution would be to assign the original result to a variable and reuse the same result in the loop, like this:

```
var links = document.getElementsByTagName("a");
if (links.length > 0) {
  for (var i=0; i<links.length; i++) {
    // do something to each link.
  }
}
```

Now the code achieves the same result but searches the DOM tree only once instead of twice.

The problem in the previous example was easy to spot. Often, these types of problems are hidden when you have multiple different functions that do similar things. If you have a function that checks for a popup class on each link and another to check for a hover class on each link, then you have the same problem. When multiple functions require you to retrieve a similar set of elements, consider refactoring to use a common global variable or pass a list of elements into the function as an argument.

Another consideration, where possible, is to minimize the markup in your document. Dozens of unnecessary elements will only increase the size of the DOM tree and the time required to traverse it looking for the appropriate elements.

Assembling and placing scripts

Most of the examples in the book use external script files that are included in the document using the <script> element, similar to this:

<script rc="script/function.js"></script>

Using external files is the best solution for including JavaScript because it's unobtrusive, it's cleanly separated from the markup, and it allows the browser to reuse the same cached script on multiple pages of your site. Ideally, however, you *don't* want to do something like this:

```
<script src="script/functionA.js"></script>
<script src="script/functionB.js"></script>
<script src="script/functionC.js"></script>
<script src="script/functionD.js"></script>
```

A much better solution would be to combine functionA.js, functionB.js, functionC.js, and functionD.js into a single file. Reducing the number of requests required to load a page is probably the number one thing you can do to improve the overall load time of your website.

The placement of your scripts in the markup also plays a big part in initial load times. Traditionally, we were told to always place scripts in the <head> portion of the document, but there's a problem with that. Scripts in the <head> block the browser's ability to download additional files (such as images or other scripts) in parallel. In general, the HTTP specification suggests that browsers download no more than two items at the same time per hostname. While a script is downloading, however, the browser won't start *any* other downloads, even on different hostnames, so everything must wait until the script has finished.

If you're following the progressive enhancement and unobtrusive methodologies discussed earlier in the chapter, then moving your <script> tags shouldn't be an issue. You can make your pages load faster simply by including all your <script> tags at the end of the document, directly before the </body> tag. When the scripts load, your window load events will still apply your changes to the document.

Minification

Once you have your scripts written, optimized, and placed accordingly in your document, there's one last thing you can do to speed things up: minification.

Minification refers to the process of taking your script and "compressing" it by removing the unnecessary bits such as whitespace and comments. Thankfully, there are tools to do this for you. Some minimizers will even rewrite portions of your code to use shorter variable names. This reduces the overall file size.

For example, suppose you have some code that looks like this:

```
function showPic(whichpic) {
  // Grab the pics href attribute.
  var source = whichpic.getAttribute("href");
  // Get the placeholder.
  var placeholder = document.getElementById("placeholder");
  // Update the placeholder source.
  placeholder.setAttribute("src",source);
  // Update the text description using the image's title attribute.
  var text = whichpic.getAttribute("title");
  var description = document.getElementById("description");
}
```

The minified version would look like this:

```
function showPic(a){var b=a.getAttribute("href");document.get
➥ElementById("placeholder").setAttribute("src",b);a.getAttribute
➥ ("title");document.getElementById("description")};
```

Minified code isn't pretty or human-readable, but it can make a big difference in file size. In most cases, you'll need to keep two copies: a working copy, in which you can make changes and comments, and the minified copy, which you serve up on your site. As a standard convention, a good idea it to include min in the file name of minified files to distinguish them from their nonminified counterparts:

```
<script src="scripts/scriptName.min.js"></script>
```

A number of different tools are available to do minification, including the following:

- Douglas Crockford's JSMin (http://www.crockford.com/javascript/jsmin.html)

- Yahoo!'s YUI Compressor (http://developer.yahoo.com/yui/compressor/)

- Google's Closure Compiler (http://closure-compiler.appspot.com/home)

Each has additional features that you can take advantage of for even more minification if required.

What's next?

This chapter introduced some important concepts and practices that should be at the heart of any DOM scripting you do:

- Graceful degradation

- Unobtrusive JavaScript

- Backward compatibility

- Performance considerations

You've seen how we can learn from other technologies like Flash and CSS to ensure that JavaScript is used wisely. A cautious, questioning attitude certainly seems to be a desirable trait when you're writing scripts.

CHAPTER 6

■ ■ ■

The Image Gallery Revisited

What this chapter covers:

- Removing inline event handlers
- Building in backward compatibility
- Ensuring accessibility

In Chapter 4, we made a JavaScript image gallery. In Chapter 5, we talked about good coding practices. In this chapter, I'm going to apply those practices to the image gallery.

"Question everything" is a good ethos for conspiracy theorists and web designers alike. Whether it's CSS, JavaScript, or visual design, a good web designer will always ask, "Is there a better way of doing this?"

As you saw in the last chapter, the questions relating to DOM scripting are all about graceful degradation, backward compatibility, and unobtrusive JavaScript. The answers to these questions can affect the usability and accessibility of your web pages.

A quick recap

In Chapter 4, I put together a script for switching out the src attribute of an image, effectively making a single-page image gallery. Here's the finished function:

```
function showPic(whichpic) {
  var source = whichpic.getAttribute("href");
  var placeholder = document.getElementById("placeholder");
  placeholder.setAttribute("src",source);
  var text = whichpic.getAttribute("title");
  var description = document.getElementById("description");
  description.firstChild.nodeValue = text;
}
```

Here's the relevant part of the HTML file that calls the function:

```
<ul>
<li>
    <a href="images/fireworks.jpg" onclick="showPic(this);return false; " title="A
➥ fireworks display">Fireworks</a>
  </li>
  <li>
    <a href="images/coffee.jpg" onclick="showPic(this); return false; "title="A cup of
➥ black coffee">Coffee</a>
  </li>
```

- Check whether this browser understands getElementsByTagName.

- Check whether this browser understands getElementById.

- Check whether an element with the ID imagegallery exists.

- Loop through all the links in the imagegallery element.

- Set the onclick event so that when the link is clicked, the following steps occur:

  - The link is passed to the showPic function.

  - The default behavior is cancelled so that the link isn't followed.

I'll begin by defining the prepareGallery function. The function won't be taking any arguments, so there won't be anything between the parentheses after the function name:

```
function prepareGallery() {
```

Checkpoints

The first thing I want to do is to find out if the browser can understand the DOM method getElementsByTagName. I'll be using this method in the function, and I want to be sure that older browsers won't execute the function if they don't understand the method:

```
if (!document.getElementsByTagName) return false;
```

This is saying, "If getElementsByTagName isn't defined, leave now." Browsers that understand that particular DOM method will continue on.

Now I'm going to do the same thing for getElementById, which will also be used by the function:

```
if (!document.getElementById) return false;
```

I could combine the two checks into one: "If either method isn't understood, go no further":

```
if (!document.getElementsByTagName || !document.getElementById)return false;
```

or

```
var supported = document.getElementsByTagName && document.getElementById;
if ( !supported ) return;
```

But that begins to look a bit unwieldy and is perhaps less readable. In fact, putting these tests on single lines isn't necessarily the best idea from a readability point of view. You might prefer to put the return statement on its own line:

```
if (!document.getElementsByTagName)
  return false;
if (!document.getElementById)
  return false;
```

In that case, I recommend enclosing the return statements within curly braces:

```
if (!document.getElementsByTagName) {
  return false;
}
if (!document.getElementById) {
  return false;
}
```

This is perhaps the clearest, most readable solution.

Whether you do these tests on single or multiple lines is entirely up to you. Use whichever one you find easiest to follow.

Once these general tests have been passed, there's a more specific test. This function is going to deal with links inside an element identified as imagegallery. If this element can't be found, then the script should go no further.

Once again, I'm going to use the NOT operator for this test:

```
if (!document.getElementById("imagegallery")) return false;
```

Or, if your prefer:

```
if (!document.getElementById("imagegallery")) {
  return false;
}
```

This is a safety check. Right now, I know that there is an "imagegallery" list in the document that's calling the JavaScript file. But that could change in the future. If, for some reason, I decided to remove the image gallery from the page, I can rest assured that related JavaScript errors won't suddenly occur. It all comes back to the importance of the separation of content from behavior. If I add behavior to a page using JavaScript, that JavaScript shouldn't make assumptions about the structure of the page.

A SHORT NOTE ABOUT STRUCTURED PROGRAMMING

There is a school of thought known as structured programming. One of its doctrines states that functions should have a single point of entry and a single exit point.

I am violating this principle by having multiple return false statements at the beginning of my function. These are all exit points. According to a principle of structured programming, there should only ever be one exit point.

In theory, I agree with this principle. In practice, it could make code very difficult to read. If I rewrote my safety checks to avoid multiple exit points, the main point of my function would be buried quite deep in a sea of curly braces:

```
function prepareGallery() {
  if (document.getElementsByTagName) {
    if (document.getElementById) {
      if (document.getElementById("imagegallery")) {
        statements go here...
      }
    }
  }
}
```

I think it is acceptable to have multiple exit points as long as they occur early on in the function.

For the sake of readability, I'm going to keep the return false statements at the start of the prepareGallery function:

```
function prepareGallery() {
  if (!document.getElementsByTagName) return false;
  if (!document.getElementById) return false;
```

```
if (!document.getElementById("imagegallery")) return false;
```

Now that all the tests and checks have been passed, I'm going to move on to the event handler's functionality.

What's in a name?

First of all, I'm going to make things a little easier for myself. Instead of writing out `document.getElementById("imagegallery")` all the time, it's going to make life a lot simpler if I just use a variable name like `gallery`:

```
var gallery = document.getElementById("imagegallery");
```

I could have chosen anything for the variable name, but `gallery` has some meaning. It's a lot easier to read code that uses recognizable words for variable names.

■ **Caution** Be careful when you're choosing your variable names. There are some words that are reserved by JavaScript. You can't give a variable the same name as a JavaScript function or method. Avoid using words like `alert`, `var`, and `if`.

I want to loop through all the links in the `imagegallery` element. I'll be using `getElementsByTagName` to do this. Because I now have the variable `gallery` at my disposal, I can simply write this:

```
gallery.getElementsByTagName("a")
```

instead of the more long-winded version:

```
document.getElementById("imagegallery").getElementsByTagName("a")
```

Once again, I'm going to make life a little easier for myself. I'm going to assign this node list to a nice short variable. I'll use the word `links`:

```
var links = gallery.getElementsByTagName("a");
```

This is what the `prepareGallery` function looks like so far:

```
function prepareGallery() {
  if (!document.getElementsByTagName) return false;
  if (!document.getElementById) return false;
  if (!document.getElementById("imagegallery")) return false;
  var gallery = document.getElementById("imagegallery");
  var links = gallery.getElementsByTagName("a");
```

Everything is set up now. I have put safety checks in place, and I have assigned variables.

Looping the loop

I want to loop through all the individual elements in the `links` set. I'm going to use a `for` loop to do this.

I'll begin by setting a counter to zero. The loop will be executed for each element in `links`, and the counter will be incremented by one. Here's the initialization of the counter:

```
var i = 0;
```

I've chosen the name i purely for traditional reasons. Using the name i for incrementing variables is a programming convention in many languages.

The test condition comes next:

```
i < links.length;
```

The loop will be executed as long as the value of i is less than the length property of the links array. The length property contains the total number of elements in an array. So if links contains four elements, then the loop will be executed as long as i is less than four.

Finally, the counter is incremented by one:

```
i++;
```

This is a shorthand way of saying:

```
i = i+1;
```

The value of i is increased by one every time the loop is executed. As soon as its value is no longer less than links.length, the loop will finish. If links contains four elements, the loop will stop once the value of i equals four. The loop will have run four times. Remember that i began with a value of zero.

Here's how the for loop opens:

```
for ( var i=0; i < links.length; i++) {
```

Changing behavior

I want to change the behavior of each element in the links array. Actually, it would be more correct to refer to links as a *node list* rather than an array. It is a set of nodes. Each node in the set has its own properties and methods.

I'm interested in the onclick method. This is how I attach a behavior for that method:

```
links[i].onclick = function() {
```

This is called an *anonymous function*. It is a way of creating a function while the code is executing. In this case, the function is created when the onclick event handler is triggered. Whatever statements I put in next will be executed when the link is clicked.

The value of links[i] will change as the value of i increases. It begins as links[0] and, if there are four elements in the links set, it will finish as links[3].

The value I'm going to pass to the showPic function is the this keyword. It refers to the element that is currently having the onclick method attached to it. So this refers to links[i], which in turn refers to a specific node in the links node list:

```
showPic(this);
```

There's one more thing I need to do. I need to cancel the default behavior. If the showPic function is successfully executed, I don't want the browser to carry out the default action for clicking on a link. Just as before, I want to cancel this default action so that the link isn't followed:

```
return false;
```

Returning the Boolean value false sends a message back to the browser saying, "Act as if this link wasn't clicked."

I just need to close up this function-within-a-function by adding a closing curly brace. This is how it looks:

```
links[i].onclick = function() {
```

```
  showPic(this);
  return false;
}
```

Closing it up

Now I need to finish the for loop by adding the closing curly brace:

```
for ( var i=0; i < links.length; i++) {
  links[i].onclick = function() {
    showPic(this);
    return false;
  }
}
```

All that remains for me to do is to close the function with one more curly brace.
This is what the final prepareGallery function looks like:

```
function prepareGallery() {
  if (!document.getElementsByTagName) return false;
  if (!document.getElementById) return false;
  if (!document.getElementById("imagegallery")) return false;
  var gallery = document.getElementById("imagegallery");
  var links = gallery.getElementsByTagName("a");
  for ( var i=0; i < links.length; i++) {
    links[i].onclick = function() {
      showPic(this);
      return false;
    }
  }
}
```

When this function is called, the onclick events will be attached to the links in the element
identified as "imagegallery".

■ **Note** For more on the ins-and-outs of JavaScript you may also want to read my AdvancED DOM Scripting:
Dynamic Web Design Techniques, cowritten with Aaron Gustafson (Apress, 2007).

Share the load

I need to execute the prepareGallery function in order to attach the onclick events.

If I simply execute the function right away, it won't work. If the JavaScript is executed before the
document has finished loading, the Document Object Model will be incomplete. By the third line of the
function (the test for the existence of imagegallery), things won't go according to plan.

I want to execute the function only when the page has finished loading. When the page loads, an
event is triggered. This event is onload and it is attached to the window object. If I attach the
prepareGallery function to this event, then everything will go smoothly:

```
window.onload = prepareGallery;
```

That's quite straightforward, but it is also potentially a little shortsighted.

Suppose I have two functions: firstFunction and secondFunction. What if I want to execute both of them when the page loads? If I attach them, one after the other, to the onload event, only the last specified function will actually be executed:

```
window.onload = firstFunction;
window.onload = secondFunction;
```

secondFunction will replace firstFunction. On the face of it, you would think that an event handler can hold only one instruction.

But here's a workaround: I could create an anonymous function to hold the other two and then execute that third function when the page loads:

```
window.onload = function() {
  firstFunction();
  secondFunction();
}
```

This works fine, and it's the simplest solution when you have a small number of functions.

There's another solution that scales very nicely, no matter how many functions you want to execute when the page loads. It takes a few more lines to set it up initially but, once it's in place, attaching functions to window.onload is an easy task.

This function is called addLoadEvent, and it was written by Simon Willison (http://simon.incutio.com/). It takes a single argument: the name of the function that you want to execute when the page loads.

Here's what addLoadEvent does:

- It stores the existing window.onload as a variable called oldonload.

- If this hasn't yet had a function attached to it, addLoadEvent simply adds the new function in the usual way.

- If there is already a function attached, addLoadEvent adds the new function after the existing instructions.

The function looks like this:

```
function addLoadEvent(func) {
  var oldonload = window.onload;
  if (typeof window.onload != 'function') {
    window.onload = func;
  } else {
    window.onload = function() {
      oldonload();
      func();
    }
  }
}
```

This effectively creates a queue of functions to be executed when the page loads. To add functions to this queue, I just need to write

```
addLoadEvent(firstFunction);
addLoadEvent(secondFunction);
```

I've found this function to be enormously useful when my code starts to get complex. No matter how many individual functions I want to execute when the page loads, I just need to add a single line for each one.

For the prepareGallery function, this might be overkill. After all, only one function needs to be executed when the page loads. Still, it's good to plan for future expansion. If I include the addLoadEvent function, this is all I need to write:

```
addLoadEvent(prepareGallery);
```

At this stage, I think the prepareGallery function is as foolproof as I can make it. It's time for me to turn my questioning gaze on the original showPic function.

Assuming too much

One of the first things I notice when I look at the showPic function is that I'm not running any checks or tests.

The showPic function is being called from prepareGallery. That function has already tested for the existence of DOM methods like getElementById and getElementsByTagName, so I know that the browser won't choke on this code.

Still, I'm making a lot of assumptions. The code contains instructions for elements identified as placeholder and description, but it never checks to see if these elements actually exist:

```
function showPic(whichpic) {
  var source = whichpic.getAttribute("href");
  var placeholder = document.getElementById("placeholder");
  placeholder.setAttribute("src",source);
  var text = whichpic.getAttribute("title");
  var description = document.getElementById("description");
  description.firstChild.nodeValue = text;
}
```

I need to introduce some checks for these elements.

Two things are happening in this function. The image identified as placeholder is having its src attribute changed, and the element identified as description is having the nodeValue of its firstChild changed. The first action is the real task of the function. The second action is a nice added extra. For that reason, I'm going to run the checks separately. If the placeholder image exists but the description element doesn't, then I still want the image to be swapped out.

Just as with the prepareGallery function, it's a simple matter to check for the existence of an element:

```
if (!document.getElementById("placeholder")) return false;
```

I can then go on to do the image swapping:

```
var source = whichpic.getAttribute("href");
var placeholder = document.getElementById("placeholder");
placeholder.setAttribute("src",source);
```

The main task has been accomplished. At this point, I can take a slightly different approach and check for the existence of the "description" element:

```
if (document.getElementById("description")) {
```

Only then do I go on to change the text:

```
  var text = whichpic.getAttribute("title");
```

```
var description = document.getElementById("description");
description.firstChild.nodeValue = text;
}
```

By enclosing the description portion in an `if` statement, I've made the `description` element optional. If it exists, it will be updated but otherwise it will be ignored.

As the last step in the function, we'll return true to report that the function executed successfully:

```
return true;
```

This is how the updated function looks with the checks built in:

```
function showPic(whichpic) {
  if (!document.getElementById("placeholder")) return false;
  var source = whichpic.getAttribute("href");
  var placeholder = document.getElementById("placeholder");
  placeholder.setAttribute("src",source);
  if (document.getElementById("description")) {
    var text = whichpic.getAttribute("title");
    var description = document.getElementById("description");
    description.firstChild.nodeValue = text;
  }
  return true;
}
```

That's better. The script no longer assumes the existence of elements in the markup. If, for some reason, the `placeholder` image isn't in the document, there won't be any JavaScript errors.

But there's a problem. Remove the `placeholder` image from the markup and refresh the page in a browser. Click on any link in the imagegallery list. You'll see that nothing happens.

This means that the script isn't degrading gracefully. In this situation, it would be better to follow the link in the browser than have nothing happen at all.

The problem lies with the `prepareGallery` function. It makes the assumption that the `showPic` function will work fine, and it cancels the default action by always returning false:

```
links[i].onclick = function() {
  showPic(this);
  return false;
}
```

The decision to return a value of false (thereby canceling the default action of following the link in the browser) should really be determined by the result of the `showPic` function.

The `showPic` function returns two possible values:

- If the image is successfully swapped out, `showPic` will return true.

- If the function is unsuccessful, `showPic` will return false.

To fix this, we just need to verify the result of `showPic` before returning, preventing the default action. If `showPic` returns true then the `placeholder` image was updated. In the `onclick` event handler we can use `!` to return the inverse of the `showPic` function:

```
links[i].onclick = function() {
  return !showPic(this)
}
```

Now if `showPic` is successful and returns true, we return false and the link won't be followed by the browser.

If showPic returns false then we assume that the image wasn't updated and return true to allow the default action to occur.

The prepareGallery function now looks like this:

```
function prepareGallery() {
  if (!document.getElementsByTagName) return false;
  if (!document.getElementById) return false;
  if (!document.getElementById("imagegallery")) return false;
  var gallery = document.getElementById("imagegallery");
  var links = gallery.getElementsByTagName("a");
  for ( var i=0; i < links.length; i++) {
    links[i].onclick = function() {
      return !showPic(this);
    }
  }
}
```

That solves the problem with our test case. If the placeholder image doesn't exist, the browser simply follows the links to the images. You can go ahead and put the placeholder image back into the markup.

Fine-tuning

The functions are looking a lot better now. They may have grown in size, but they now assume much less about the markup.

I can still see some assumptions being made in the showPic function that I may need to tackle.

For instance, I am assuming that the link has a title attribute:

```
var text = whichpic.getAttribute("title");
```

To find out if there is a title attribute, I can test to see if it isn't equal to null:

```
if (whichpic.getAttribute("title") != null)
```

This if statement will evaluate to true if there is a title attribute. It will return a value of false if there is no title attribute, because the value of whichpic.getAttribute("title") will be equal to null.

I can save some space by simply writing

```
if (whichpic.getAttribue("title"))
```

The if statement will still return a value of true as long as there is a title attribute.

As a simple fallback, I could set the value of text to be empty if there is no title attribute:

```
if (whichpic.getAttribute("title")) {
  var text = whichpic.getAttribute("title");
} else {
  var text = "";
}
```

Here's another way of doing the same thing:

```
var text = whichpic.getAttribute("title") ? whichpic.getAttribute("title") : "";
```

The getAttribute test is followed by a question mark. This is called a *ternary operator*. Two possible values for the variable text are provided after the question mark. The first value will be assigned if `getAttribute("title")` returns a value. The second value will be returned if `getAttribute("title")` returns a value of null:

```
variable = condition ? if true : if false;
```

If a title attribute exists, the variable text will contain `whichpic.getAttribute("title")`. If there is no `title` attribute, the variable text will be an empty string, "".

A ternary operator is just another way of performing `if`/`else` statements. It's shorter, but if you find it confusing, you can always use the more verbose `if`/`else` statement.

Try removing the `title` attribute from one of the links in the `imagegallery` list. If you click on that link, the "`description`" element will be filled with an empty string.

If I wanted to be really thorough, I could introduce checks for just about everything.

For example, I'm checking for the existence of an element called `placeholder`, but I'm just assuming that it is an image. I could run a further check, using the `nodeName` property, to verify this:

```
if (placeholder.nodeName != "IMG") return false;
```

Notice that in HTML documents, `nodeName` always a returns an uppercase value, even if the element is lowercase in the markup.

There are further checks I could introduce. I'm assuming that the `firstChild` of the `description` element is a text node, but I should really check to make sure.

I can use the `nodeType` property for this test. If you recall, text nodes have a `nodeType` value of 3:

```
if (description.firstChild.nodeType == 3) {
  description.firstChild.nodeValue = text;
}
```

This is how the `showPic` function would look with these extra tests:

```
function showPic(whichpic) {
  if (!document.getElementById("placeholder")) return false;
  var source = whichpic.getAttribute("href");
  var placeholder = document.getElementById("placeholder");
  if (placeholder.nodeName != "IMG") return false;
  placeholder.setAttribute("src",source);
  if (document.getElementById("description")) {
    var text = whichpic.getAttribute("title") ? whichpic.getAttribute("title") : "";
    var description = document.getElementById("description");
    if (description.firstChild.nodeType == 3) {
      description.firstChild.nodeValue = text;
    }
  }
  return true;
}
```

The function is much more verbose when it's done in this way. In a real-world situation, you may decide that all these checks aren't necessary. They are intended to account for situations where the markup might be beyond your control. Ideally, your scripts shouldn't assume too much about the content and structure of the markup.

That said, these kinds of decisions need to be made on a case-by-case basis.

Keyboard access

There is one last piece of fine-tuning that often arises with any scripts that are attached to the onclick event handler.

Take a look at the heart of the prepareGallery function:

```
links[i].onclick = function() {
  if (showPic(this)) {
    return false;
  } else {
    return true;
  }
}
```

First, for brevity in the examples, let's change this to use the ternary operator instead:

```
links[i].onclick = function() {
  return showPic(this) ? false : true;
}
```

This works fine. When the link is clicked, the showPic function is executed. It looks like I'm assuming that the user will be clicking on the link with a mouse.

But remember, not everybody navigates using a mouse. People with visual disabilities, for example, aren't going to move a small icon around their screen. Instead, they are likely to navigate using a keyboard.

You don't need a mouse to browse the web. You can use the Tab key on your keyboard to move from link to link. Pressing the Return key will activate the currently selected link.

There is an event handler specifically for the action of pressing any key on the keyboard. It is called onkeypress.

If I want to execute the same behavior for onkeypress as onclick, I could simply duplicate the instructions:

```
links[i].onclick = function() {
  return showPic(this) ? false : true;
}
links[i].onkeypress = function() {
  return showPic(this) ? false : true;
}
```

There's an easier way to ensure that onkeypress imitates onclick, however:

```
links[i].onkeypress = links[i].onclick;
```

This assigns all the functionality from the onclick event to the onkeypress event as well:

```
links[i].onclick = function() {
  return showPic(this) ? false : true;
}
links[i].onkeypress = links[i].onclick;
```

That brings us right back to the benefits of unobtrusive JavaScript.

By keeping all your functions and event handlers in external files, you can change them without tinkering with the markup. You can always revisit your scripts and refine them, knowing that those refinements will automatically be applied to every web page that references the JavaScript file.

If I were still using inline event handlers, I would have needed to make a lot of changes to my markup as the JavaScript functionality changed. I used to have inline event handlers like this:

```
<li>
  <a href="images/fireworks.jpg" onclick="showPic(this);return false;"title="A
➡fireworks display">Fireworks</a>
</li>
```

When I changed the showPic function to return either true or false, I would have needed to update the event handlers accordingly:

```
<li>
  <a href="images/fireworks.jpg" onclick="return showPic(this) ? false : true;"
➡ title="A fireworks display">Fireworks</a>
</li>
```

If my image gallery were more than a few links long, this would have been quite tiresome.

Suppose I wanted to add the onkeypress event handler. I would have to go through all the links and add another inline event handler to each one:

```
<li>
  <a href="images/fireworks.jpg" onclick="return showPic(this) ? false : true;"
➡ onkeypress="return showPic(this) ? false : true;"
➡ title="A fireworks display">Fireworks</a>
</li>
```

That would have been a lot of drudgery. It's so much simpler to tweak and adjust a few lines of JavaScript in an external file.

Beware of onkeypress

As it turns out, I'm not going to add the onkeypress event handler at all. This event handler is quite problematic. It is triggered whenever a key is pressed. In some browsers, that includes the Tab key! That means that a user navigating with a keyboard can never tab past a link if a function associated with onkeypress returns false. That's exactly what's happening with the image gallery. The showPic function, if it is successful, returns false.

So where does that leave users navigating with a keyboard?

Fortunately, the onclick event handler turns out to be smarter than it sounds. With a name like onclick, it gives the impression of being tied to the action of clicking a button on a mouse. In fact, in nearly all browsers, the onclick event handler is also triggered if you press Return while tabbing from link to link. It would be more accurate if it were named something like onactivate.

There is a lot of confusion surrounding onclick and onkeypress, which is hardly surprising given the terminology. Some accessibility guidelines recommend using onkeypress whenever you use onclick. In reality, this could cause more harm than good.

Avoid using onkeypress. The onclick event handler is all that's needed. In spite of its name, onclick supports keyboard access perfectly well.

The finished functions look like this:

```
function prepareGallery() {
  if (!document.getElementsByTagName) return false;
  if (!document.getElementById) return false;
  if (!document.getElementById("imagegallery")) return false;
  var gallery = document.getElementById("imagegallery");
  var links = gallery.getElementsByTagName("a");
  for ( var i=0; i < links.length; i++) {
```

```
    links[i].onclick = function() {
      return showPic(this) ? false : true;
    }
  }
}
function showPic(whichpic) {
  if (!document.getElementById("placeholder")) return false;
  var source = whichpic.getAttribute("href");
  var placeholder = document.getElementById("placeholder");
  if (placeholder.nodeName != "IMG") return false;
  placeholder.setAttribute("src",source);
  if (document.getElementById("description")) {
    var text = whichpic.getAttribute("title") ? whichpic.getAttribute("title") : "";
    var description = document.getElementById("description");
    if (description.firstChild.nodeType == 3) {
      description.firstChild.nodeValue = text;
    }
  }
  return true;
}
```

■ **Note** You can download the completed functions from this book's page from the friends of ED website,
http://www.friendsofed.com/.

Sharing hooks with CSS

There's another benefit to unobtrusive JavaScript. Since removing the inline event handlers from my markup, I've added one hook for my JavaScript:

```
<ul id="imagegallery">
```

There's no reason why I can't also use that hook for my CSS.

For instance, I might not want the list to have bullet points. I can use the imagegallery identifier to specify this in the CSS:

```
#imagegallery {
  list-style: none;
}
```

I can put this CSS in an external file, say layout.css, and reference it from the <head> of my gallery.html file:

```
<link rel="stylesheet" href="styles/layout.css" type="text/css" media="screen" />
```

Using CSS, I can even make the list run horizontally instead of vertically:

```
#imagegallery li {
  display: inline;
}
```

Here's what my page looks like now:

This also works if I decide to use thumbnail images instead of text for my links:

```
<ul id="imagegallery">
  <li>
    <a href="images/fireworks.jpg" title="A fireworks display">
      <img src="images/thumbnail_fireworks.jpg" alt="Fireworks" />
    </a>
  </li>
  <li>
    <a href="images/coffee.jpg" title="A cup of black coffee" >
      <img src="images/thumbnail_coffee.jpg" alt="Coffee" />
    </a>
  </li>
  <li>
    <a href="images/rose.jpg" title="A red, red rose">
      <img src="images/thumbnail_rose.jpg" alt="Rose" />
    </a>
  </li>
  <li>
    <a href="images/bigben.jpg" title="The famous clock">
      <img src="images/thumbnail_bigben.jpg" alt="Big Ben" />
    </a>
  </li>
</ul>
```

Here's my web page with thumbnails rather than text:

The complete layout.css file looks like this:

```css
body {
  font-family: "Helvetica","Arial",serif;
  color: #333;
  background-color: #ccc;
  margin: 1em 10%;
}
h1 {
  color: #333;
  background-color: transparent;
}
a {
  color: #c60;
  background-color: transparent;
  font-weight: bold;
  text-decoration: none;
}
ul {
  padding: 0;
}
li {
  float: left;
  padding: 1em;
  list-style: none;
}
#imagegallery {
  list-style: none;
}
```

```
#imagegallery li {
  display: inline;
}
#imagegallery li a img {
  border: 0;
}
```

Applying that style sheet will give the image gallery a nice sheen:

DOM Core and HTML-DOM

So far, I've been using a small set of methods to accomplish everything I want to do, including

- getElementById

- getElementsByTagName

- getAttribute

- setAttribute

These methods are all part of the *DOM Core*. They aren't specific to JavaScript, and they can be used by any programming language with DOM support. They aren't just for web pages, either. These methods can be used on documents written in any markup language (XML, for instance).

When you are using JavaScript and the DOM with HTML files, you have many more properties at your disposal. For example, I've actually used one of these properties, onclick, for event management in the image gallery. These properties belong to the *HTML-DOM*, which has been around longer than the DOM Core.

For instance, the HTML-DOM provides a forms object. That means that instead of writing

```
document.getElementsByTagName("form")
```

you can use

```
document.forms
```

Similarly, the HTML-DOM provides properties to represent attributes of elements. Images, for instance, have a `src` property. Instead of writing

```
element.getAttribute("src")
```

you can write

```
element.src
```

These methods and properties are interchangeable. It doesn't really matter whether you decide to use the DOM Core exclusively or use the HTML-DOM. As you can see, the HTML-DOM is generally shorter. However, it's worth remembering that it is specific to web documents, so you'll need to bear that in mind if you ever find yourself using the DOM with other kinds of documents.

If I were to use the HTML-DOM, I could shorten a few lines from the `showPic` function.

This line uses the DOM Core to retrieve the `href` attribute of the `whichpic` element and assign its value to the variable `source`:

```
var source = whichpic.getAttribute("href");
```

Here's the same thing using HTML-DOM:

```
var source = whichpic.href;
```

Here's another example of the DOM Core. This time, the `src` attribute of the `placeholder` element is being set to the value of the variable `source`:

```
placeholder.setAttribute("src",source);
```

Here it is using HTML-DOM:

```
placeholder.src = source;
```

Even if you decide to use DOM Core methods exclusively, you should still be aware of the HTML-DOM. You're bound to come across these shorthand methods when you're looking at the source code for other people's scripts. It's good to at least be able to recognize them.

For the most part, I'm going to stick to using DOM Core. I find it easier to use a small arsenal of DOM methods, even if that means slightly more verbose code. However, you don't have to do the same. Wherever possible, I'll point out where you can use HTML-DOM to shorten your code.

What's next?

In this chapter I've made plenty of tweaks to the image gallery. The markup is now tidier. I've introduced some basic CSS. Most of all, I've improved the JavaScript. Here are some of the main things I accomplished:

Wherever possible, I've tried to avoid making unwarranted assumptions in my code. I've introduced lots of tests and checks. The JavaScript is more likely to degrade gracefully in unforeseen situations.

- I've ensured the accessibility of the JavaScript by avoiding the `onkeypress` event handler.

- Perhaps most importantly of all, I've moved the event handling from the markup to the JavaScript. This is unobtrusive JavaScript.

Here's my final product after all of the tweaks I've made through this chapter:

And my mantra: the more separation there is between structure and behavior, the better.

Something about the markup of the image gallery is still bothering me. I have two elements, `placeholder` and `description`, that exist solely for the `showPic` function to use. For visitors without JavaScript, these elements are, at best, meaningless. At worst, they could be downright confusing.

Ideally, these elements should only appear in the document if the visitor has a DOM-capable browser. In the next chapter, I'm going to show how you can use the DOM to create elements and insert them into your markup.

Creating Markup on the Fly

What this chapter covers:

- A quick look at the "old-school" techniques: `document.write` and `innerHTML`

- An in-depth look at the DOM methods `createElement`, `createTextNode`, `appendChild`, and `insertBefore`

- An introduction to Ajax and asynchronous requests

Most of the DOM methods you've seen so far are useful for identifying elements. Both `getElementById` and `getElementsByTagName` allow you to quickly and easily target specific element nodes in a document. These elements can then be manipulated using methods and properties like `setAttribute` (to change the value of an attribute) or `nodeValue` (to change the text contained by an element node). That's how the image gallery works. The `showPic` function identifies two elements, with the IDs `"placeholder"` and `"description"`, and then updates their contents. The `src` attribute of the `"placeholder"` element is changed using `setAttribute`. The text within `"description"` is changed using `nodeValue`. In both cases, changes are being made to elements that already exist.

This is the way that the majority of JavaScript functions work. The structure of the web page is created with markup. JavaScript is then used to change some of the details without altering the underlying structure. It is also possible to use JavaScript to change the structure and contents of a web page. In this chapter, you'll learn about some DOM methods that can alter the structure of a web page by creating new elements and modifying existing ones.

Some old-school methods

Before we look at DOM methods for adding markup to a document in the web browser, let's briefly review a couple techniques that developers have used in the past: `document.write` and `innerHTML`.

document.write

The `write` method of the `document` object provides a quick and easy way to insert a string into a document. Let's see how this works.

Save the following markup as a file. Call it something like test.html.

```
<!DOCTYPE html>
<html lang="en">
<head>
  <meta charset="utf-8" />
  <title>Test</title>
```

```
</head>
<body>
  <script>
    document.write("<p>This is inserted.</p>");
  </script>
</body>
</html>
```

If you load test.html in a web browser, you will see a paragraph of text that reads **This is inserted.**

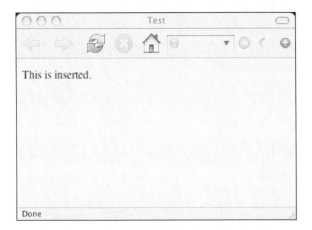

The major drawback to using document.write is that it goes against the principle of *unobtrusive JavaScript*. Even if you place the document.write statement in an external function, you'll still need to insert <script> tags into the body of your markup in order to call the function in the location where you want the write to occur.

The following is a function that takes a string as its argument. This function concatenates an opening <p> tag, the string, and a closing </p> tag. This concatenated string is stored in a variable called str, which is then written out.

```
function insertParagraph(text) {
  var str = "<p>";
  str += text;
  str += "</p>";
  document.write(str);
}
```

You can store this function in an external file called example.js. In order to call this function, you need to insert <script> tags into your markup:

```
<!DOCTYPE html>
<html lang="en">
<head>
  <meta charset="utf-8" />
  <title>Test</title>
  </script>
</head>
<body>
  <script src="example.js">
```

```
  <script>
    insertParagraph("This is inserted.");
  </script>
</body>
</html>
```

Mixing up JavaScript and markup like this is a bad idea. Editing the markup becomes trickier, and the benefits of separating behavior from structure are lost.

You could also very easily introduce validation errors. For instance, in the first example, it appears as though a <p> tag has been opened after a <script> tag, which is invalid. In fact, the <p> and </p> form part of the string being inserted into the document.

If you are writing XHTML documents that are being served up with the MIME type application/xhtml+xml, then document.write simply won't work.

In some ways, using document.write is a bit like using <font> tags to specify font size and color. Both techniques work fine in HTML documents, but neither of them is very elegant.

It's always a good idea to separate structure, behavior, and style. It's much better to specify and maintain styling information by using external CSS files instead of <font> tags. It's also much better to control behavior with external JavaScript files. You should avoid cluttering your markup with <script> tags in your <body>. That rules out using document.write.

innerHTML

Most browsers today include support for a property called innerHTML. This property is not part of the DOM specification from the W3C, although it has been included in the current HTML5 specification. It was first introduced by Microsoft, in Internet Explorer 4, and has since been adopted by other browsers.

innerHTML can be used to read and write the HTML in an element. To see how this works, insert the following piece of markup into the <body> of test.html:

```
<div id="testdiv">
<p>This is <em>my</em> content.</p>
</div>
```

This is how the DOM sees the markup inside "testdiv".

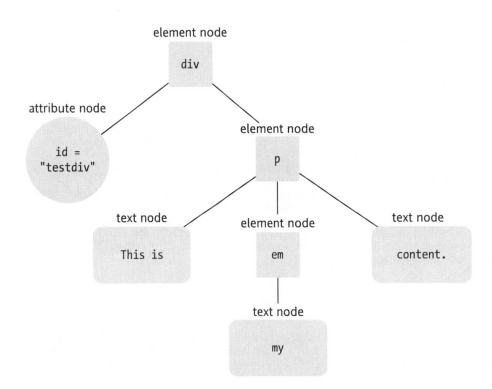

The div element with the id attribute "testdiv" contains an element node—the p element. This p element, in turn, has a number of child nodes. There are two text nodes. These text nodes have the values This is and content. There's also an element node, em, which itself contains a text node with the value my.

The DOM provides a very detailed picture of the markup. Using DOM methods and properties, you can access any of those nodes individually. The innerHTML property takes a much simpler view. As shown in the following diagram, it sees the markup inside "testdiv" as a string of HTML with the value <p>This is my content.</p>.

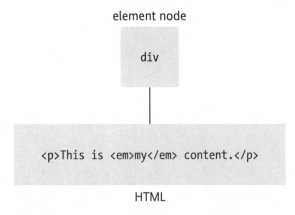

You can test this by updating example.js with a new function, as follows:

```
window.onload = function() {
  var testdiv = document.getElementById("testdiv");
  alert(testdiv.innerHTML);
}
```

Refresh test.html in a web browser. You will see an alert box with the innerHTML value of "testdiv".

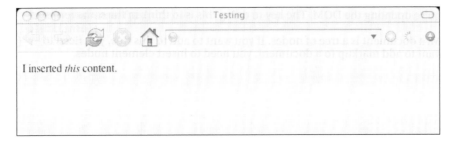

Clearly, innerHTML doesn't offer the fine detail that you can get from DOM methods and properties. Using the standardized DOM is like using a scalpel. Using innerHTML is like using a sledgehammer.

There are times when you might want to use a sledgehammer. If you have a chunk of HTML that you would like to insert verbatim into a web page, innerHTML can do that. It is a read/write property, which means you can use it not only to *get* the HTML inside an element, but also to *set* the HTML inside an element.

Edit the test.html file so that the element with the id value of "testdiv" is empty:

```
<div id="testdiv">
</div>
```

If you put this JavaScript into example.js, you can insert a chunk of HTML into the <div>:

```
window.onload = function() {
  var testdiv = document.getElementById("testdiv");
  testdiv.innerHTML = "<p>I inserted <em>this</em> content.</p>";
}
```

To view the result, refresh test.html in a web browser.

This technique makes no distinction between inserting a chunk of HTML and replacing a chunk of HTML. It doesn't matter whether or not the testdiv element has HTML inside it. Once you use innerHTML, its entire contents will be replaced.

You can then translate the plan into JavaScript:

```javascript
window.onload = function() {
  var para = document.createElement("p");
  var txt1 = document.createTextNode("This is ");
  para.appendChild(txt1);
  var emphasis = document.createElement("em");
  var txt2 = document.createTextNode("my");
  emphasis.appendChild(txt2);
  para.appendChild(emphasis);
  var txt3 = document.createTextNode(" content.");
  para.appendChild(txt3);
  var testdiv = document.getElementById("testdiv");
  testdiv.appendChild(para);
}
```

Write that code into example.js and reload test.html in a browser.

You can use a different approach if you like. You could do all the creating first, and then do all the appending. In that case, your plan of action would look this:

1. Create an element node "p" assigned to the variable para.

2. Create a text node assigned to the variable txt1.

3. Create an element node "em" assigned to the variable emphasis.

4. Create a text node assigned to the variable txt2.

5. Create a text node assigned to the variable txt3.

6. Append txt1 to para.

7. Append txt2 to emphasis.

8. Append emphasis to para.

9. Append txt3 to para.

10. Append para to the element "testdiv" in the document.

That plan translates into this JavaScript code:

```javascript
window.onload = function() {
  var para = document.createElement("p");
  var txt1 = document.createTextNode("This is ");
  var emphasis = document.createElement("em");
  var txt2 = document.createTextNode("my");
  var txt3 = document.createTextNode(" content.");
  para.appendChild(txt1);
  emphasis.appendChild(txt2);
  para.appendChild(emphasis);
  para.appendChild(txt3);
  var testdiv = document.getElementById("testdiv");
  testdiv.appendChild(para);
}
```

If you write that code into the example.js file and then refresh test.html, you will see the same result as before.

As you can see, there's more than one way of adding to the node tree of a document. Even if you decide to never use document.write or innerHTML, you still have a lot of choices and flexibility in how you implement the DOM methods for creating and appending nodes.

Revisiting the image gallery

Now let's look at a practical example of creating markup on the fly. In the previous chapter, we made a lot of improvements to the image gallery script. The JavaScript is unobtrusive and degrades gracefully. We also made some accessibility enhancements.

There's still something that bothers me though. Take a look at the markup in gallery.html:

```
<!DOCTYPE html>
<html lang="en">
<head>
  <meta charset="utf-8" />
  <title>Image Gallery</title>
  <link rel="stylesheet" href="styles/layout.css" media="screen" />
</head>
<body>
  <h1>Snapshots</h1>
  <ul id="imagegallery">
    <li>
      <a href="images/fireworks.jpg" title="A fireworks display">
        <img src="images/thumbnail_fireworks.jpg" alt="Fireworks" />
      </a>
    </li>
    <li>
      <a href="images/coffee.jpg" title="A cup of black coffee" >
        <img src="images/thumbnail_coffee.jpg" alt="Coffee" />
      </a>
    </li>
    <li>
      <a href="images/rose.jpg" title="A red, red rose">
        <img src="images/thumbnail_rose.jpg" alt="Rose" />
      </a>
    </li>
    <li>
      <a href="images/bigben.jpg" title="The famous clock">
        <img src="images/thumbnail_bigben.jpg" alt="Big Ben" />
      </a>
    </li>
  </ul>
  <img id="placeholder" src="images/placeholder.gif" alt="my image gallery" />
  <p id="description">Choose an image.</p>
  <script src="scripts/showPic.js"></script>
</body>
</html>
```

The XHTML file contains an image and a paragraph solely for the use of the showPic script. It's preferable to separate the structure and the behavior entirely. If these elements exist just to be manipulated by DOM methods, then it makes sense to also create them using DOM methods.

The first step is straightforward: remove those elements from the gallery.html document. For the next step, let's create those elements using JavaScript.

Let's write a function called preparePlaceholder and place it into the showPic.js file. We'll call this function when the document loads. This is what the function is going to do:

1. Create an image element node.

2. Give this node an id attribute.

3. Give this node a src attribute.

4. Give this node an alt attribute.

5. Create a paragraph element node.

6. Give this node an id attribute.

7. Create a text node.

8. Append the text node to the paragraph element.

9. Insert the image and paragraph into the document.

Creating the elements and giving them attributes is relatively straightforward. We can use a combination of createElement, createTextNode, and setAttribute:

```
var placeholder = document.createElement("img");
placeholder.setAttribute("id","placeholder");
placeholder.setAttribute("src","images/placeholder.gif");
placeholder.setAttribute("alt","my image gallery");
var description = document.createElement("p");
description.setAttribute("id","description");
var desctext = document.createTextNode("Choose an image");
```

We can then put the text node inside the paragraph node using appendChild:

```
description.appendChild(desctext);
```

The final step is to insert the newly created elements into the document. As it happens, the gallery list is currently the last content element in the document. If we append the placeholder and description elements to the body element, they will then appear after the gallery list. We can reference the body tag as the first (and only) element with the tag name "body":

```
document.getElementsByTagName("body")[0].appendChild(placeholder);
document.getElementsByTagName("body")[0].appendChild(description);
```

Alternatively, we could use the HTML-DOM shortcut body:

```
document.body.appendChild(placeholder);
document.body.appendChild(description);
```

In either case, the placeholder and description elements will be inserted before the closing </body> tag.

This works, but only because the image gallery list is the last content element in the body. What if there was some more content after the image gallery list? What we would like to do is insert the newly created elements after the image gallery list, no matter where the list appears in the document.

Inserting a new element before an existing one

There is a DOM method called `insertBefore`. You can use it to insert a new element before an existing element. You must specify three things:

- The new element you want to insert
- The target element you want to insert it before
- The parent of both elements

Here's the syntax:

```
parentElement.insertBefore(newElement,targetElement)
```

You might not know what the parent element is. That's okay. You can always use the `parentNode` property of the target element. The parent of any element node must be another element node. (Attribute nodes and text nodes can't have element nodes as children.)

For instance, this is how you could insert the `placeholder` element before the image gallery list, which has the id `"imagegallery"`:

```
var gallery = document.getElementById("imagegallery");
gallery.parentNode.insertBefore(placeholder,gallery);
```

At the moment, the `parentNode` of gallery is the body element. The `placeholder` element will be inserted as a new child of the body element. It will be inserted before its sibling element, gallery.

You can also insert the `description` element as a sibling of the gallery element:

```
gallery.parentNode.insertBefore(description,gallery);
```

The placeholder image and description paragraph are inserted before the image gallery list.

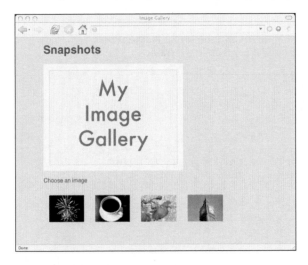

That's all well and good, but we want to add the newly created elements *after* the image gallery, not before it.

Inserting a new element after an existing one

Seeing as there is an insertBefore method, you might expect to be able to use a corresponding insertAfter method. Unfortunately, no such DOM method exists.

Writing the insertAfter function

Although the DOM hasn't provided a method called insertAfter, it does have all the tools you need to insert a node after another node. You can use existing DOM methods and properties to create a function called insertAfter:

```
function insertAfter(newElement,targetElement) {
  var parent = targetElement.parentNode;
  if (parent.lastChild == targetElement) {
    parent.appendChild(newElement);
  } else {
    parent.insertBefore(newElement,targetElement.nextSibling);
  }
}
```

This function is using quite a few DOM methods and properties:

- parentNode property
- lastChild property
- appendChild method
- insertBefore method
- nextSibling property

This is what the function is doing, step by step:

1. The function takes two arguments: the new element and the target element the new element should be inserted after. These are passed as the variables newElement and targetElement:

```
function insertAfter(newElement,targetElement)
```

2. Get the parentNode property of the target element and assign it to the variable parent:

```
var parent = targetElement.parentNode
```

3. Find out if the target element happens to be the last child of parent. Compare the lastChild property of parent with the target element:

```
if (parent.lastChild == targetElement)
```

4. If this is true, then append the new element to parent using appendChild. The new element will be inserted directly after the target element:

```
parent.appendChild(newElement)
```

5. Otherwise, the new element needs to be inserted between the target element and the next child of parent. The next node after the target element is the nextSibling property of the target element. Use the insertBefore method to place the new element before the target element's next sibling:

```
parent.insertBefore(newElement.targetElement.nextSibling)
```

On the face of it, insertBefore is quite a complex function. But if you break it down into its individual components, it's relatively straightforward. Don't worry if isn't completely clear to you right now. As you become more familiar with the DOM methods and properties that insertAfter uses, it will make more sense.

Like addLoadEvent from Chapter 6, insertAfter is a handy function to include in your scripts.

Using the insertAfter function

We can use the insertAfter function in the preparePlaceholder function. First, we need a reference to the image gallery list:

```
var gallery = document.getElementById("imagegallery");
```

Now we can insert placeholder, which refers to the newly created image, right after gallery:

```
insertAfter(placeholder,gallery);
```

The placeholder image is now part of the node tree of gallery.html. We want to insert the description paragraph directly after it. We already have the variable description for this node. We can use the insertAfter function again to insert description after placeholder:

```
insertAfter(description, placeholder);
```

With those lines added, this is how the preparePlaceholder function looks:

```
function preparePlaceholder() {
  var placeholder = document.createElement("img");
  placeholder.setAttribute("id","placeholder");
  placeholder.setAttribute("src","images/placeholder.gif");
  placeholder.setAttribute("alt","my image gallery");
  var description = document.createElement("p");
  description.setAttribute("id","description");
  var desctext = document.createTextNode("Choose an image");
  description.appendChild(desctext);
  var gallery = document.getElementById("imagegallery");
  insertAfter(placeholder,gallery);
  insertAfter(description,placeholder);
}
```

There's just one problem with the function: we haven't tested whether the browser supports the DOM methods it's using. To ensure that the function degrades gracefully, we need to add just a few extra lines:

```
function preparePlaceholder() {
  if (!document.createElement) return false;
  if (!document.createTextNode) return false;
  if (!document.getElementById) return false;
  if (!document.getElementById("imagegallery")) return false;
  var placeholder = document.createElement("img");
```

```
    placeholder.setAttribute("id","placeholder");
    placeholder.setAttribute("src","images/placeholder.gif");
    placeholder.setAttribute("alt","my image gallery");
    var description = document.createElement("p");
    description.setAttribute("id","description");
    var desctext = document.createTextNode("Choose an image");
    description.appendChild(desctext);
    var gallery = document.getElementById("imagegallery");
    insertAfter(placeholder,gallery);
    insertAfter(description,placeholder);
}
```

The finished image gallery

The showPic.js file now contains five functions:

- addLoadEvent
- insertAfter
- preparePlaceholder
- prepareGallery
- showPic

Both addLoadEvent and insertAfter are general-purpose functions that you can use in many situations.

The preparePlaceholder function creates an image element and a paragraph element. The function then inserts these newly created elements into the node tree, immediately after the image gallery list.

The prepareGallery function handles events. The function loops through all the links in the image gallery list. When one of these links is activated, the showPic function is called.

The showPic swaps out the placeholder image for one of the images linked from the gallery list.

To initiate the functionality, the two functions preparePlaceholder and prepareGallery are called using the addLoadEvent function:

```
addLoadEvent(preparePlaceholder);
addLoadEvent(prepareGallery);
```

This is how the finished showPic.js file looks:

```
function addLoadEvent(func) {
  var oldonload = window.onload;
  if (typeof window.onload != 'function') {
    window.onload = func;
  } else {
    window.onload = function() {
      oldonload();
      func();
    }
  }
}

function insertAfter(newElement,targetElement) {
  var parent = targetElement.parentNode;
  if (parent.lastChild == targetElement) {
    parent.appendChild(newElement);
```

```
  } else {
    parent.insertBefore(newElement,targetElement.nextSibling);
  }
}

function preparePlaceholder() {
  if (!document.createElement) return false;
  if (!document.createTextNode) return false;
  if (!document.getElementById) return false;
  if (!document.getElementById("imagegallery")) return false;
  var placeholder = document.createElement("img");
  placeholder.setAttribute("id","placeholder");
  placeholder.setAttribute("src","images/placeholder.gif");
  placeholder.setAttribute("alt","my image gallery");
  var description = document.createElement("p");
  description.setAttribute("id","description");
  var desctext = document.createTextNode("Choose an image");
  description.appendChild(desctext);
  var gallery = document.getElementById("imagegallery");
  insertAfter(placeholder,gallery);
  insertAfter(description,placeholder);
}

function prepareGallery() {
  if (!document.getElementsByTagName) return false;
  if (!document.getElementById) return false;
  if (!document.getElementById("imagegallery")) return false;
  var gallery = document.getElementById("imagegallery");
  var links = gallery.getElementsByTagName("a");
  for ( var i=0; i < links.length; i++) {
    links[i].onclick = function() {
      return showPic(this);
    }
    links[i].onkeypress = links[i].onclick;
  }
}

function showPic(whichpic) {
  if (!document.getElementById("placeholder")) return true;
  var source = whichpic.getAttribute("href");
  var placeholder = document.getElementById("placeholder");
  placeholder.setAttribute("src",source);
  if (!document.getElementById("description")) return false;
  if (whichpic.getAttribute("title")) {
    var text = whichpic.getAttribute("title");
  } else {
    var text = "";
  }
  var description = document.getElementById("description");
  if (description.firstChild.nodeType == 3) {
    description.firstChild.nodeValue = text;
  }
  return false;
}
```

```
addLoadEvent(preparePlaceholder);
addLoadEvent(prepareGallery);
```

While the JavaScript file has grown, the amount of markup has diminished. The gallery.html file now contains just a single hook, which is being used by the JavaScript and the CSS. This hook is the id attribute of the image gallery list:

```
<!DOCTYPE html>
<html>
<head>
  <meta http-equiv="content-type" content="text/html; charset=utf-8" />
  <title>Image Gallery</title>
  <link rel="stylesheet" href="styles/layout.css" media="screen" />
</head>
<body>
  <h1>Snapshots</h1>
  <ul id="imagegallery">
    <li>
      <a href="images/fireworks.jpg" title="A fireworks display">
<img src="images/thumbnail_fireworks.jpg" alt="Fireworks" />
      </a>
    </li>
    <li>
      <a href="images/coffee.jpg" title="A cup of black coffee" >
        <img src="images/thumbnail_coffee.jpg" alt="Coffee" />
      </a>
    </li>
    <li>
      <a href="images/rose.jpg" title="A red, red rose">
        <img src="images/thumbnail_rose.jpg" alt="Rose" />
      </a>
    </li>
    <li>
      <a href="images/bigben.jpg" title="The famous clock">
        <img src="images/thumbnail_bigben.jpg" alt="Big Ben" />
      </a>
    </li>
  </ul>
  <script src="scripts/showPic.js"></script>
</body>
</html>
```

The structure, style, and behavior are now separated.

Load gallery.html in a web browser. You will see the placeholder image and the description paragraph. They have been inserted after the imagegallery list.

The JavaScript has created markup on the fly and added the markup to the document. The JavaScript has also prepared all the links in the image gallery list. Click any of the thumbnails to see the image gallery in action.

So far, the new content we've been creating has not really been all that new to the page. The `title` attributes already existed in our markup when the page loaded. The new paragraphs we added with `createElement` were based on markup embedded in our scripts. Everything that we created was included in the initial page load; we just rearranged a few things with our scripts. So what if we want to retrieve new content that was not part of the original page load? Let's see how that's also possible.

Ajax

In 2005, Jesse James Garrett of Adaptive Path coined the term *Ajax* to describe an asynchronous method of loading page content. Traditionally, web applications involved a lot of page refreshes. The user made a choice, that information was sent back to the server, and then the server responded with a new page based on the user's actions. Even if the user saw only a small change to one area of the page, a whole new page was served with all the branding, navigation, header, and footer elements around the obligatory change.

Using Ajax, only the appropriate portion of the page changes. Everything else—the branding, the navigation, header, and footer—remains the same. The user still makes a choice, but this time, a small change appears within the page that is already loaded in the browser, rather than the full page being served again.

The advantage of using Ajax is that with Ajax, the request to the server occurs asynchronously to the page. Instead of serving up a whole new page every time the user sends a request, the browser can process requests in the background while the user continues to view and interact with the page. This allows your scripts to retrieve and create new content without loading a whole new page and interrupting the user experience With Ajax, web applications can offer content rich interfaces and a much more interactive, "desktop-like" experience, as you can see in applications such as Google Maps.

Like any new technology however, Ajax must be used appropriately. Ajax relies on JavaScript and therefore won't work in some browsers or search engine spiders.

The XMLHttpRequest object

The magic of Ajax is achieved by using the XMLHttpRequest object. This object acts as an intermediary between your script in the web browser (client) and the server. Instead of the web browser, JavaScript initiates the requests, and as a result, must also handle the response.

The XMLHttpRequest object it is a relatively new standard (part of HTML5), however, it has a long history and is widely supported in modern web browsers. Unfortunately, different browsers implement XMLHttpRequest in different ways. So for the best results, you'll need to branch your code.

To work with an example, start by creating the following HTML file and call it ajax.html:

```
<!DOCTYPE html>
<html lang="en">
<head>
<meta charset="utf-8" />
  <title>Ajax</title>
</head>
<body>

  <div id="new"></div>

  <script src="scripts/addLoadEvent.js"></script>
  <script src="scripts/getHTTPObject.js"></script>
  <script src="scripts/getNewContent.js"></script>
</body>
</html>
```

This HTML file includes a scripts folder with the addLoadEvent.js, as well as two new scripts: getHTTPObject.js and getNewContent.js.

To simulate the server response, alongside the ajax.html file, create a response.txt file with the following text content:

```
This was loaded asynchronously!
```

This file will act as our server-side script. In most cases, you'll probably have some script that does something fancy with the request, but this will do for the example. Now let's fill the getHTTPObject.js and getNewContent.js scripts.

Microsoft first implemented something called XMLHTTP as one of its proprietary ActiveX objects in Internet Explorer 5. Here's how you would create a new instance of the object in Internet Explorer:

```
var request = new ActiveXObject("Msxml2.XMLHTTP.3.0");
```

Other browsers achieve the same result by using XMLHttpRequest:

```
var request = new XMLHttpRequest();
```

To add to the confusion, different versions of Internet Explorer used slightly different XMLHTTP object initializations. In order to satisfy all implementations, add this getHTTPObject function to your getHTTPObject.js file:

```
function getHTTPObject() {
  if (typeof XMLHttpRequest == "undefined")
    XMLHttpRequest = function () {
      try { return new ActiveXObject("Msxml2.XMLHTTP.6.0"); }
        catch (e) {}
      try { return new ActiveXObject("Msxml2.XMLHTTP.3.0"); }
        catch (e) {}
      try { return new ActiveXObject("Msxml2.XMLHTTP"); }
        catch (e) {}
      return false;
    }
  return new XMLHttpRequest();
}
```

The getHTTPObject function uses object detection to check for the XMLHttpRequest object. If that fails, it tries various other methods before returning false or a reference to a new XMLHttpRequest object (or the equivalent XMLHTTP object).

Now, to use an XMLHttpRequest object in one of your scripts, you can assign the resulting XMLHttpRequest object to a variable:

```
var request = getHTTPObject();
```

The XMLHttpRequest object has a number of methods. The most useful of these is open, which is used to point the object at a file on the server. You can also specify what sort of HTTP request you want to make: GET, POST, or SEND. A third parameter specifies whether the request should be processed asynchronously.

Add the following to your getNewContent.js file:

```
function getNewContent() {
  var request = getHTTPObject();
  if (request) {
    request.open( "GET", "example.txt", true );
    request.onreadystatechange = function() {
      if (request.readyState == 4) {
      var para = document.createElement("p");
      var txt = document.createTextNode(request.responseText);
      para.appendChild(txt);
      document.getElementById('new').appendChild(para);
      }
    };
    request.send(null);
```

```
    } else {
      alert('Sorry, your browser doesn\'t support XMLHttpRequest');
    }
}
addLoadEvent(getNewContent);
```

When the page loads, this will initiate a GET request to a file called example.txt in the same directory as the ajax.html file:

```
request.open( "GET", "example.txt", true );
```

The onreadystatechange property is the event handler that is triggered when the server sends a response back to the XMLHttpRequest object. You can use it to specify what happens with the response from the server.

You can specify a function directly, as in the example:

```
request.onreadystatechange = function() {
  // Process the response…
};
```

Alternatively, you can reference a function. The following code will cause a function called doSomething to be executed when onreadystatechange is triggered:

■ **Note** When assigning to the onreadystatechange property, remember not to include the parentheses on the end of the function. You want to assign a reference to the function itself, not to the function's result.

```
request.onreadystatechange = doSomething;
```

After you've specified where the object should send a request and what it should do once it receives a response, you can start the process using the send method:

```
request.send(null);
```

When a browser doesn't support the XMLHttpRequest object, the getHTTPObject function returns false, so you'll need to handle that case as well.

When the server sends a response back to the XMLHttpRequest object, a number of properties are made available. The readyState property is a numeric value that is updated while the server deals with the request. There are five possible values:

- 0 for uninitialized

- 1 for loading

- 2 for loaded

- 3 for interactive

- 4 for complete

Once the readyState property has a value of 4, you have access to the data sent by the server.

You can access this data as a string of text provided by the responseText property. If the data is sent back with a Content-Type header of "text/xml", you can also access the responseXML property, which is effectively a DocumentFragment. You can use all the usual DOM methods to manipulate this DocumentFragment. This is where the XML part of XMLHttpRequest comes from.

In the example, the onreadystatechange handler waits for a readyState value of 4, and then dumps the entire responseText property into a paragraph and appends it to the DOM:

```
request.onreadystatechange = function() {
  if (request.readyState == 4) {
    var para = document.createElement("p");
    var txt = document.createTextNode(request.responseText);
    para.appendChild(txt);
    document.getElementById('new').appendChild(para);
  }
}
```

The text in the example.txt file then appears in the div with the id attribute of new.

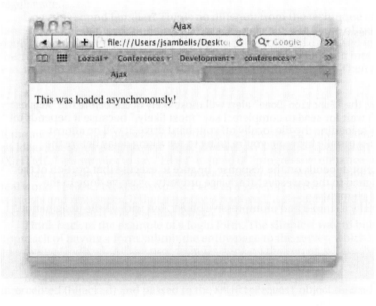

Caution One important thing to remember is the same origin security policy. Requests using the XMLHttpRequest object are limited to the same domain where the HTML file resides. You can't make a request from one domain to another. Also, some browsers restrict requests by protocol. In Chrome, the example produces an error "Cross origin requests are only supported for HTTP" if you're trying to load example.txt from your hard drive using the file:// protocol.

An easy thing to forget is the asynchronous aspect of the request. Once the XMLHttpRequest request has been sent, the script will continue to execute, without waiting for the response to return. To see this

What's next?

In this chapter, you've seen different ways of adding markup to a document in the web browser. We began with some quick examples of the old-school techniques:

- `document.write`
- `innerHTML`

Then you saw more in-depth examples using the DOM methods:

- `createElement`
- `createTextNode`
- `appendChild`
- `insertBefore`

The key to using these methods is to see a web document as a tree of nodes. Whenever you use `createElement` or `createTextNode`, you are creating a node that floats around in JavaScript limbo. Using `appendChild` and `insertBefore`, you can take these `DocumentFragment` objects and insert them into the node tree of a document.

You've seen the image gallery example refined. Along the way, you've seen the construction of a very handy function called `insertAfter`. You'll be able to use this function in many situations where you need to add markup to a document.

You also got a quick introduction to Ajax and asynchronous requests, which you'll see more of in Chapter 12.

The next chapter presents some more examples of adding markup to documents. You'll see how to create little nuggets of useful information that you can add to a document on the fly.

CHAPTER 8

■ ■ ■

Enhancing Content

What this chapter covers:

- A function that creates a list of abbreviations used in a document

- A function that adds links to the sources of quotes in a document

- A function that creates a list of access keys available in a document

In the previous chapter, you saw how you can use the DOM to create markup on the fly. In this chapter, you're going to put those techniques into practice. You'll use the DOM to create discrete chunks of markup that can be added to a web page. You can find the finished function files on the downloads page for this book at the friends of ED website, `http://friendsofed.com/`.

What not to do

In theory, you could use JavaScript to add important content to a web page. However, that would be a very bad idea, because there would be no room for graceful degradation. Visitors lacking the necessary JavaScript support would never see the content. At the time of writing, that includes searchbots.

If you find yourself using the DOM to insert important content into a web page, you should probably reexamine your process. You may find that you are using the DOM inappropriately.

As discussed in Chapter 5, you should always consider two issues associated with JavaScript:

- **Progressive enhancement**: The principle of progressive enhancement is based on the idea that you should begin with your core content. The content is structured using markup. The marked-up content is then enhanced. The enhancement might be stylistic, using CSS, or it might be behavioral, using DOM scripting. If you are adding core content with the DOM, you are adding it too late. The content should be part of the initial document.

- **Graceful degradation**: The corollary to progressive enhancement is graceful degradation. If you have progressively enhanced your content, then it follows that your stylistic and behavioral enhancements will degrade gracefully. Visitors to your website who lack the means to benefit from your CSS and DOM scripting will still be able to get to your core content. If you add important content using JavaScript, it won't degrade gracefully—no JavaScript, no content. This may seem like a restriction, but it isn't. There are plenty of other uses for generating content with the DOM.

Making the invisible visible

Web designers today have a great amount of control over how web pages are displayed. CSS is a very powerful tool for styling the content contained between HTML tags. The techniques go far beyond simply changing the fonts and colors used to display content. Using CSS, you can make block-level elements display as if they were inline. That was demonstrated with the list containing the thumbnail images in the markup for the JavaScript image gallery in Chapter 6. The list items, contained within `<li>` tags, would normally be displayed on separate lines. By specifying a value of `inline` for the `display` property of each list item, the list items appear horizontally instead of vertically.

The reverse is also possible. By declaring `display:block` for an element that is normally inline, you can put that element on its own line. You can even use CSS to hide content completely. By specifying `display:none`, you can completely remove elements from the flow of the document. These elements are still part of the DOM's node tree—the browser simply doesn't display them.

Along with the content between the tags, markup can also contain semantic information within the tag attributes. Placing information in attributes is an important part of marking up content.

Web browsers don't display the content of most attributes. When exceptional attributes are displayed, the presentation can vary from browser to browser. For example, some browsers display the content of the `title` attribute as a tool tip, and others display it in the status bar. Some browsers display the content of the `alt` attribute as a tool tip, which has led to widespread abuse of an attribute intended to provide an *alternative* description of an image.

When it comes to displaying attributes, you're at the mercy of the browser right now. With a little bit of DOM scripting, you can wrest control back into your own hands.

Let's look at a few variations on the concept of creating "widgets" for web pages using the DOM:

- Retrieve information that is hidden in attributes.

- Create markup to wrap around this information.

- Insert this markup into the document.

This approach is different from simply creating content with the DOM. In this scenario, the content already exists in the markup. You use JavaScript and the DOM to duplicate content and present it in a different structure.

The content

As always, the starting point for any web page is the content. Take the following text as your starting point:

```
What is the Document Object Model?
The W3C defines the DOM as:
A platform- and language-neutral interface that will allow programs
and scripts to dynamically access and update the
content, structure  and style of documents.
It is an API that can be used to navigate HTML and XML documents.
```

This is how you might mark it up:

```
<h1>What is the Document Object Model?</h1>
<p>
The <abbr title="World Wide Web Consortium">W3C</abbr> defines
➥the <abbr title="Document Object Model">DOM</abbr> as:
</p>
```

```
<blockquote cite="http://www.w3.org/DOM/">
  <p>
A platform- and language-neutral interface that will allow programs
➥and scripts to dynamically access and update the
➥content, structure and style of documents.
  </p>
</blockquote>
<p>
It is an <abbr title="Application Programming Interface">API</abbr>
➥that can be used to navigate <abbr title="HyperText Markup Language">
➥HTML</abbr> and <abbr title="eXtensible Markup Language">XML
➥</abbr> documents.
</p>
```

There are quite a few abbreviations in there. They are marked up using the `<abbr>` tag.

■ **Note** There's a lot of confusion surrounding the difference between the `<abbr>` tag and the `<acronym>` tag. An abbreviation is any shortened version of a word or phrase. An acronym is an abbreviation that is spoken as a single word. DOM is an acronym if you are saying it as a word, "dom", rather than saying each letter, "D.O.M." All acronyms are abbreviations, but not all abbreviations are acronyms. As a result, the `<acronym>` tag has become obsolete in HTML5, and `<abbr>` should be used instead.

Now that you have your content structured in a fragment of markup, you can put it into context. This fragment goes inside a `<body>` tag. This body element, along with a corresponding head element, goes inside the `<html>` tag.

The markup: HTML, XHTML, or HTML5

For the markup, it's up to you whether to use HTML or XHTML. The important thing is that whichever document type you choose, the markup validates to the specified DOCTYPE declaration.

Personally, I like to stick to the rules of XHTML and use a DOCTYPE that tells the browser to employ a more strict rendering method. It is stricter about the markup it allows, so it encourages me to write cleaner markup. For instance, with HTML you can write tags and attributes in uppercase or lowercase: `<p>` or `<P>`; XHTML insists on lowercase for all tags and attributes.

HTML also allows you to sometimes leave off the closing tags. You can omit closing `</p>` and `</li>` tags. This may seem to offer flexibility, but it actually makes it harder to track down problems when browsers render your documents in unexpected ways. With XHTML, all tags must be closed. That includes stand-alone elements like `<img>` and `<br>`, which must be written with a closing slash: `<img />` and `<br />`. For backward compatibility with very old browsers, you should put a space before the closing slash. By using a stricter DOCTYPE, validation tools can become more useful in tracking down errors.

To use the XHTML DOCTYPE, you include this at the beginning of your document:

```
<!DOCTYPE html
  PUBLIC "-//W3C//DTD XHTML 1.0 Strict//EN"
  "http://www.w3.org/TR/xhtml1/DTD/xhtml1-strict.dtd">
```

Another option that you may like even better is to use the HTML5 DOCTYPE. The HTML5 DOCTYPE is simple:

```
<!DOCTYPE html>
```

It's just 15 characters. Besides being short enough to remember and type by hand, it also supports both the HTML and XHTML markup methodologies. For more on HTML5, see Chapter 11.

Note In some browsers the DOCTYPE is used to determine if the browser should use standards mode or quirks mode when it renders the page. Quirks mode tells the browser to emulate some "quirky" behaviors introduced by legacy browsers and allows poorly written pages to still function properly in newer browsers. As a general rule, you should stick to standards mode and avoid quirks mode. Thankfully, the HTML5 DOCTYPE defaults to standards mode.

XHTML5

If you want to be really strict about things, you can go the XHTML5 route and serve your pages with the application/xhtml+xml MIME type, but be forewarned.

XHTML5 is basically HTML5 written using strict XML rules. Technically, web browsers should treat any XHTML5 documents as XML rather than HTML. In practice, you need to send the correct MIME type, application/xhtml+xml, in the headers of your document. Some browsers don't understand this MIME type, so it is usually sent only after some server-side browser sniffing. or in the worst case, the page won't render at all. As a result, most XHTML pages are still served as HTML anyway.

If you are using XHTML5 with the correct MIME type, remember that besides not working in some browsers, some HTML-DOM methods and properties, like document.write, will no longer work. The core DOM methods will continue to work just fine. They will work on any valid XML document, not just XHTML5.

This is how the content looks when it is marked up as a complete HTML5 document:

```
<!DOCTYPE html>
<html lang="en">
  <head>
    <meta charset="utf-8" />
    <title>Explaining the Document Object Model</title>
  </head>
  <body>
    <h1>What is the Document Object Model?</h1>
    <p>
The <abbr title="World Wide Web Consortium">W3C</abbr> defines the <abbr title="Document
Object Model">DOM</abbr> as:
    </p>
    <blockquote cite="http://www.w3.org/DOM/">
      <p>
A platform- and language-neutral interface that will allow programs
➥and scripts to dynamically access and update the
```

```
➥content, structure and style of documents.
      </p>
    </blockquote>
    <p>
It is an <abbr title="Application Programming Interface">API</abbr>
➥that can be used to navigate <abbr title="HyperText Markup Language">
➥HTML</abbr> and <abbr title="eXtensible Markup Language">XML
➥</abbr> documents.
      </p>
  </body>
</html>
```

Save this page as explanation.html.

If you load the page in a web browser, you will see the how the browser displays the marked-up content. (Some browsers will render the abbreviations with dotted underlines; others will show them italicized.)

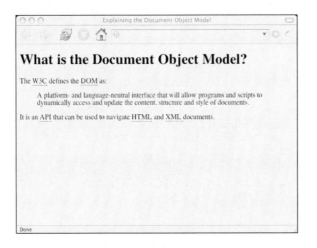

The CSS

Even though there is no style sheet attached to this document, styles are still being applied. Every browser applies its own default styling.

You can override the browser's default styles by applying your own style sheet. Here's an example:

```
body {
  font-family: "Helvetica","Arial",sans-serif;
  font-size: 10pt;
}
abbr {
  text-decoration: none;
  border: 0;
  font-style: normal;
}
```

Save this as typography.css and put it in a folder called styles.

Now add this line to the <head> of explanation.html:

```
<link rel="stylesheet" media="screen" href="styles/typography.css" />
```

If you load explanation.html in a web browser, you should see a difference. The text is now displayed with a different font, and abbreviations no longer stand out.

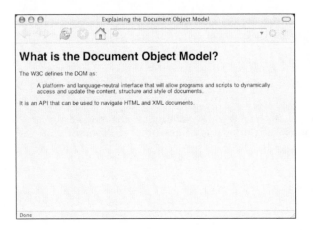

The JavaScript

The title attributes for the abbreviations in the document are hidden. Some browsers will display the titles as tool tips when you mouse over the abbreviations. The default browser behavior for abbreviations is as unpredictable as the default browser styling.

In the same way that you can override the default styles with CSS, you can override the default behavior with the DOM.

Displaying abbreviations

It would be nice to gather all the title values from the <abbr> tags and display them on the page. A *definition list* would be the perfect way to display the titles and the values contained in the <abbr> tags. This is how the definition list would be written:

```
<dl>
  <dt>W3C</dt>
  <dd>World Wide Web Consortium</dd>
  <dt>DOM</dt>
  <dd>Document Object Model</dd>
  <dt>API</dt>
  <dd>Application Programming Interface</dd>
  <dt>HTML</dt>
  <dd>HyperText Markup Language</dd>
  <dt>XML</dt>
  <dd>eXtensible Markup Language</dd>
</dl>
```

You can create this list using the DOM. This is how:

1. Loop through all the abbr elements in the document.
2. Store the title attributes from each abbr element.
3. Store the values from each abbr element.
4. Create a definition list element.
5. Loop through the stored titles and values.
6. Create a definition title element.
7. Insert the value into the definition title.
8. Create a definition description element.
9. Insert the title into the definition description.
10. Append the definition title to the definition list.
11. Append the definition description to the definition list.
12. Append the definition list to the body of the document.

Let's write a function to do this.

Writing the displayAbbreviations function

Our function will be called displayAbbreviations. Create a file called displayAbbreviations.js and store it in a folder called scripts.

Begin by defining the function. It doesn't need to take any arguments, so the parentheses will be empty:

```
function displayAbbreviations() {
```

Before we can begin looping through all the abbreviations in the document, we must first find them. This is easily done with getElementsByTagName. Pass this method the value " abbr". The method will return a node set containing all the abbr element nodes in the document. (As mentioned in previous chapters, a *node set* is an array of nodes.) Store this array in a variable called abbreviations:

```
var abbreviations = document.getElementsByTagName("abbr");
```

Now we can start looping through the abbreviations array. But before we do that, let's run a little test. We know that there are abbreviations in this particular document. But that won't be the case for all documents. If you want to use this function for another document, you should probably check to see if that document contains any abbreviations before going further.

We can find out how many abbreviations are in the document by querying the length property of the abbreviations array. If abbreviations.length is less than one, there are no abbr elements in the document. If that is the case, the function should return a Boolean value:

```
if (abbreviations.length < 1) return false;
```

If there are no abbr elements in the document, the function will finish at this point.

The next step is to store information from each abbr element. We'll need to store the text within the <abbr> tags as well as the value of each title attribute. When you want to store a series of values like this, an array is the ideal storage medium. Define a new array called defs:

```
var defs = new Array();
```

Now loop through the abbreviations array:

```
for (var i=0; i<abbreviations.length; i++) {
```

To get the definition provided by the current abbreviation, use the getAttribute method on the title attribute. Store the value in a variable called definition:

```
var definition = abbreviations[i].getAttribute("title");
```

To get the abbreviation within the abbr tag, use the nodeValue property. We want the value of the text node within the abbr element. In all the occurrences of the abbr element in explanation.html, the text node is the first (and only) node within the element; in other words, the text node is the first child of the abbr element node:

```
abbreviations[i].firstChild
```

However, it's possible that the text node could be nested within other elements. Consider this piece of markup:

```
<abbr title="Document Object Model"><em>DOM</em></abbr>
```

In this case, the first child of the abbr element node is the em element node. The text node is the second (and last) node within the abbr element. Instead of using the firstChild property, it's safer to use the lastChild property:

```
abbreviations[i].lastChild
```

Get the nodeValue property of this text node and assign it to the variable key:

```
var key = abbreviations[i].lastChild.nodeValue;
```

Now we have two variables: definition and key. These are the values that we want to store in the defs array. We can store both values by setting one of them as the key and the other as the value:

```
defs[key] = definition;
```

The first element of the defs array has the key " W3C" and the value "World Wide Web Consortium", the second element of the defs array has the key "DOM" and the value "Document Object Model", and so on.

This is the finished loop:

```
for (var i=0; i<abbreviations.length; i++) {
  var definition = abbreviations[i].getAttribute("title");
  var key = abbreviations[i].lastChild.nodeValue;
  defs[key] = definition;
}
```

To improve the readability of the loop, you could assign the value of abbreviations[i], the current iteration of the abbreviations array, to a variable called current_abbr:

```
for (var i=0; i<abbreviations.length; i++) {
  var current_abbr = abbreviations[i];
  var definition = current_abbr.getAttribute("title");
  var key = current_abbr.lastChild.nodeValue;
  defs[key] = definition;
}
```

If you find that the current_abbr variable helps you to follow the code more easily, then I recommend using it. Adding one extra line is a small price to pay.

In theory, you could write the entire loop in one line, but that would be very hard to read:

```
for (var i=0; i<abbreviations.length; i++) {
  defs[abbreviations[i].lastChild.nodeValue] = abbreviations[i].getAttribute("title");
}
```

Again, there's always more than one way of doing things in JavaScript. You've just seen three different ways of writing the same loop. Choose the one that makes the most sense to you. If it seems confusing to you when you write it, there's a good chance that it will confuse you even more when you come back to it later.

Now that we have our definitions stored in the defs array, we can create the markup in which to display them.

Creating the markup

A definition list is the ideal way to structure a list of abbreviations and their meanings. A definition list (<dl>) contains a series of definition titles (<dt>) and definition descriptions (<dd>):

```
<dl>
  <dt>Title 1</dt>
  <dd>Description 1</dd>
  <dt>Title 2</dt>
  <dd>Description 2</dd>
</dl>
```

Create the definition list using the createElement method. Assign the newly created element to a variable called dlist:

```
var dlist = document.createElement("dl");
```

The new dl element is a DocumentFragment floating in JavaScript limbo for now. Later, we'll be able to insert it into the document by referencing the dlist variable.

It's time for another loop. This time, we'll be looping through the defs array that we created earlier. Once again, we'll be using a for loop, but this time it will be slightly different.

You can use a for/in loop to temporarily assign the key of an array to a variable:

```
for (variable in array)
```

On the first iteration of the for loop, the variable has the value of the key of the first element in the array. The next time around, the variable has the value of the key of the second element in the array. The loop will run through all the keys of the array. This is how we can loop through the associative array, defs:

```
for (key in defs) {
```

This means "For each key in the defs associative array, assign its value to the variable key." We can then use the variable key in the subsequent block of code. Because we have the key for the current iteration of the defs array, we can retrieve the corresponding value:

```
var definition = defs[key];
```

On the first iteration of the for/in loop, the variable key has the value "W3C" and the variable definition has the value "World Wide Web Consortium". The next time around, key has the value "DOM" and definition has the value "Document Object Model".

On each iteration of the loop, we'll need to create a dt element and a dd element. We'll also need to create text nodes to put inside them.

Start by creating the dt element:

```
var dtitle = document.createElement("dt");
```

131

Create a text node with the value of key:

```
var dtitle_text = document.createTextNode(key);
```

We have created two nodes. The element node is assigned to the variable dtitle. The text node is assigned to the variable dtitle_text. Use the appendChild method to put the text node inside the element node:

```
dtitle.appendChild(dtitle_text);
```

Repeat the process for the dd element:

```
var ddesc = document.createElement("dd");
```

This time, create a text node with the value of the variable definition:

```
var ddesc_text = document.createTextNode(definition);
```

Again, append the text node to the element node:

```
ddesc.appendChild(ddesc_text);
```

Now we have two element nodes: dtitle and ddesc. These element nodes contain the text nodes dtitle_text and ddesc_text.

Before finishing the loop, append your newly created dt and dd elements to the dl element you created earlier. The dl element has been assigned to the variable dlist:

```
dlist.appendChild(dtitle);
dlist.appendChild(ddesc);
```

Here is the finished for/in loop:

```
for (key in defs) {
  var definition = defs[key];
  var dtitle = document.createElement("dt");
  var dtitle_text = document.createTextNode(key);
  dtitle.appendChild(dtitle_text);
  var ddesc = document.createElement("dd");
  var ddesc_text = document.createTextNode(definition);
  ddesc.appendChild(ddesc_text);
  dlist.appendChild(dtitle);
  dlist.appendChild(ddesc);
}
```

At this stage, our definition list is complete. It exists in JavaScript as a DocumentFragment. All that remains to do is to insert it into the document.

Inserting the definition list

Rather than inserting the list of abbreviations unannounced, it would be a good idea to place them under a descriptive heading.

Create an h2 element node:

```
var header = document.createElement("h2");
```

Create a text node with the value "Abbreviations":

```
var header_text = document.createTextNode("Abbreviations");
```

Place the text node inside the element node:

```
header.appendChild(header_text);
```

In a complicated document, you would probably want to insert the newly created elements into a specific part of the document, probably identified with an id. In the case of explanation.html, which is quite a straightforward document, we can just append them to the body tag.

There are two ways you could reference the body tag:

- Using the DOM Core, you can reference the first (and only) body tag in the document:

```
document.getElementsByTagName("body")[0]
```

- Using HTML-DOM, you can simply reference the body property of the document:

```
document.body
```

First, insert the header:

```
document.body.appendChild(header);
```

Then insert the definition list:

```
document.body.appendChild(dlist);
```

The displayAbbreviations function is complete:

```
function displayAbbreviations() {
  var abbreviations = document.getElementsByTagName("abbr");
  if (abbreviations.length < 1) return false;
  var defs = new Array();
  for (var i=0; i<abbreviations.length; i++) {
    var current_abbr = abbreviations[i];
    var definition = current_abbr.getAttribute("title");
    var key = current_abbr.lastChild.nodeValue;
    defs[key] = definition;
  }
  var dlist = document.createElement("dl");
  for (key in defs) {
    var definition = defs[key];
    var dtitle = document.createElement("dt");
    var dtitle_text = document.createTextNode(key);
    dtitle.appendChild(dtitle_text);
    var ddesc = document.createElement("dd");
    var ddesc_text = document.createTextNode(definition);
    ddesc.appendChild(ddesc_text);
    dlist.appendChild(dtitle);
    dlist.appendChild(ddesc);
  }
  var header = document.createElement("h2");
  var header_text = document.createTextNode("Abbreviations");
  header.appendChild(header_text);
  document.body.appendChild(header);
  document.body.appendChild(dlist);
}
```

As usual, there's some room for improvement.

133

```
// create the definition description
  var ddesc = document.createElement("dd");
  var ddesc_text = document.createTextNode(definition);
  ddesc.appendChild(ddesc_text);
// add them to the definition list
  dlist.appendChild(dtitle);
  dlist.appendChild(ddesc);
}
if (dlist.childNodes.length < 1) return false;
```

Again, this runs counter to the principles of structured programming because there is now an additional exit point in the middle of the function. But this is probably the simplest way of dealing with Internet Explorer's quirk without altering the existing function significantly.

The finished function looks like this:

```
function displayAbbreviations() {
  if (!document.getElementsByTagName || !document.createElement
➥ || !document.createTextNode) return false;
// get all the abbreviations
  var abbreviations = document.getElementsByTagName("abbr");
  if (abbreviations.length < 1) return false;
  var defs = new Array();
// loop through the abbreviations
  for (var i=0; i<abbreviations.length; i++) {
    var current_abbr = abbreviations[i];
    if (current_abbr.childNodes.length < 1) continue;
    var definition = current_abbr.getAttribute("title");
    var key = current_abbr.lastChild.nodeValue;
    defs[key] = definition;
  }
// create the definition list
  var dlist = document.createElement("dl");
// loop through the definitions
  for (key in defs) {
    var definition = defs[key];
// create the definition title
    var dtitle = document.createElement("dt");
    var dtitle_text = document.createTextNode(key);
    dtitle.appendChild(dtitle_text);
// create the definition description
    var ddesc = document.createElement("dd");
    var ddesc_text = document.createTextNode(definition);
    ddesc.appendChild(ddesc_text);
// add them to the definition list
    dlist.appendChild(dtitle);
    dlist.appendChild(ddesc);
  }
  if (dlist.childNodes.length < 1) return false;
// create a headline
  var header = document.createElement("h2");
  var header_text = document.createTextNode("Abbreviations");
  header.appendChild(header_text);
// add the headline to the body
  document.body.appendChild(header);
```

```
// add the definition list to the body
  document.body.appendChild(dlist);
}
```

The two new lines will ensure that there will be no errors even if the abbr element isn't understood. They act as safety checks, much like the object detection at the start of the script.

■ **Note** Notice that even though the problem was caused by a specific browser, there's still no need to use browser-sniffing code. Sniffing for a specific browser name and number is bound to cause problems and result in very convoluted code.

We have successfully defused a nasty surprise left over from the legacy of the browser wars. If nothing else, it serves as a reminder of the importance of standards. Because their browser doesn't support the abbr element, users of Internet Explorer won't get the benefit of seeing a generated list of abbreviations. But they will still be able to view the core content. The definition list of abbreviations provides a nice enhancement, but it is by no means a vital part of the page. If it were, it would have been included in the markup to begin with.

Displaying citations

The displayAbbreviations function is a good example of content enhancement (at least in any browser other than Internet Explorer). It takes content that is already part of the document structure and displays it in a clearer way. The information contained in the title attributes of the abbr tags appears directly in the browser. Now, let's work through another example of content enhancement.

Take a look at this piece of markup in explanation.html:

```
<blockquote cite="http://www.w3.org/DOM/">
  <p>
A platform- and language-neutral interface that will allow programs
➥and scripts to dynamically access and update the
➥content, structure and style of documents.
  </p>
</blockquote>
```

The blockquote element contains an attribute called cite. This is an optional attribute you can use to specify a URL where the contents of the blockquote can be found. In theory, this is a useful way of linking quotes with relevant web pages. In practice, browsers tend to ignore the cite attribute completely. The information is there, but it isn't being acted upon. Using JavaScript and the DOM, you can take that information and display it in a more meaningful way.

Here is a plan of action for displaying these kind of citations as links:

1. Loop through all the blockquote elements in the document.

2. Get the value of the cite attribute from the blockquote.

3. Create a link with the text "source".

4. Give this link the value of the cite attribute from the blockquote.

5. Insert this link at the end of the quoted text.

As with the display of abbreviations, we'll put this plan into action in a JavaScript function.

Writing the displayCitations function

We'll call our new JavaScript function displayCitations, and store it in a file called displayCitations.js.

First, the function won't take any arguments, so the parentheses after the function name are empty:

```
function displayCitations() {
```

The first step is to gather all the blockquote elements in the document. Use getElementsByTagName and store the resultant node set as the variable quotes:

```
var quotes = document.getElementsByTagName("blockquote");
```

Now start looping through this set:

```
for (var i=0; i<quotes.length; i ++) {
```

Inside the loop, we're interested in only quotes that have a cite attribute. We can perform a simple test to see if the current quote in the loop has this attribute.

Run the test on the current element of the quotes node set, which is quotes[i]. Use getAttribute to perform the test on this node. If the result of getAttribute("cite") is true, there is a cite attribute. If the result of !getAttribute("cite") is true, there is no cite attribute. If that's the case, the keyword continue will cause the loop to jump forward to the next iteration. All the subsequent statements inside the loop will be ignored during the current iteration:

```
if (!quotes[i].getAttribute("cite")) {
    continue;
}
```

You could also write it like this:

```
if (!quotes[i].getAttribute("cite")) continue;
```

The following statements will be performed on only blockquote element nodes that have cite attribute nodes.

First, get the value of the cite attribute of the current blockquote and store it in a variable called url:

```
var url = quotes[i].getAttribute("cite");
```

The next step involves figuring out where to put the link. At first, this might seem very straightforward.

Finding your element

A blockquote element must contain block-level elements, such as paragraphs, to hold the text being quoted. We want to place the link at the end of the last child element node contained by the blockquote element. The obvious thing to do is find the lastChild property of the current blockquote element:

```
quotes[i].lastChild
```

But if we do this, we could potentially run into a problem. Take a look at the markup again:

```
<blockquote cite="http://www.w3.org/DOM/">
    <p>
A platform- and language-neutral interface that will allow programs
➥and scripts to dynamically access and update the
```

➥content, structure and style of documents.
```
  </p>
</blockquote>
```

At first glance, it appears as though the last child of the blockquote element is the p element. You might expect the lastChild property to return the p element node. In reality, this won't necessarily be the case.

It's true that the paragraph is the last *element* node contained by the blockquote element. However, between the end of the p element and the end of the blockquote element, there is a line break. Some browsers will treat this line break as a text node. That means that the lastChild property of the blockquote element node isn't the p element node, it's a text node.

■ **Caution** A common mistake in DOM scripting is assuming that a node is an element node. When in doubt, always check the nodeType value. There are certain methods that can be performed only on element nodes. If you try to perform them on text nodes, you could get an error.

It would be great if there was a DOM property called lastChildElement in addition to the existing lastChild property. Unfortunately, there isn't. However, using existing DOM methods, you can write some statements to perform the required task.

You can find all the element nodes within the current blockquote. If you use getElementsByTagName with the wildcard character (*), it will return every element regardless of its tag name:

```
var quoteElements = quotes[i].getElementsByTagName("*");
```

The variable quoteElements is an array containing all the element nodes contained by the current blockquote element, quotes[i].

To find the last element node contained by the blockquote, retrieve the last element in the quoteElements array. The last element of the array has an index that is one less than the length of the array. Remember that arrays begin counting from zero. That's why the index of the last element isn't equal to the length of the array; it is equal to the length of the array minus one:

```
var elem = quoteElements[quoteElements.length - 1];
```

The variable elem refers to the last element node within the blockquote.

Getting back to our loop in the displayCitations function, this is what we have so far:

```
for (var i=0; i<quotes.length; i++) {
  if (!quotes[i].getAttribute("cite")) continue;
  var url = quotes[i].getAttribute("cite");
  var quoteChildren = quotes[i].getElementsByTagName('*');
  var elem = quoteChildren[quoteChildren.length - 1];
```

Rather than assuming that quoteChildren will return an array of element nodes, run a little check to see if its length is less than one. If that's the case, use the continue keyword again to break out of the current loop:

```
for (var i=0; i<quotes.length; i++) {
  if (!quotes[i].getAttribute("cite")) continue;
  var url = quotes[i].getAttribute("cite");
  var quoteChildren = quotes[i].getElementsByTagName('*');
  if (quoteChildren.length < 1) continue;
```

```
var elem = quoteChildren[quoteChildren.length - 1];
```

We have all the values we need to create a link. The variable url contains the information required for the href value of the link we will make. The elem variable contains the node where we want to place the link.

Creating the link

Create the link by using createElement to make an a element:

```
var link = document.createElement("a");
```

Now create the text that will go within the link. Use the createTextNode method to create some text with the value "source":

```
var link_text = document.createTextNode("source");
```

The newly created a element has been assigned to the variable link. The newly created text node has been assigned to the variable link_text.

Put the text inside the link using the appendChild method:

```
link.appendChild(link_text);
```

Add the href attribute to the link. Set it to the value of the variable url using setAttribute:

```
link.setAttribute("href",url);
```

The link is ready to insert into the document.

Inserting the link

You could insert it into the document as is. You could also wrap it in another element like sup so that the link appears as superscript.

Create a sup element node, giving it the variable superscript:

```
var superscript = document.createElement("sup");
```

Place the link inside this element:

```
superscript.appendChild(link);
```

You now have a DocumentFragment created in JavaScript that isn't connected to the document:

```
<sup><a href="http://www.w3.org/DOM/">source</a></sup>
```

Insert this markup into the document by making it the last child of elem. The variable elem refers to the last element node contained by the blockquote, so the superscripted link will be inserted directly after the quoted text:

```
elem.appendChild(superscript);
```

Close the loop with a closing curly brace, and finish the function by adding a closing curly brace. Here's the finished displayAbbreviations function:

```
function displayCitations() {
  var quotes = document.getElementsByTagName("blockquote");
  for (var i=0; i<quotes.length; i++) {
    if (!quotes[i].getAttribute("cite")) continue;
```

```
        var url = quotes[i].getAttribute("cite");
        var quoteChildren = quotes[i].getElementsByTagName('*');
        if (quoteChildren.length < 1) continue;
        var elem = quoteChildren[quoteChildren.length - 1];
        var link = document.createElement("a");
        var link_text = document.createTextNode("source");
        link.appendChild(link_text);
        link.setAttribute("href",url);
        var superscript = document.createElement("sup");
        superscript.appendChild(link);
        elem.appendChild(superscript);
    }
}
```

Improving the script

As always, there's room for improvement. Add a test at the start of the function to ensure that the browser will understand the DOM methods you're using. You can also add some comments to the make the code clearer.

```
function displayCitations() {
    if (!document.getElementsByTagName || !document.createElement
å|| !document.createTextNode) return false;
// get all the blockquotes
    var quotes = document.getElementsByTagName("blockquote");
// loop through all the blockquotes
    for (var i=0; i<quotes.length; i++) {
// if there is no cite attribute, continue the loop
        if (!quotes[i].getAttribute("cite")) continue;
// store the cite attribute
        var url = quotes[i].getAttribute("cite");
// get all the element nodes in the blockquote
        var quoteChildren = quotes[i].getElementsByTagName('*');
// if there are no element nodes, continue the loop
        if (quoteChildren.length < 1) continue;
// get the last element node in the blockquote
        var elem = quoteChildren[quoteChildren.length - 1];
// create the markup
        var link = document.createElement("a");
        var link_text = document.createTextNode("source");
        link.appendChild(link_text);
        link.setAttribute("href",url);
        var superscript = document.createElement("sup");
        superscript.appendChild(link);
// add the markup to the last element node in the blockquote
        elem.appendChild(superscript);
    }
}
```

Call the displayCitations function using the addLoadEvent function:

```
addLoadEvent(displayCitations);
```

The final markup

Call the displayCitations.js file from explanation.html by adding a new set of `<script>` tags to the end of the document:

```html
<!DOCTYPE html>
<html lang="en">
  <head>
    <meta charset="utf-8" />
    <title>Explaining the Document Object Model</title>
    <link rel="stylesheet" media="screen"
➥href="styles/typography.css" />
</head>
<body>
    <h1>What is the Document Object Model?</h1>
    <p>
The <abbr title="World Wide Web Consortium">W3C</abbr> defines
➥the <abbr title="Document Object Model">DOM</abbr> as:
    </p>
    <blockquote cite="http://www.w3.org/DOM/">
<p>
A platform- and language-neutral interface that will allow programs
➥and scripts to dynamically access and update the
➥content, structure and style of documents.
    </p>
    </blockquote>
    <p>
It is an <abbr title="Application Programming Interface">API</abbr>
➥that can be used to navigate <abbr title="HyperText Markup Language">
➥HTML</abbr> and <abbr title="eXtensible Markup Language">XML
➥</abbr> documents.
    </p>
    <script src="scripts/addLoadEvent.js"></script>
    <script src="scripts/displayAbbreviations.js"></script>
    <script src="scripts/displayCitations.js"></script>
  </body>
</html>
```

Load explanation.html in a web browser to see the result.

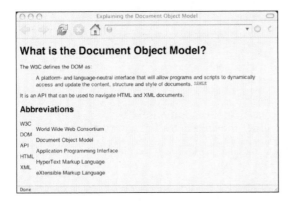

Displaying access keys

The two functions that we've written, `displayAbbreviations` and `displayCitations`, have a lot in common. They both begin by creating a node set of a certain element (`abbr` or `blockquote`). Then they loop through this node set, creating some markup during each iteration of the loop. This markup is then inserted into the document.

Let's look at one more example that follows this pattern. We'll write a function to display all the access keys used in a document.

The `accesskey` attribute associates an element, such as a link, with a specific key on a keyboard. This can be useful for people who don't navigate with a mouse. If you are visually impaired, for instance, it's very handy to have keyboard shortcuts.

On many Windows browsers, you can press Alt+*access key*; on many Mac browsers, you can press Ctrl+*access key*.

Here's an example of an `accesskey` attribute:

```
<a href="index.html" accesskey="1">Home</a>
```

■ **Caution** It's usually not a good idea to use too many access keys. There is a danger that they could clash with the keyboard shortcuts built into the browser.

While many browsers support the functionality of the `accesskey` attribute, it is left to you to indicate which access keys have been assigned. This is often done in an *accessibility statement*, which is a page that lists the accessibility features of a website.

A loose convention has arisen for some basic access key settings (see `http://www.clagnut.com/blog/193/`):

- An `accesskey` value of 1 is used for a link back to the home page of a site.

- An `accesskey` value of 2 is used for "skip navigation" links.

- An `accesskey` value of 4 is used for a link to a search form or page.

- An `accesskey` value of 9 is used for a link to contact information.

- An `accesskey` value of 0 is used for a link to an accessibility statement.

145

Here's an example of a site navigation list that uses access keys:

```
<ul id="navigation">
  <li><a href="index.html" accesskey="1">Home</a></li>
  <li><a href="search.html" accesskey="4">Search</a></li>
  <li><a href="contact.html" accesskey="9">Contact</a></li>
</ul>
```

Add that markup right after the opening of the <body> tag in explanation.html.

If you load explanation.html in a web browser, you will see the links in the list. But you won't see anything to indicate that there are accesskey attributes present.

Using the DOM, you can create a list of access keys on the fly. Here's how:

1. Get a node set of all the links in the document.

2. Loop through all these links.

3. If a link has an accesskey attribute, store its value.

4. Store the link text as well.

5. Create a list.

6. For each link with an access key, create a list item.

7. Add the list item to the list.

8. Add the list to the document.

As in the previous examples, we'll put these steps in a function.

Name the function displayAccesskeys and store it in a file called displayAccesskeys.js.

This function works very similarly to the displayAbbreviations function. The accesskey values and the corresponding link texts are stored in an associative array. A for/in loop is then used to loop through this array and create list items.

Rather than going through each line, let's just look at the finished function. The comments give an indication of what's happening at each stage:

```
function displayAccesskeys() {
  if (!document.getElementsByTagName || !document.createElement ||
➥!document.createTextNode) return false;
// get all the links in the document
  var links = document.getElementsByTagName("a");
// create an array to store the access keys
  var akeys = new Array();
// loop through the links
  for (var i=0; i<links.length; i++) {
    var current_link = links[i];
// if there is no accesskey attribute, continue the loop
    if (!current_link.getAttribute("accesskey")) continue;
// get the value of the accesskey
    var key = current_link.getAttribute("accesskey");
// get the value of the link text
    var text = current_link.lastChild.nodeValue;
// add them to the array
    akeys[key] = text;
  }
// create the list
  var list = document.createElement("ul");
```

```
// loop through the access keys
  for (key in akeys) {
    var text = akeys[key];
// create the string to put in the list item
    var str = key + ": "+text;
// create the list item
    var item = document.createElement("li");
    var item_text = document.createTextNode(str);
    item.appendChild(item_text);
// add the list item to the list
    list.appendChild(item);
  }
// create a headline
  var header = document.createElement("h3");
  var header_text = document.createTextNode("Accesskeys");
  header.appendChild(header_text);
// add the headline to the body
  document.body.appendChild(header);
// add the list to the body
  document.body.appendChild(list);
}
addLoadEvent(displayAccesskeys);
```

Reference the displayAccesskeys.js file with a new set of <script> tags in explanation.html:

```
<script src="scripts/displayAccesskeys.js"></script>
```

Load explanation.html in a web browser to see the newly created list of access keys.

Retrieving and attaching information

In the course of this chapter, we've created several useful DOM scripts that you can attach to just about any web page. They all perform different tasks, but the underlying principle is the same for each one. The JavaScript functions examine the document structure, extract information from it, and then insert that information back into the document in a clear and meaningful way.

These functions can improve the clarity and usability of web pages:

- Displaying a definition list of abbreviations used in a document

- Linking to the source of quoted texts

- Displaying a list of access keys used in a document

You can alter these scripts if you like. For example, instead of displaying the source of quoted text with each blockquote, you could display all of the sources as a list at the end of the document, just like footnotes. Also, you could indicate which access key has been assigned to a link by appending the access key directly to the link text.

Following the pattern described in this chapter, you can write useful scripts. For example, you could create a table of contents for a document. Loop through all the h1 or h2 elements in a document and put them into a list. Attach that list to the start of the document. You could even make each item in the list an internal link to the corresponding header.

You can create useful scripts like these using just a handful of DOM methods and properties. Having well-structured markup is an important prerequisite when you are enhancing content with DOM scripts.

As a recap, these are the most useful methods for retrieving information from a document:

- getElementById
- getElementsByTagName
- getAttribute

These are the most useful methods for attaching information to a document:

- createElement
- createTextNode
- appendChild
- insertBefore
- setAttribute

By combining those methods, you can create very powerful DOM scripts.

Always remember to use JavaScript to enhance the content of your documents, rather than creating any core content directly with the DOM.

What's next?

So far, we've been using JavaScript and the DOM to manipulate or create markup. In the next chapter, you're going to see a whole new side to the DOM. It shows you how you can use the DOM to manipulate styles, such as colors, fonts, and so on. Not only can the DOM alter the structure of a web page, it can update the CSS attached to elements in the page!

CSS-DOM

What this chapter covers:

- Introducing the style property
- How to retrieve style information
- How to change styles

In this chapter, the presentation layer and the behavior layer will meet head-on. You'll see how the DOM can be used to get and set styles by reading and writing CSS.

Three sheets to the Web

Content on the Web can be wrapped up in three successive layers that web browsers can read:

- Structure
- Presentation
- Behavior

Structure

First and foremost, the *structural layer* is created with a markup language, such as HTML or XHTML. The *tags*, or words contained in angle brackets, describe the semantic meaning of content. For example, the `<p>` tag conveys the information, "This content is a paragraph." But the tag doesn't include any information about how the content should be displayed:

```
<p>An example of a paragraph</p>
```

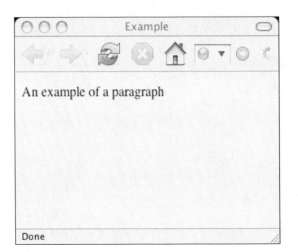

Presentation

The *presentation layer*, achieved with Cascading Style Sheets, describes how the content should be displayed. You can use CSS to declare, "Paragraphs should be colored grey and use Arial or some other sans-serif font":

```
p {
  color: grey;
  font-family: "Arial", sans-serif;
}
```

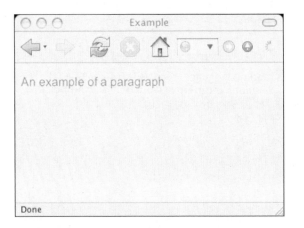

Behavior

Finally, the *behavior layer* describes how the content should react to events. This is where JavaScript and the DOM rule the roost. Using the DOM, you can specify, "When the user clicks on a paragraph, display an alert dialog":

```
var paras = document.getElementsByTagName("p");
for (var i=0; i<paras.length; i++) {
  paras[i].onclick = function() {
    alert("You clicked on a paragraph.");
  }
}
```

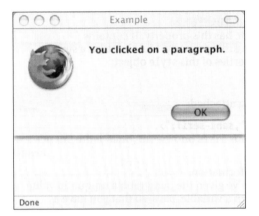

Presentation and behavior are always present, even if you don't give any specific instructions. Web browsers will apply their own default styles and event handlers. Browsers will apply margins to paragraph elements. Many browsers will display the contents of title attributes as tool tips when the user hovers over an element.

Separation

A good rule of thumb in any design discipline is to use the right tool for the task at hand. For web design, that means:

- Use (X)HTML to structure your documents.
- Use CSS to attach presentational information.
- Use DOM scripting to apply behavioral instructions.

However, there is a certain amount of potential crossover between these three technologies. You've already seen one example of this. Using the DOM, you can alter the structure of a web page. Methods like createElement and appendChild allow you to create and add markup on the fly.

Another example of technologies crossing over can be found in CSS. Pseudo-classes like :hover and :focus allow you to change the appearance of elements based on user-triggered events. Changing the appearance of elements certainly belongs in the presentation layer, but reacting to user-triggered events is part of the behavior layer. This is a situation where presentation and behavior overlap, creating a grey area.

It's true that CSS is stepping on the DOM's toes with pseudo-classes. But the Document Object Model can step right back. You can use the DOM to attach presentational information to elements.

```
<!DOCTYPE html>
<html lang="en">
<head>
  <meta charset="utf-8" />
  <title>Example</title>
  <script>
window.onload = function() {
  var para = document.getElementById("example");
  alert("The font size is " + para.style.fontSize);
}
  </script>
</head>
<body>
  <p id="example" style="color: grey; font-family: 'Arial',sans-serif;
➥ font-size: 1em;">
An example of a paragraph
  </p>
</body>
</html>
```

Here, the fontSize property has been set using the em unit:

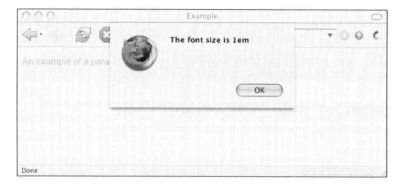

If an element's CSS font-size property has a value of "1em", the DOM fontSize property will return a value of "1em". If "12px" is applied with CSS, the DOM will return "12px".

Using CSS shorthand properties, you can combine a number of styles into one declaration. If you declare font: 12px 'Arial',sans-serif, the CSS font-size property is set to 12px and the CSS font-family will have a value of 'Arial',sans-serif":

```
<p id="example" style="color: grey; font: 12px 'Arial',sans-serif;">
```

The DOM is able to parse shorthand properties like font. If you query the fontSize property, you will get a value of "12px":

```
alert("The font size is " + para.style.fontSize);
```

Here, the fontSize property has been set using pixels.

Inline only

There's a big caveat to retrieving stylistic information with the style property.

The style property only returns inline style information. If you apply styling information by inserting style attributes into your markup, you can query that information using the DOM style property:

```
<p id="example" style="color: grey; font: 12px 'Arial',sans-serif;">
```

This is not a very good way of applying styles. Presentational information is mixed in with structure. It's much better to apply styles in an external style sheet:

```
p#example {
  color: grey;
  font: 12px 'Arial', sans-serif;
}
```

Save that CSS in a file called styles.css in the styles folder. Now update example.html, removing the inline styling to leave the following instead:

```
<p id="example">
An example of a paragraph
</p>
```

Add a link element to the head of example.html, pointing to the styles.css file:

```
<link rel="stylesheet" media="screen" href="styles/styles.css" />
```

The style information is applied to the markup, just as before. But the linked styles, unlike those assigned in a style attribute, won't be picked up by the DOM style property:

```
alert("The font size is " + para.style.fontSize);
```

The DOM style property doesn't retrieve styles declared externally, as you can see here.

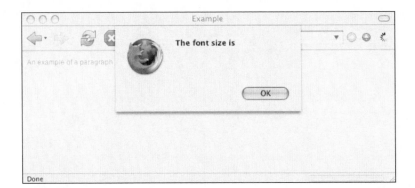

You'll see the same result (or lack thereof) if you add style information between <style> tags in the head of example.html:

```
<style>
  p#example {
    color: grey;
    font: 12px 'Arial', sans-serif;
  }
</style>
```

The DOM style property won't pick up that information.

The style object doesn't include stylistic information that has been declared in an external style sheet. It also doesn't include stylistic information that has been declared in the head of a document.

The style object does pick up stylistic information that has been declared inline using the style attribute. But this is of little practical use, because styles should be applied separately from the markup.

At this point, you might be thinking that using the DOM to manipulate CSS seems next to useless. However, there is one other situation where the DOM style object correctly reflects stylistic information that you have applied. If you apply styles using the DOM, you will be able to retrieve those styles.

Setting styles

Many DOM properties are read-only. That means you can use them to retrieve information, but you can't use them to set or update information. Properties like previousSibling, nextSibling, parentNode, firstChild, and lastChild are invaluable for gathering information about an element's position in the document's node tree, but they can't be used to update information.

The properties of the style object, on the other hand, are read/write. That means you can use an element's style property to retrieve information, and you can also use it to update information. You can do this using the assignment operator, the equal sign:

```
element.style.property = value
```

The value of a style property is always a string. Update the example.html file with some JavaScript that overrides the inline CSS. Set the color property of para to the string "black":

```
<!DOCTYPE html>
<html lang="en">
<head>
  <meta charset="utf-8" />
  <title>Example</title>
  <script>
```

```
window.onload = function() {
  var para = document.getElementById("example");
  para.style.color = "black";
}
  </script>
</head>
<body>
  <p id="example" style="color: grey; font-family: 'Arial',sans-serif;">
An example of a paragraph
  </p>
</body>
</html>
```

The color property has been changed to "black," as shown here.

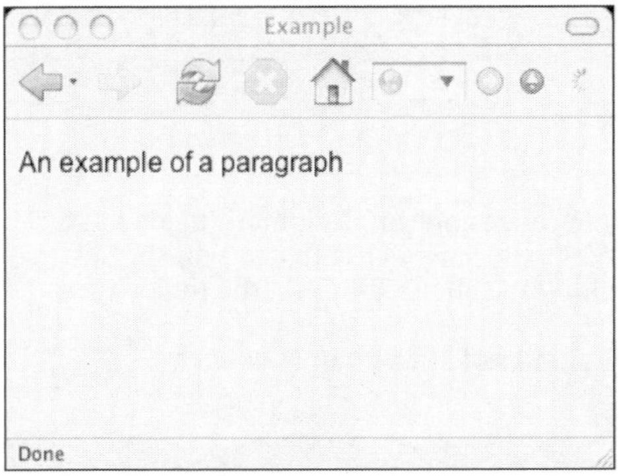

The value must be placed within quotes. You can use either double quotes or single quotes, whichever you prefer:

```
para.style.color = 'black';
```

If you don't use quotes, JavaScript will assume that the value is a variable:

```
para.style.color = black;
```

If you haven't defined a variable called black, the code won't work.

You can set any style property using the assignment operator. You can even use shorthand properties like font:

```
para.style.font = "2em 'Times',serif";
```

This will set the fontSize property to 2em and the fontFamily property to 'Times',serif:

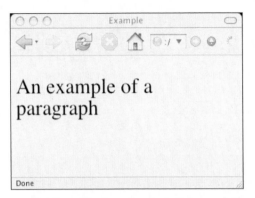

Setting styles is quite straightforward. I've shown you how. But perhaps the more important question is, "Why?"

Knowing when to use DOM styling

You've seen how easy it is to set styles using the DOM. But just because you can do something doesn't mean you should. Nine times out of ten, you should be using CSS to declare styles. Just as you should never use the DOM to create important content, you also shouldn't use the DOM to set the majority of styles for a document.

Occasionally, however, you can use the DOM to add some small stylistic enhancements to documents where it would be unwieldy to use CSS.

Styling elements in the node tree

CSS can be used in several different ways to apply styles. You can apply styles to all occurrences of a particular element, such as paragraphs:

```
p {
    font-size: 1em;
}
```

You can apply styles to all elements that have a particular class attribute:

```
.fineprint {
    font-size: .8em;
}
```

You can apply styles to an element with a unique id attribute:

```
#intro {
    font-size: 1.2em;
}
```

You can apply styles to elements with similar attributes:

```
input[type*="text"] {
    font-size:1.2em;
}
```

In modern browsers, you can even apply styles to an element based on some aspects of its position:

```
p:first-of-type {
  font-size:2em;
  font-weight:bold;
}
```

CSS2 introduced a number of position-based selectors such as :first-child and :last-child, while CSS3 includes position selectors such as :nth-child() and :nth-of-type(), but it's still sometimes difficult to apply styles to an element based on its position in the document's node tree. For instance, with CSS3 you could say, "Apply the following styles to the next sibling of all h1 elements" by using the h1 ~ * selector. The problem, however, is that many browsers don't support all the nice CSS3 position selectors.

The DOM, on the other hand, makes it quite easy to target elements based on their familial relationships with other elements. Using the DOM, you could quite easily imitate the CSS3 sibling selector and find all the h1 elements in a document and then find out what element immediately follows each h1 and apply styles specifically to those elements.

First of all, get all the h1 elements using getElementsByTagName:

```
var headers = document.getElementsByTagName("h1");
```

Loop through all the elements in the node set:

```
for (var i=0; i<headers.length; i++) {
```

You can find the next node in the document using nextSibling:

```
headers[i].nextSibling
```

But in this case you actually want to find not just the next node, but specifically the next element node. This is easily done using a function called getNextElement:

```
function getNextElement(node) {
  if(node.nodeType == 1) {
   return node;
  }
  if (node.nextSibling) {
    return getNextElement(node.nextSibling);
  }
  return null;
}
```

Pass this function the nextSibling node of an h1 element as the argument. Assign the result to a variable called elem:

```
var elem = getNextElement(headers[i].nextSibling);
```

Now you can style this element any way you want:

```
elem.style.fontWeight = "bold";
elem.style.fontSize = "1.2em";
```

Wrap the whole thing up in a function called styleHeaderSiblings. Be sure to throw in a test to make sure that the browser understands the DOM methods being used:

```
function styleHeaderSiblings() {
  if (!document.getElementsByTagName) return false;
  var headers = document.getElementsByTagName("h1");
  var elem;
  for (var i=0; i<headers.length; i++) {
    elem = getNextElement(headers[i].nextSibling);
```

```
      elem.style.fontWeight = "bold";
      elem.style.fontSize = "1.2em";
    }
  }
  function getNextElement(node) {
    if(node.nodeType == 1) {
     return node;
    }
    if (node.nextSibling) {
      return getNextElement(node.nextSibling);
    }
    return null;
  }
```

You can call the function using the window.onload event:

```
window.onload = styleHeaderSiblings;
```

Better yet, use the addLoadEvent function so that you can always add more functions to the same event:

```
addLoadEvent(styleHeaderSiblings);
```

Here's the addLoadEvent function, which you can store in an external file:

```
function addLoadEvent(func) {
  var oldonload = window.onload;
  if (typeof window.onload != 'function') {
    window.onload = func;
  } else {
    window.onload = function() {
      oldonload();
      func();
    }
  }
}
```

To see the styleHeaderSiblings function in action, write a document that uses level one headings:

```
<!DOCTYPE html>
<html lang="en">
<head>
  <meta charset="utf-8" />
  <title>Man bites dog</title>
</head>
<body>
  <h1>Hold the front page</h1>
  <p>This first paragraph leads you in.</p>
  <p>Now you get the nitty-gritty of the story.</p>
  <p>The most important information is delivered first.</p>
  <h1>Extra! Extra!</h1>
  <p>Further developments are unfolding.</p>
  <p>You can read all about it here.</p>
</body>
</html>
```

Save this document as story.html; here's what it looks like in a browser.

Create a folder called scripts where you can put your JavaScript files. Then, write a file for the addLoadEvent function and place it in this folder. Call it addLoadEvent.js. Write the styleHeaderSiblings function to a file called styleHeaderSiblings.js and place it in the same folder.

Insert <script> tags before the closing </body> tag of story.html to reference your JavaScript files:

```
<script src="scripts/addLoadEvent.js"></script>
<script src="scripts/styleHeaderSiblings.js"></script>
```

Load story.html in a web browser to see the results of the DOM-generated styles. The element immediately following every h1 has been styled.

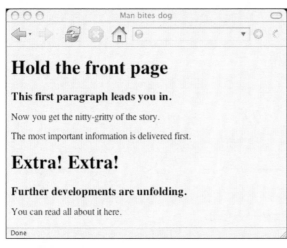

Ideally, this kind of styling should be handled by CSS alone. In reality, that isn't always practical or possible depending on the browser. In this case, you would have to add a class attribute to every element following a level one heading. In a situation where you are regularly editing and updating your content, that can quickly become tiresome. If you are using a Content Management System (CMS) to handle your content, it may not be possible to add classes or other style information to individual parts of the content.

Repetitive styling

Let's say you have a list of dates and places. It could be a list of concert dates or an itinerary for a road trip. In any case, there is a direct relationship between each date and place. This is tabular data. The ideal tag for marking up this data is the <table> tag.

■ **Note** If you're using CSS to lay out your web pages, don't fall into the trap of thinking that all tables are bad. Using tables for layout isn't a good idea. But you should definitely use tables to display tabular data.

Here's how your markup might look:

```
<!DOCTYPE html>
<html lang="en">
<head>
  <meta charset="utf-8" />
  <title>Cities</title>
</head>
<body>
  <table>
    <caption>Itinerary</caption>
    <thead>
    <tr>
      <th>When</th>
      <th>Where</th>
    </tr>
    </thead>
    <tbody>
    <tr>
      <td>June 9th</td>
      <td>Portland, <abbr title="Oregon">OR</abbr></td>
    </tr>
    <tr>
      <td>June 10th</td>
      <td>Seattle, <abbr title="Washington">WA</abbr></td>
    </tr>
    <tr>
      <td>June 12th</td>
      <td>Sacramento, <abbr title="California">CA</abbr></td>
    </tr>
    </tbody>
  </table>
</body>
</html>
```

Save this as `itinerary.html`. If you load this file in a web browser, you will see a perfectly functional, but somewhat dull, table of information.

Write a style sheet so that the data is presented in a more readable format:

```css
body {
    font-family: "Helvetica","Arial",sans-serif;
    background-color: #fff;
    color: #000;
}
table {
    margin: auto;
    border: 1px solid #699;
}
caption {
    margin: auto;
    padding: .2em;
    font-size: 1.2em;
    font-weight: bold;
}
th {
    font-weight: normal;
    font-style: italic;
    text-align: left;
    border: 1px dotted #699;
    background-color: #9cc;
    color: #000;
}
th,td {
    width: 10em;
    padding: .5em;
}
```

Save this file as `format.css` and place it in a folder called `styles`. Add a `link` in the head of `itinerary.html` pointing to this file:

```html
<link rel="stylesheet" media="screen" href="styles/format.css" />
```

Refresh `itinerary.html` in a web browser to see the effects of the CSS:

A common technique for making table rows more readable is to alternate the background colors. The resulting striped effect helps to separate individual rows. This can be done by applying styles to every second row. If the browser supports CSS3, it's as easy as this:

```
tr:nth-child(odd)    { background-color:# ffc; }
tr:nth-child(even)   { background-color:#fff; }
```

To get this same effect when `:nth-child()` isn't available, you'll need a different technique. In the case of `itinerary.html`, this could be easily done by assigning a `class` attribute to each odd or even row. However, this isn't very convenient, especially for larger tables—if a row is added to or removed from the middle of the table, you would have to painstakingly update the `class` attributes by hand.

JavaScript is very good at handling repetitive tasks. You can easily loop through a long list using a `while` or `for` loop.

You can write a function to stripe your tables by applying styles to every second row:

1. Get all the table elements in the document.

2. For each table, create a variable called odd set to false.

3. Loop through all the rows in the table.

4. If odd is true, apply styles and change odd to false.

5. If odd is false, don't apply styles but change odd to true.

Call the function `stripeTables`. The function doesn't need to take any arguments, so the parentheses after the function name will be empty. Don't forget to start your function by testing the DOM compliance of the browser:

```
function stripeTables() {
  if (!document.getElementsByTagName) return false;
  var tables = document.getElementsByTagName("table");
  var odd, rows;
  for (var i=0; i<tables.length; i++) {
    odd = false;
    rows = tables[i].getElementsByTagName("tr");
    for (var j=0; j<rows.length; j++) {
      if (odd == true) {
```

```
        rows[j].style.backgroundColor = "#ffc";
        odd = false;
      } else {
        odd = true;
      }
    }
  }
}
```

Run the function when the page loads. The best way to do this is using the addLoadEvent function again:

```
addLoadEvent(stripeTables);
```

Save the JavaScript to a file called stripeTables.js in a folder called scripts, together with the addLoadEvent.js file.

Add <script> tags to include both the following JavaScript files right before the closing </body> tag in itinerary.html:

```
<script src="scripts/addLoadEvent.js"></script>
<script src="scripts/stripeTables.js"></script>
```

Load itinerary.html in a web browser. You'll see that every second row in the table has been styled with a background color.

Incidentally, you could also use the displayAbbreviations function from the previous chapter for this document. Drop the displayAbbreviations.js file into the scripts folder and add one more set of <script> tags to itinerary.html. Refresh the page in a web browser to see the generated definition list.

Responding to events

Wherever possible, it's best to use CSS to set styles for a document. That said, you've just seen some situations where CSS could be unwieldy or tedious to deploy. In those situations, the DOM can help.

It's not always easy to know when to use CSS and when to use DOM scripting to set styles. The biggest grey area concerns the changing of styles based on events.

CSS provides pseudo-classes like :hover that allow you to change the styles of elements based on their state. The DOM also responds to changes of state using event handlers like onmouseover. It's difficult to know when to use :hover and when to use onmouseover.

The simplest solution is to follow the path of least resistance. If you simply want to change the color of your links when they're moused over, then you should definitely use CSS:

```
a:hover {
  color: #c60;
}
```

The :hover pseudo-class is widely supported, at least when it is used for styling links. If you want to style any other elements when they are moused over, browser support isn't quite so widespread.

Take the example of the table in itinerary.html. If you wanted to highlight a row when it is moused over, you could use CSS:

```
tr:hover {
  font-weight: bold;
}
```

In theory, this should bold the text in any table row whenever it is moused over. In practice, this will only work in certain browsers.

In situations like that, the DOM can be used to level the playing field. While support for CSS pseudo-classes remains patchy, the DOM is well supported in most modern browsers. Until CSS support improves, it makes sense to use the DOM to apply styles based on events.

Here's a short function called highlightRows that will bold text whenever a table row is moused over:

```
function highlightRows() {
  if(!document.getElementsByTagName) return false;
  var rows = document.getElementsByTagName("tr");
  for (var i=0; i<rows.length; i++) {
    rows[i].onmouseover = function() {
      this.style.fontWeight = "bold";
    }
    rows[i].onmouseout = function() {
      this.style.fontWeight = "normal";
    }
  }
}
addLoadEvent(highlightRows);
```

Save it to a file called highlightRows.js in the scripts folder. Add another set of <script> tags before the closing </body> tag of itinerary.html:

```
<script src="scripts/highlightRows.js"></script>
```

Refresh itinerary.html in a web browser. Now hover over one of the rows in the table. The text will turn bold:

In situations like these, you'll need to decide whether to use a purely CSS solution or use the DOM to set styles. You'll need to consider factors like

- What's the simplest solution to this problem?
- Which solution has greater browser support?

To make an informed decision, you'll need to be well versed in both CSS and DOM Scripting. If all you have is a hammer, then everything looks like a nail. If you only feel comfortable using CSS, then you might choose a CSS solution where JavaScript would actually be better. On the other hand, if you only know DOM scripting, then you may find yourself writing functions to accomplish tasks that are quicker and easier to implement with CSS.

If you want to apply presentation to elements, use CSS. If you want to apply behavior to elements, use the DOM. If you want to apply presentation based on behavior, use your best judgment. There is no "one size fits all" solution.

className

In the examples you've seen so far in this chapter, the DOM has been used to explicitly set stylistic information. This is less than ideal because the behavior layer is doing the work of the presentation layer. If you change your mind about the styles being set, you'll need to dig down into your JavaScript functions and update the relevant statements. It would be better if you could make those kinds of changes in your style sheets.

There's a simple solution. Instead of changing the presentation of an element directly with the DOM, use JavaScript to update the class attribute attached to that element.

Take a look at how the styleHeaderSiblings function is adding stylistic information:

```
function styleHeaderSiblings() {
  if (!document.getElementsByTagName) return false;
  var headers = document.getElementsByTagName("h1");
  var elem;
  for (var i=0; i<headers.length; i++) {
    elem = getNextElement(headers[i].nextSibling);
    elem.style.fontWeight = "bold";
    elem.style.fontSize = "1.2em";
  }
}
```

If you ever decided that the elements following level one headings should have a CSS font-size value of "1.4em" instead of "1.2em", you would have to update the styleHeaderSiblings function.

It would be better if you were to include a style sheet with a declaration for a class named something like intro:

```
.intro {
  font-weight: bold;
  font-size: 1.2em;
}
```

Now all that the styleHeaderSiblings function needs to do is to apply this class to the element immediately following a level one heading.

You can do this using the setAttribute method.

```
elem.setAttribute("class","intro");
```

An easier solution is to update a property called className. This is a read/write property of any element node.

You can use className to get the class of an element.

```
element.className
```

You can use the assignment operator to set the class of an element.

```
element.className = value
```

This is how the styleHeaderSiblings function looks when you use className instead of setting styles directly with the style property:

```
function styleHeaderSiblings() {
  if (!document.getElementsByTagName) return false;
  var headers = document.getElementsByTagName("h1");
  var elem;
  for (var i=0; i<headers.length; i++) {
    elem = getNextElement(headers[i].nextSibling);
    elem.className = "intro";
  }
}
```

Now, whenever you want to update the presentation of elements that follow level-one headings, you can do so by updating the style declarations for the intro class:

```
.intro {
  font-weight: bold;
  font-size: 1.4em;
}
```

There's just one drawback to this technique. If you assign a class using the className property, you will overwrite any classes that are already attached to that element:

```
<h1>Man bites dog</h1>
<p class="disclaimer">This is not a true story</p>
```

If you run the styleHeaderSiblings function on a document containing that piece of markup, the class attribute of the paragraph will be changed from disclaimer to intro. What you really want to do is update the class attribute so that it reads disclaimer intro. That way the styles for the disclaimer and intro classes will both be applied.

You can do this by concatenating a space and the name of the new class to the className property:

```
elem.className += " intro";
```

But you really only want to do this when there are existing classes. If there are no existing classes, you can just use the assignment operator with className.

Whenever you want to add a new class to an element, you can run through these steps:

1. Is the value of className null?

2. If so, assign the class value to the className property.

3. If not, concatenate a space and the class value to the className property.

You can encapsulate those steps in a function. Call the function addClass. It will need to take two arguments: the element to which you want to add the class and the name of the class you want to add. You can call these arguments element and value:

```
function addClass(element,value) {
  if (!element.className) {
    element.className = value;
  } else {
    newClassName = element.className;
    newClassName+= " ";
    newClassName+= value;
```

```
    element.className = newClassName;
  }
}
```

Call the addClass function from the styleHeaderSiblings function:

```
function styleHeaderSiblings() {
  if (!document.getElementsByTagName) return false;
  var headers = document.getElementsByTagName("h1");
  var elem;
  for (var i=0; i<headers.length; i++) {
    elem = getNextElement(headers[i].nextSibling);
    addClass(elem,"intro");
  }
}
```

You could also update the stripeTables function. Right now, the background color of every second row in every table is being changed directly with JavaScript:

```
function stripeTables() {
  if (!document.getElementsByTagName) return false;
  var tables = document.getElementsByTagName("table");
  var odd, rows;
  for (var i=0; i<tables.length; i++) {
    odd = false;
    rows = tables[i].getElementsByTagName("tr");
    for (var j=0; j<rows.length; j++) {
      if (odd == true) {
        rows[j].style.backgroundColor = "#ffc";
        odd = false;
      } else {
        odd = true;
      }
    }
  }
}
```

Update format.css with a new class named odd:

```
.odd {
  background-color: #ffc;
}
```

Now use the addClass function from within stripeTables:

```
function stripeTables() {
  if (!document.getElementsByTagName) return false;
  var tables = document.getElementsByTagName("table");
  var odd, rows;
  for (var i=0; i<tables.length; i++) {
    odd = false;
    rows = tables[i].getElementsByTagName("tr");
    for (var j=0; j<rows.length; j++) {
      if (odd == true) {
        addClass(rows[j],"odd");
        odd = false;
```

```
    } else {
      odd = true;
    }
  }
}
}
```

The final result will be exactly the same as before. The difference is that now presentational information is being set using CSS rather than being set by the DOM. The JavaScript functions are updating the className property and the style property is left untouched. This ensures better separation between presentation and behavior.

Abstracting a function

All of your functions are working fine and you can leave them as they are. However, you can make some small changes that will make your functions easier to reuse in the future. The process of taking something very specific and turning it into something more general is called *abstraction*.

If you look at the styleHeaderSiblings function, you'll see that it is very specific to h1 elements. The className value of intro is also hard-coded into the function:

```
function styleHeaderSiblings() {
  if (!document.getElementsByTagName) return false;
  var headers = document.getElementsByTagName("h1");
  var elem;
  for (var i=0; i<headers.length; i++) {
    elem = getNextElement(headers[i].nextSibling);
    addClass(elem,"intro");
  }
}
```

If you wanted to turn this into a more generic function, you could make those values into arguments. Call the new function styleElementSiblings and give it two arguments, tag and theclass:

```
function styleElementSiblings(tag,theclass)
```

Now, replace the string h1 with the argument tag and replace the string intro with the argument theclass. You might also want to change the name of the variable headers to something more descriptive, like elems:

```
function styleElementSiblings(tag,theclass) {
  if (!document.getElementsByTagName) return false;
  var elems = document.getElementsByTagName(tag);
  var elem;
  for (var i=0; i<elems.length; i++) {
    elem = getNextElement(elems[i].nextSibling);
    addClass(elem,theclass);
  }
}
```

You can achieve the same effect as before by passing this function the values h1 and intro:

```
addloadEvent(function(){
  styleElementSiblings("h1","intro");
});
```

173

Whenever you spot a chance to abstract a function like this, it's usually a good idea to do so. You may find yourself needing to accomplish a similar effect to `styleHeaderSiblings`, but on a different element or with a different class. That's when a generic function like `styleElementSiblings` will come in useful.

What's next?

In this chapter, you've seen a whole new side to the Document Object Model. You have previously been introduced to methods and properties that belonged either to the DOM Core or to HTML-DOM. This chapter introduced CSS-DOM, which involves getting and setting properties of the `style` object. The `style` object is itself a property of every element node in a document.

The biggest limitation to using the `style` property is that it doesn't pick up styles that have been set in an external style sheet. But you can still use `style` to alter the presentation of elements. This can be useful in situations where it would be too unwieldy or unpredictable to use CSS. Wherever possible, it's best to update the `className` property rather than updating properties of the `style` object directly.

You've seen a few short examples of CSS-DOM in action:

- Styling an element based on its position in the node tree (`styleHeaderSiblings`)
- Styling elements by looping through a node set (`stripeTables`)
- Styling an element in response to an event (`highlightRows`)

These are situations where JavaScript takes over from CSS, either because CSS can't target elements in the same way, or because CSS support for that level of targeting isn't yet widely supported. In the future, it may be possible to discard a lot of this kind of DOM scripting in favor of advanced CSS techniques.

There's one area where CSS is unlikely to ever be in competition with the DOM. JavaScript can repeat actions at regular intervals. By making incremental changes to style information over time, you can create effects that would be impossible using just CSS.

In the next chapter, you're going to see an example of that. You will write a function that will update an element's position over time. Simply put, you're going to create animation.

An Animated Slideshow

What this chapter covers:

- The basics of animation
- Web page enhancement with animation

In this chapter, you'll see one of the most dynamic applications of CSS-DOM: the ability to animate elements.

Animation basics

The previous chapter introduced the DOM's ability to update the styles attached to a document. Using JavaScript to add presentational information can save you time and effort, but, for the most part, CSS remains the best tool for the job.

There's one area, however, where CSS can't really help much. If you want to change an element's style information over time, you'll probably need to use JavaScript. CSS3 introduces a number of different transition methods that allow you to animate elements. However, currently, browser support without vendor-specific prefixes is minimal. JavaScript, on the other hand, allows you to execute functions at set intervals. This means that you can alter an element's style with the passage of time.

Animation is the perfect example of this kind of change. In a nutshell, animation involves changing an element's position over time.

Position

An element's position in the browser window is presentational information. As such, it is usually added using CSS. Here's an example that sets an element's position on the page:

```
element {
  position: absolute;
  top: 50px;
  left: 100px;
}
```

That will position the element 100 pixels from the left of the browser window and 50 pixels from the top. Here's the DOM equivalent of the same information:

```
element.style.position = "absolute";
element.style.left = "100px";
element.style.top = "50px";
```

Valid values for the position property are "static", "fixed", "relative", and "absolute". Elements have a position value of "static" by default, which simply means that they appear one after the other in the same sequence as they occur in the markup. The "relative" value is similar. The difference is that relatively positioned elements can be taken out of the regular flow of the document by applying the float property.

By applying a value of "absolute" to an element's position, you can place the element wherever you want in relation to its container. The container is either the document itself or a parent element with a position of "fixed" or "absolute". It doesn't matter where the element appears in the original markup, because its position will be determined by properties like top, left, right, and bottom. You can set any of those properties using pixels or percentages.

Setting an element's top property will place the element a specified distance from the top of the document. An element's bottom property will place it a specified distance from the bottom of the document. Similarly, left and right can be used to place the element a specified distance from the left and right edges of the document, respectively. It's a good idea to use either top or bottom, but not both. Likewise with left and right.

Positioning an element in the document is relatively straightforward. Say you had an element like this:

```
<p id="message">Whee!</p>
```

You could set the message element's position in JavaScript with a function like this:

```
function positionMessage() {
  if (!document.getElementById) return false;
  if (!document.getElementById("message")) return false;
  var elem = document.getElementById("message");
  elem.style.position = "absolute";
  elem.style.left = "50px";
  elem.style.top = "100px";
}
```

Calling the positionMessage function when the page loads will position the paragraph 50 pixels from the left and 100 pixels from the top of the browser window:

```
window.onload = positionMessage;
```

Better yet, use the addLoadEvent function:

```
function addLoadEvent(func) {
  var oldonload = window.onload;
  if (typeof window.onload != 'function') {
    window.onload = func;
  } else {
    window.onload = function() {
      oldonload();
      func();
    }
  }
}
addLoadEvent(positionMessage);
```

Here, the element has been positioned absolutely.

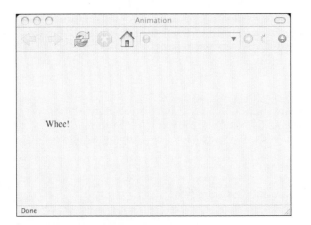

Updating an element's position is also quite easy. You just need to run a function that updates a style property like top or left:

```
function moveMessage() {
  if (!document.getElementById) return false;
  if (!document.getElementById("message")) return false;
  var elem = document.getElementById("message");
  elem.style.left = "200px";
}
```

But how do you activate that function? If you execute moveMessage when the page loads, the element's position will be updated instantaneously. The original positioning, as specified by positionMessage, will be overridden instantly:

```
addLoadEvent(positionMessage);
addLoadEvent(moveMessage);
```

Now the element's position has been changed.

The change in position is immediate. This isn't true animation. Animation involves changing an element's position over time.

The problem in this situation is that JavaScript is too efficient. Functions are executed one after another without any noticeable pause. To create animation, you need to create delays, which is what we will look at next.

Time

The JavaScript function setTimeout allows you to execute a function after a specified amount of time has elapsed. It takes two arguments. The first argument is a string containing the function you want to execute. The second argument is the number of milliseconds that will elapse before the first argument is executed.

```
setTimeout("function",interval)
```

It's a good idea to always assign the result of this function to a variable:

```
variable = setTimeout("function",interval)
```

You'll need to do this if you want to cancel the action that has been queued up. You can cancel a pending action using a function called clearTimeout. This function takes one argument, which is a variable that has been assigned to the result of a setTimeout function:

```
clearTimeout(variable)
```

Let's update the positionMessage function so that it calls moveMessage after 5 seconds (5,000 milliseconds):

```
function positionMessage() {
  if (!document.getElementById) return false;
  if (!document.getElementById("message")) return false;
  var elem = document.getElementById("message");
  elem.style.position = "absolute";
  elem.style.left = "50px";
  elem.style.top = "100px";
  movement = setTimeout("moveMessage()",5000);
}
```

The positionMessage function is called when the page loads:

```
addLoadEvent(positionMessage);
```

At first, the message appears at its specified coordinates. After five seconds, the message jumps 150 pixels to the right.

If you want to cancel that action any time before the five seconds elapse, you could do so with this statement:

```
clearTimeout(movement);
```

The movement variable refers to the setTimeout function defined in positionMessage. It's a global variable; it wasn't declared with the var keyword. This means the action can be canceled outside the positionMessage function.

Incremental movement

Moving an element by 150 pixels after an interval of five seconds is a sort of animation, albeit a very primitive one. Effective animation uses *incremental movement*. Moving from the starting position to the final location should happen in a series of steps rather than one quick jump.

Let's update the moveMessage function so that movement occurs incrementally. Here's the logic behind the new function:

1. Get the element's current position.

2. If the element has reached its final destination, leave the function.

3. Otherwise, move the element closer to its destination.

4. Repeat from step 1 after a pause.

The first step is getting the element's current position. We can do this by querying properties of the element's style property. We want to find the left and top properties. We'll assign them to the variables xpos and ypos, respectively:

```
var xpos = elem.style.left;
var ypos = elem.style.top;
```

When the moveMessage function is called after the positionMessage function, xpos will have a value of "50px". The ypos variable will have a value of "100px". These values are strings, which presents a bit of a problem. The next step in the function involves arithmetical comparison operators. We need to work with numbers, not strings.

The JavaScript function parseInt can extract numeric information from a string. If you pass it a string that begins with a number, it will return the number:

```
parseInt(string)
```

Here's an example:

```
parseInt("39 steps");
```

That will return the number 39.

The parseInt function will return whole numbers (integers). If you need to extract numbers with decimal places (floating-point numbers), there is a corresponding parseFloat function:

```
parseFloat(string)
```

We're dealing with integers in the moveMessage function, so we'll use parseInt:

```
var xpos = parseInt(elem.style.left);
var ypos = parseInt(elem.style.top);
```

The parseInt function converts the string "50px" to the number 50. The string "100px" becomes the number 100. Now the xpos and ypos variables contain those numbers.

◼ **Note** The use of the parseInt function shown here works only when the elements have been assigned a position using a DOM script or the style property.

The next few steps in the moveMessage function require the use of a lot of comparison operators.

The first comparison is a test for equality. We want to find out if xpos is equal to the final left position and if ypos is equal to the final top position. If they are, we'll exit the function. We can do this test by using the comparison operator, which consists of two equal signs (remember that a single equal sign is used for assignment).

```
if (xpos == 200 && ypos == 100) {
  return true;
}
```

Everything after this line will be executed only if the `message` element has not reached its final position.

Next, we'll update the xpos and ypos numbers based on their relationship to the final position. We want to bring them both closer to the final coordinates. If the value of xpos is less than the final left position, increase it by one:

```
if (xpos < 200) {
  xpos++;
}
```

If it's greater than the final left position, decrease it:

```
if (xpos > 200) {
  xpos--;
}
```

The same applies for the relationship between the ypos variable and the final top position:

```
if (ypos < 100) {
  ypos++;
}
if (ypos > 100) {
  ypos--;
}
```

You can see why we need xpos and ypos to be numbers rather than strings. We're using the less-than and greater-than operators to compare numerical values and update the variables accordingly.

Now we want to apply the xpos and ypos variables to the `style` property of the element. We do this by adding the string "px" to their values and applying them to the `left` and `top` properties:

```
elem.style.left = xpos + "px";
elem.style.top = ypos + "px";
```

Finally, we want to repeat the whole function afresh after a slight pause. We'll make the pause one hundredth of a second, which is ten milliseconds:

```
movement = setTimeout("moveMessage()",10);
```

The finished `moveMessage` function looks like this:

```
function moveMessage() {
  if (!document.getElementById) return false;
  if (!document.getElementById("message")) return false;
  var elem = document.getElementById("message");
  var xpos = parseInt(elem.style.left);
  var ypos = parseInt(elem.style.top);
  if (xpos == 200 && ypos == 100) {
    return true;
  }
  if (xpos < 200) {
    xpos++;
  }
  if (xpos > 200) {
    xpos--;
```

```
  }
  if (ypos < 100) {
    ypos++;
  }
  if (ypos > 100) {
    ypos--;
  }
  elem.style.left = xpos + "px";
  elem.style.top = ypos + "px";
  movement = setTimeout("moveMessage()",10);
}
```

The message moves across the screen, one pixel at a time. Once the `top` property is `"100px"` and the `left` property is `"200px"`, the function stops. That's animation. It's pretty pointless, but it's animation nonetheless. We will be applying the same principles to something much more useful later in this chapter.

Abstraction

As it stands, the `moveMessage` function accomplishes a very specific task. It moves a specific element to a specific place, pausing for a specific amount of time between movements. All of that information is hard-coded into the function:

```
function moveMessage() {
  if (!document.getElementById) return false;
  if (!document.getElementById("message"))
return false;
  var elem = document.getElementById("message");
  var xpos = parseInt(elem.style.left);
  var ypos = parseInt(elem.style.top);
  if (xpos == 200 && ypos == 100) {
    return true;
  }
  if (xpos < 200) {
    xpos++;
  }
  if (xpos > 200) {
    xpos--;
  }
  if (ypos < 100) {
    ypos++;
  }
  if (ypos > 100) {
    ypos--;
  }
  elem.style.left = xpos + "px";
  elem.style.top = ypos + "px";
  movement = setTimeout("moveMessage()",10);
}
```

If all of those things were variables, the function would be a lot more flexible. By abstracting the `moveMessage` function, you can create something more portable and reusable.

Creating the moveElement function

Call your new function moveElement. Unlike moveMessage, this function will take a number of arguments. These are the things that you can vary each time you call the function:

1. The ID of the element you want to move
2. The left position to which you want to move the element
3. The top position to which you want to move the element
4. How long to wait between each movement

These arguments should all have descriptive names:

1. elementID
2. final_x
3. final_y
4. interval

Begin the moveElement function with these arguments:

```
function moveElement(elementID,final_x,final_y,interval) {
```

Substitute these for the values that were previously hard-coded into moveMessage. The moveMessage function began with these lines:

```
if (!document.getElementById) return false;
if (!document.getElementById("message")) return false;
var elem = document.getElementById("message");
```

Replace all the instances of getElementById("message") with getElementById(elementID):

```
if (!document.getElementById) return false;
if (!document.getElementById(elementID)) return false;
var elem = document.getElementById(elementID);
```

The variable elem now refers to whichever element you want to move.

The next step of the function remains the same. The left and top properties of the element are converted to numbers and assigned to the variables xpos and ypos, respectively:

```
var xpos = parseInt(elem.style.left);
var ypos = parseInt(elem.style.top);
```

Next, check to see if the element has reached its final position. In moveMessage, these coordinates were the values 200 (for the left position) and 100 (for the top position):

```
if (xpos == 200 && ypos == 100) {
  return true;
}
```

In moveElement, these coordinates are provided by the arguments final_x and final_y:

```
if (xpos == final_x && ypos == final_y) {
  return true;
}
```

Update the values of the xpos and ypos variables. If xpos is less than the final left position, increase its value by one.

The final left position used to be hard-coded as 200:

```
if (xpos < 200) {
  xpos++;
}
```

Now the final left position is contained in the final_x argument:

```
if (xpos < final_x) {
  xpos++;
}
```

Likewise, if the value of xpos is greater than the final left position, decrease the value of xpos by one:

```
if (xpos > final_x) {
  xpos--;
}
```

Do the same for ypos. If its value is less than final_y, increase it by one. If it is greater than final_y, decrease it by one:

```
if (ypos < final_y) {
  ypos++;
}
if (ypos > final_y) {
  ypos--;
}
```

The next step remains the same. Update the left and top style properties of the element elem. Assign the values of xpos and ypos with the string "px" attached:

```
elem.style.left = xpos + "px";
elem.style.top = ypos + "px";
```

Finally, we want to call the function again after a suitable interval. In moveMessage, this was quite straightforward. The moveMessage function is called after ten milliseconds:

```
movement = setTimeout("moveMessage()",10);
```

In moveElement, it gets a little trickier. As well as calling the function again, we need to pass it the same arguments: elementID, final_x, final_y, and interval. The whole thing needs to be contained as a string:

```
"moveElement('"+elementID+"',"+final_x+","+final_y+","+interval+")"
```

That's a lot of concatenating! Rather than inserting that long string directly into the setTimeout function, assign the string to a variable called repeat:

```
var repeat = "moveElement('"+elementID+"',"+final_x+","+final_y+","+interval+")";
```

Now we can simply insert repeat as the first argument of the setTimeout function. The second argument is the length of the pause before the first argument is called. This used to be hard-coded as ten milliseconds. Now it's whatever value is contained by the variable interval:

```
movement = setTimeout(repeat,interval);
```

Close the function with a curly brace:

```
}
```

The finished moveElement function looks like this:

```
function moveElement(elementID,final_x,final_y,interval) {
  if (!document.getElementById) return false;
  if (!document.getElementById(elementID)) return false;
  var elem = document.getElementById(elementID);
  var xpos = parseInt(elem.style.left);
  var ypos = parseInt(elem.style.top);
  if (xpos == final_x && ypos == final_y) {
    return true;
  }
  if (xpos < final_x) {
    xpos++;
  }
  if (xpos > final_x) {
    xpos--;
  }
  if (ypos < final_y) {
    ypos++;
  }
  if (ypos > final_y) {
    ypos--;
  }
  elem.style.left = xpos + "px";
  elem.style.top = ypos + "px";
  var repeat = "moveElement('"+elementID+"',"+final_x+","+final_y+","+interval+")";
  movement = setTimeout(repeat,interval);
}
```

Save the moveElement function to a file called moveElement.js. Place this file in a folder called scripts, along with that old workhorse, addLoadEvent.js.

Using the moveElement function

Let's take this function for a test drive.

Start by re-creating the previous example. Create a document called message.html, which contains a paragraph identified as "message":

```
<!DOCTYPE html>
<html lang="en">
<head>
  <meta charset="utf-8" />
  <title>Message</title>
</head>
<body>
  <p id="message">Whee!</p>
</body>
</html>
```

Before we can animate the message, we need to position it. Write another JavaScript file called positionMessage.js. At the end of the positionMessage function, call the moveElement function:

```
function positionMessage() {
```

```
  if (!document.getElementById) return false;
  if (!document.getElementById("message")) return false;
  var elem = document.getElementById("message");
  elem.style.position = "absolute";
  elem.style.left = "50px";
  elem.style.top = "100px";
  moveElement("message",200,100,10);
}
addLoadEvent(positionMessage);
```

We are passing the string "message" as the value of the elementID argument. The final_x argument is 200. The final_y argument is 100. The value of interval is 10.

Now you have three files in your scripts folder: addLoadEvent.js, positionMessage.js, and moveElement.js. Reference those files from message.html using <script> tags:

```html
<!DOCTYPE html>
<html lang="en">
<head>
  <meta charset="utf-8" />
  <title>Message</title>
</head>
<body>
  <p id="message">Whee!</p>
  <script src="scripts/addLoadEvent.js"></script>
  <script src="scripts/positionMessage.js"></script>
  <script src="scripts/moveElement.js"></script>
</body>
</html>
```

Load message.html in a web browser to see the animation in action. The element moves horizontally across the screen.

So far, so good. The moveElement function is working exactly like the moveMessage function. You abstracted the function so that you could send it any arguments you like. By altering the values of final_x and final_y, you can change the direction of the animation. Altering the value of interval changes the speed of the animation:

```
function moveElement(elementID,final_x,final_y,interval)
```

Update the last line of the positionMessage function in positionMessage.js so that these three values are changed:

185

```
function positionMessage() {
  if (!document.getElementById) return false;
  if (!document.getElementById("message")) return false;
  var elem = document.getElementById("message");
  elem.style.position = "absolute";
  elem.style.left = "50px";
  elem.style.top = "100px";
  moveElement("message",125,25,20);
}
addLoadEvent(positionMessage);
```

Refresh message.html in a web browser to see the change. The element now moves diagonally and more slowly.

The other argument that you can change in moveElement is the value of elementID:

```
function moveElement(elementID,final_x,final_y,interval)
```

Add a new element to message.html. Give it an id attribute of "message2":

```
<!DOCTYPE html>
<html lang="en">
<head>
  <meta charset="utf-8" />
  <title>Message</title>
</head>
<body>
  <p id="message">Whee!</p>
  <p id="message2">Whoa!</p>
  <script src="scripts/addLoadEvent.js"></script>
  <script src="scripts/positionMessage.js"></script>
  <script src="scripts/moveElement.js"></script>
</body>
</html>
```

Now update positionMessage.js. Set the initial position of "message2" and call the moveElement function again, this time passing it "message2" as the first argument:

```
function positionMessage() {
  if (!document.getElementById) return false;
  if (!document.getElementById("message")) return false;
  var elem = document.getElementById("message");
  elem.style.position = "absolute";
  elem.style.left = "50px";
  elem.style.top = "100px";
  moveElement("message",125,25,20);
  if (!document.getElementById("message2")) return false;
  var elem = document.getElementById("message2");
  elem.style.position = "absolute";
  elem.style.left = "50px";
  elem.style.top = "50px";
  moveElement("message2",125,125,20);
}
addLoadEvent(positionMessage);
```

Reload message.html to see the new animation. Both elements move in different directions at the same time.

The moveElement function is doing all the work in both cases. By simply changing the arguments that you send to the function, you can reuse it as often as you like. This is the great advantage of using arguments instead of hard-coding values.

Practical animation

With moveElement, you have a reusable function that you can use to move page elements in any direction. From a programming point of view, that's quite impressive. From a practical standpoint, it seems fairly pointless.

Arbitrarily animating elements in a web page is the ideal way to annoy your visitors. It's also frowned upon from an accessibility point of view. Checkpoint 7.2 of the W3C's Web Content Accessibility Guidelines states, "Until user agents allow users to freeze moving content, avoid movement in pages. [Priority 2] When a page includes moving content, provide a mechanism within a script or applet to allow users to freeze motion or updates."

The key issue here is one of user control. Animating a page element based on an action initiated by the user could potentially enhance a web page. Let's look at an example of this kind of enhancement.

The situation

We have a web page that contains a list of links. When the user hovers over one of these links, we want to provide some kind of sneak preview of where the link will lead—we would like to show an image.

The document is called list.html. Here's the markup:

```html
<!DOCTYPE html>
<html lang="en">
<head>
  <meta charset="utf-8" />
  <title>Web Design</title>
</head>
<body>
  <h1>Web Design</h1>
  <p>These are the things you should know.</p>
  <ol id="linklist">
    <li>
      <a href="structure.html">Structure</a>
    </li>
    <li>
      <a href="presentation.html">Presentation</a>
    </li>
    <li>
      <a href="behavior.html">Behavior</a>
    </li>
  </ol>
</body>
</html>
```

Each link leads to a page covering a particular aspect of web design. The text within each link succinctly describes the content of the linked page.

As it stands, this document is perfectly fine. That said, showing a visual clue about the destination documents would be a nice touch.

In some ways, this situation is similar to that of the JavaScript image gallery presented in earlier chapters. Both contain lists of links. In both cases, we want to show an image. The difference is that here, we want to show the image when an onmouseover event handler is triggered, instead of an onclick event.

We could adapt the image gallery script. All we would need to do is change the event handler for each link from onclick to onmouseover. That would work, but it wouldn't be very smooth. The first time that the user hovers over a link, the new image would be loaded. Even on a fast connection, this will take a little time. We want a more immediate response.

The solution

If we use a different image for the visual preview of each link, there will be delays in swapping out the images. Besides, simply swapping out the images isn't the effect we want. We're looking for something with a bit more pizzazz.

Here's what we'll do:

1. Make a composite image of all the previews.

2. Hide most of this image.

3. When the user hovers over a link, display just a part of the image.

I've made a composite image of the three previews plus one default view.

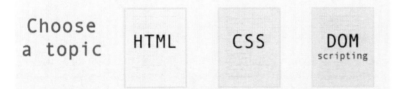

The image is called topics.gif. It is 400 pixels wide and 100 pixels tall.

We'll insert the topics.gif image into list.html, giving it an id of "preview":

```
<!DOCTYPE html>
<html lang="en">
<head>
  <meta charset="utf-8" />
  <title>Web Design</title>
</head>
<body>
  <h1>Web Design</h1>
  <p>These are the things you should know.</p>
  <ol id="linklist">
    <li>
      <a href="structure.html">Structure</a>
    </li>
    <li>
      <a href="presentation.html">Presentation</a>
    </li>
    <li>
      <a href="behavior.html">Behavior</a>
    </li>
```

```
    </ol>
    <img src="images/topics.gif" alt="building blocks of web design" id="preview" />
</body>
</html>
```

The web page now contains the list of links and the composite image.

Right now, the entire image is visible. We want only a 100-by-100 pixel portion to be visible at any one time. We can't do that with JavaScript, but we can do it with CSS.

CSS

The CSS overflow property dictates how content within an element should be displayed when the content is larger than its container element. When an element contains content that is larger than itself, there is an overflow. In that situation, you can clip the content so that only a portion of it is visible. You can also specify whether or not the web browser should display scrollbars, allowing the user to see the rest of the content.

There are four possible values for the overflow property:

- "visible": If the overflow of an element is set to "visible", then no clipping occurs. The content overflows and is rendered outside the element.

- "hidden": A value of "hidden" will cause the excess content to be clipped. Only a portion of the content will be visible.

- "scroll": The "scroll" value is similar to "hidden". The content will be clipped, but the web browser will display scrollbars so that the rest of the content can be viewed.

- "auto": A value of "auto" is just like "scroll", except that the scrollbars will be displayed only if the content overflows its container element. If there is no overflow, no scrollbars appear.

Of these four values, "hidden" sounds like the most promising for our purposes. We want to display just a 100-by-100 pixel portion of an image that is 400-by-100 pixels in size.

First, let's wrap the image in a container element. We'll put it in a div element with an id of "slideshow":

```
<div id="slideshow">
 <img src="images/topics.gif" alt="building blocks of web design"  id="preview" />
</div>
```

Now, we'll create a style sheet called layout.css. Put this file in a folder called styles.

In layout.css, we can set the size of the "slideshow" div:

```
#slideshow {
  width: 100px;
  height: 100px;
  position: relative;
}
```

Setting the position to relative is important because we want to use an absolute position for the child image. By using relative, the 0,0 position for children elements will be the upper-left corner of the slideshow div.

By applying an overflow value of "hidden", we can ensure that the content within the div will be clipped:

```
#slideshow {
  width: 100px;
  height: 100px;
  position: relative;
  overflow: hidden;
}
```

We're attaching the layout.css style sheet to list.html using a <link> in the head of the document:

```
<!DOCTYPE html>
<html lang="en">
<head>
  <meta charset="utf-8" />
  <title>Web Design</title>
  <link rel="stylesheet" href="styles/layout.css" media="screen" />
</head>
<body>
  <h1>Web Design</h1>
  <p>These are the things you should know.</p>
  <ol id="linklist">
    <li>
<a href="structure.html">Structure</a>
    </li>
    <li>
      <a href="presentation.html">Presentation</a>
    </li>
    <li>
      <a href="behavior.html">Behavior</a>
    </li>
  </ol>
  <div id="slideshow">
    <img src="images/topics.gif" alt="building blocks of web design" id="preview" />
```

```
    </div>
  </body>
</html>
```

Load list.html in a web browser to see the difference. The image has been clipped. Now only a portion of topics.gif—only the first 100 pixels—is visible.

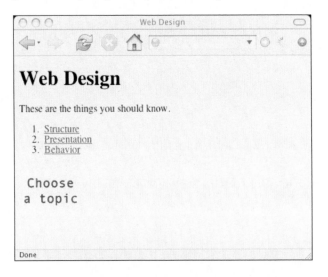

The next part of the plan revolves around the actions of the user. We want to display a different portion of topics.gif in the "slideshow" div depending on which link the user hovers the mouse over. This is a behavioral change and definitely a job for JavaScript and the DOM.

JavaScript

We'll use the moveElement function to move the topics.gif image around. We'll move the image to the left or to the right, depending on which link the user is currently hovering over.

We need to attach that behavior (calling the moveElement function) to the onmouseover event of each link in the link list.

Here's a function called prepareSlideshow, which does just that:

```
function prepareSlideshow() {
// Make sure the browser understands the DOM methods
  if (!document.getElementsByTagName) return false;
  if (!document.getElementById) return false;
// Make sure the elements exist
  if (!document.getElementById("linklist")) return false;
  if (!document.getElementById("preview")) return false;
// Apply styles to the preview image
  var preview = document.getElementById("preview");
  preview.style.position = "absolute";
  preview.style.left = "0px";
  preview.style.top = "0px";
// Get all the links in the list
  var list = document.getElementById("linklist");
```

```
  var links = list.getElementsByTagName("a");
// Attach the animation behavior to the mouseover event
  links[0].onmouseover = function() {
    moveElement("preview",-100,0,10);
  }
  links[1].onmouseover = function() {
    moveElement("preview",-200,0,10);
  }
  links[2].onmouseover = function() {
    moveElement("preview",-300,0,10);
  }
}
```

First, the prepareSlideshow function checks for browser compatibility with the DOM methods that will be used:

```
if (!document.getElementsByTagName) return false;
if (!document.getElementById) return false;
```

Next, there's a check to make sure that the "linklist" and "preview" elements exist. Remember that "preview" is the id value of the topics.gif image.

```
if (!document.getElementById("linklist")) return false;
if (!document.getElementById("preview")) return false;
```

After that, a default position is given to the "preview" image. We're setting the left property to "0px" and the top property to "0px":

```
var preview = document.getElementById("preview");
preview.style.position = "absolute";
preview.style.left = "0px";
preview.style.top = "0px";
```

This doesn't mean that the topics.gif image will appear in the top-left corner of the screen. Instead, it will appear in the top-left corner of its container element, the "slideshow" div. That's because the CSS position value of the div is "relative". Any absolutely positioned elements contained by a relatively positioned element will be placed in relation to that container element. In other words, the "preview" image will appear zero pixels to the left and zero pixels from the top of the "slideshow" element.

Finally, we're attaching the onmouseover behaviors to the links in the list. The variable links contains a node set of all the a elements contained within the "linklist" element. The first link is links[0], the second link is links[1], and the third link is links[2].

```
var list = document.getElementById("linklist");
var links = list.getElementsByTagName("a");
```

When the user hovers over the first link, the moveElement function is called. The elementID argument has a value of "preview". The final_x argument has a value of -100. The final_y argument has a value of 0. The interval argument is ten milliseconds.

```
links[0].onmouseover = function() {
  moveElement("preview",-100,0,10);
}
```

The same behavior applies for the second link, except that the final_x argument is -200:

```
links[1].onmouseover = function() {
  moveElement("preview",-200,0,10);
}
```

The third link will move the "preview" element -300 pixels to the left:

```
links[2].onmouseover = function() {
  moveElement("preview",-300,0,10);
}
```

The prepareSlideshow function is called using the addLoadEvent function. The behaviors are attached when the page loads.

```
addLoadEvent(prepareSlideshow);
```

Save the prepareSlideshow function to a file called prepareSlideshow.js in a folder called scripts. Place the moveElement.js and addLoadEvent.js files in the same folder.

We can reference all three scripts from list.html by adding <script> tags immediately before the closing </body> tag:

```
<!DOCTYPE html>
<html lang="en">
<head>
  <meta charset="utf-8" />
  <title>Web Design</title>
  <link rel="stylesheet" href="styles/layout.css" media="screen" />
</head>
<body>
  <h1>Web Design</h1>
  <p>These are the things you should know.</p>
  <ol id="linklist">
    <li>
      <a href="structure.html">Structure</a>
    </li>
    <li>
      <a href="presentation.html">Presentation</a>
    </li>
    <li>
      <a href="behavior.html">Behavior</a>
    </li>
  </ol>
  <div id="slideshow">
    <img src="images/topics.gif" alt="building blocks of web design" id="preview" />
  </div>
  <script src="scripts/addLoadEvent.js"></script>
  <script src="scripts/moveElement.js"></script>
  <script src="scripts/prepareSlideshow.js"></script>
</body>
</html>
```

Load list.html in a web browser. Hover over one of the links in the list to see the slideshow in action.

Depending on which link in the list you hover over, a different portion of the topics.gif image will slide into view.

But something is not quite right. If you move quickly from link to the link, the animation becomes confused. There's something wrong with the moveElement function.

A question of scope

The animation problem is being caused by a global variable. When we abstracted the moveMessage function and turned it into the moveElement function, we left the variable movement as it was:

```
function moveElement(elementID,final_x,final_y,interval) {
  if (!document.getElementById) return false;
  if (!document.getElementById(elementID)) return false;
  var elem = document.getElementById(elementID);
  var xpos = parseInt(elem.style.left);
  var ypos = parseInt(elem.style.top);
  if (xpos == final_x && ypos == final_y) {
    return true;
  }
  if (xpos < final_x) {
    xpos++;
  }
  if (xpos > final_x) {
    xpos--;
  }
  if (ypos < final_y) {
    ypos++;
  }
  if (ypos > final_y) {
    ypos--;
  }
  elem.style.left = xpos + "px";
  elem.style.top = ypos + "px";
```

```
  var repeat = "moveElement('"+elementID+"',"+final_x+","+final_y+","+interval+")";
  movement = setTimeout(repeat,interval);
}
```

This is causing a problem now that the moveElement function is being called whenever the user hovers over a link. Regardless of whether or not the previous call to the function has finished moving the image, the function is being asked to move the same element somewhere else. In other words, the moveElement function is attempting to move the same element to two different places at once, and the movement variable has become the rope in a tug of war.

As the user quickly moves from link to link, there is a backlog of events building up in the setTimeout queue. We can flush out this backlog by using clearTimeout:

```
clearTimeout(movement);
```

But if this statement is executed before movement has been set, we'll get an error.

We can't use a local variable:

```
var movement = setTimeout(repeat,interval);
```

If we do that, the clearTimeout statement won't work; the movement variable will no longer exist.

We can't use a global variable. We can't use a local variable. We need something in between. We need a variable that applies just to the element being moved.

Element-specific variables do exist. In fact, we've been using them all the time. What I've just described is a *property*.

Until now, we've used properties provided by the DOM: *element*.firstChild, *element*.style, and so on. You can also assign your own properties:

```
element.property = value
```

If you wanted, you could create a property called foo with a value of "bar":

```
element.foo = "bar";
```

It's just like creating a variable. The difference is that the variable belongs just to that element.

Let's change movement from being a global variable to a property of the element being moved, elem. That way, we can test for its existence and, if it exists, use clearTimeout.

```
function moveElement(elementID,final_x,final_y,interval) {
  if (!document.getElementById) return false;
  if (!document.getElementById(elementID)) return false;
  var elem = document.getElementById(elementID);
  if (elem.movement) {
    clearTimeout(elem.movement);
  }
  var xpos = parseInt(elem.style.left);
  var ypos = parseInt(elem.style.top);

  if (xpos == final_x && ypos == final_y) {
    return true;
  }
  if (xpos < final_x) {
    xpos++;
  }
  if (xpos > final_x) {
    xpos--;
  }
  if (ypos < final_y) {
```

```
    ypos++;
  }
  if (ypos > final_y) {
    ypos--;
  }
  elem.style.left = xpos + "px";
  elem.style.top = ypos + "px";
  var repeat = "moveElement('"+elementID+"',"+final_x+","+final_y+","+interval+")";
  elem.movement = setTimeout(repeat,interval);
}
```

Whichever element is currently being moved by the moveElement function is assigned a property called movement. If the element already has this property at the start of the function, it is reset using clearTimeout. This means that even if the same element is being told to move in different directions, there is only ever one setTimeout statement.

Reload list.html. Moving quickly from link to link no longer creates a problem. There is no backlog of events being queued up. The animation changes direction as you move up and down the list of links. Still, the animation is a bit lackluster.

Refining the animation

The moveElement function moves an element one pixel at a time until it reaches the coordinates specified by the final_x and final_y arguments. The movement is smooth, but it's also kind of boring. Let's spice up the animation a bit.

Take a look at this simple bit of code in moveElement.js:

```
if (xpos < final_x) {
  xpos++;
}
```

The variable xpos is the element's current left position. The variable final_x is the element's final left position. This piece of code states, "If the variable xpos is less than the variable final_x, increase the value of xpos by one." No matter how far away the element is from its final position, it will always move toward it one pixel at a time. To add some interest, we'll change that.

If the element is far away from its final position, we want it to move a large distance. If the element is near to its final position, we want it to move a short distance.

First, we need to figure out how far the element is from its final destination. If xpos is less than final_x, we want to know by how much. We can find out by subtracting xpos, the current left position, from final_x, the desired left position:

```
dist = final_x - xpos;
```

That's the distance that the element needs to travel. We'll move the element one-tenth of this distance.

```
dist = (final_x - xpos)/10;
xpos = xpos + dist;
```

This will move the element one-tenth of the distance it needs to go. I've chosen one-tenth as a nice round fraction. You can try other values if you like,

If xpos is 500 pixels away from final_x, the variable dist will have a value of 50. The value of xpos is increased by 50. If xpos is 100 pixels less than final_x, xpos is increased by ten.

A problem occurs when the distance between xpos and final_x is less than ten. When that value is divided by ten, the result will be less than one. You can't move an element by less than one pixel.

197

Using the ceil property of the Math object, you can round up the value of the variable dist. The ceil property has the following syntax:

```
Math.ceil(number)
```

This will round up any floating-point number to the nearest integer. There is a corresponding floor property that will round any floating-point number down to the nearest integer. The round property will round any floating-point number to whichever whole number is closest:

```
Math.floor(number)
Math.round(number)
```

For the moveElement function, we'll round upward. If we used floor or round, the element might never reach its final destination.

```
dist = Match.ceil((final_x - xpos)/10);
xpos = xpos + dist;
```

This covers the situation when xpos is less than final_x:

```
if (xpos < final_x) {
  dist = Math.ceil((final_x - xpos)/10);
  xpos = xpos + dist;
}
```

If xpos is greater than final_x, then the distance to travel is calculated by subtracting final_x from xpos. This value is divided by ten and rounded up to the nearest whole number to give the variable dist. This is then subtracted from xpos to bring the element closer to its final destination.

```
if (xpos > final_x) {
  dist = Math.ceil((xpos - final_x)/10);
  xpos = xpos - dist;
}
```

The same logic applies for ypos and final_y:

```
if (ypos < final_y) {
  dist = Math.ceil((final_y - ypos)/10);
  ypos = ypos + dist;
}
if (ypos > final_y) {
  dist = Math.ceil((ypos - final_y)/10);
  ypos = ypos - dist;
}
```

For good measure, don't forget to declare the dist variable alongside xpos and ypos:

```
var xpos = parseInt(elem.style.left);
var ypos = parseInt(elem.style.top);
var dist = 0;
```

The updated moveElement function looks like this:

```
function moveElement(elementID,final_x,final_y,interval) {
  if (!document.getElementById) return false;
  if (!document.getElementById(elementID)) return false;
  var elem = document.getElementById(elementID);
  if (elem.movement) {
    clearTimeout(elem.movement);
```

```
}
var xpos = parseInt(elem.style.left);
var ypos = parseInt(elem.style.top);
var dist = 0;
if (xpos == final_x && ypos == final_y) {
  return true;
}
if (xpos < final_x) {
  dist = Math.ceil((final_x - xpos)/10);
  xpos = xpos + dist;
}
if (xpos > final_x) {
  dist = Math.ceil((xpos - final_x)/10);
  xpos = xpos - dist;
}
if (ypos < final_y) {
  dist = Math.ceil((final_y - ypos)/10);
  ypos = ypos + dist;
}
if (ypos > final_y) {
  dist = Math.ceil((ypos - final_y)/10);
  ypos = ypos - dist;
}
elem.style.left = xpos + "px";
elem.style.top = ypos + "px";
var repeat = "moveElement('"+elementID+"',"+final_x+","+final_y+","+interval+")";
elem.movement = setTimeout(repeat,interval);
}
```

Save these changes to moveElement.js. Reload list.html to see the difference.

The animation now feels much smoother and snappier. When you first hover over a link, the image jumps quite a distance. As the image approaches its final destination, it "eases" into place.

The markup, the CSS, and the JavaScript all come together to create this slideshow effect. Everything is working fine, but there's always room for some small tweaks.

Adding a safety check

The moveElement function is working really well now. There's just one thing that bothers me. There is an assumption being made near the start of the function:

```
var xpos = parseInt(elem.style.left);
var ypos = parseInt(elem.style.top);
```

It's assuming that the element elem has a left style property and a top style property. We should really check to make sure that this is the case.

If the left or top properties haven't been set, we have a couple of options. We could simply exit the function there and then:

```
if (!elem.style.left || !elem.style.top) {
  return false;
}
```

If JavaScript can't read those properties, then the function stops without throwing up an error message.

Another solution is to apply default left and top properties in the moveElement function. If either property hasn't been set, we can give them a default value of "0px":

```
if (!elem.style.left) {
  elem.style.left = "0px";
}
if (!elem.style.top) {
  elem.style.top = "0px";
}
```

The moveElement function now looks like this:

```
function moveElement(elementID,final_x,final_y,interval) {
  if (!document.getElementById) return false;
  if (!document.getElementById(elementID)) return false;
  var elem = document.getElementById(elementID);
  if (elem.movement) {
    clearTimeout(elem.movement);
  }
  if (!elem.style.left) {
    elem.style.left = "0px";
  }
  if (!elem.style.top) {
    elem.style.top = "0px";
  }
  var xpos = parseInt(elem.style.left);
  var ypos = parseInt(elem.style.top);
  var dist = 0;
  if (xpos == final_x && ypos == final_y) {
    return true;
  }
  if (xpos < final_x) {
    dist = Math.ceil((final_x - xpos)/10);
```

```
    xpos = xpos + dist;
  }
  if (xpos > final_x) {
    dist = Math.ceil((xpos - final_x)/10);
    xpos = xpos - dist;
  }
  if (ypos < final_y) {
    dist = Math.ceil((final_y - ypos)/10);
    ypos = ypos + dist;
  }
  if (ypos > final_y) {
    dist = Math.ceil((ypos - final_y)/10);
    ypos = ypos - dist;
  }
  elem.style.left = xpos + "px";
  elem.style.top = ypos + "px";
  var repeat = "moveElement('"+elementID+"','"+final_x+"','"+final_y+"','"+interval+"')";
  elem.movement = setTimeout(repeat,interval);
}
```

With that safety check in place, we no longer need to explicitly set the position of the "preview" element. Right now, we're doing that in the prepareSlideshow function. Remove these lines:

```
preview.style.left = "0px";
preview.style.top = "0px";
```

While we're at it, let's overhaul the prepareSlideshow function.

Generating markup

The list.html document contains some markup that exists just for the JavaScript slideshow:

```
<div id="slideshow">
  <img src="images/topics.gif" alt="building blocks of web design" id="preview" />
</div>
```

If the user doesn't have JavaScript enabled, this content is somewhat superfluous. The div and the img element are there purely for the slideshow effect. Instead of hard-coding these elements into the document, it makes sense to use JavaScript to generate them. Let's do that in prepareSlideshow.js.

First, create the div element:

```
var slideshow = document.createElement("div");
slideshow.setAttribute("id","slideshow");
```

Next, create the img element:

```
var preview = document.createElement("img");
preview.setAttribute("src","images/topics.gif");
preview.setAttribute("alt","building blocks of web design");
preview.setAttribute("id","preview");
```

Place the img inside the div:

```
slideshow.appendChild(preview);
```

Finally, we want these newly created elements to appear directly after the list of links. For this, we'll use the insertAfter function from Chapter 7:

```
var list = document.getElementById("linklist");
insertAfter(slideshow,list);
```

The finished prepareSlideshow function looks like this:

```
function prepareSlideshow() {
// Make sure the browser understands the DOM methods
  if (!document.getElementsByTagName) return false;
  if (!document.getElementById) return false;
// Make sure the elements exist
  if (!document.getElementById("linklist")) return false;
  var slideshow = document.createElement("div");
  slideshow.setAttribute("id","slideshow");
  var preview = document.createElement("img");
  preview.setAttribute("src","images/topics.gif");
  preview.setAttribute("alt","building blocks of web design");
  preview.setAttribute("id","preview");
  slideshow.appendChild(preview);
  var list = document.getElementById("linklist");
  insertAfter(slideshow,list);
// Get all the links in the list
  var links = list.getElementsByTagName("a");
// Attach the animation behavior to the mouseover event
  links[0].onmouseover = function() {
    moveElement("preview",-100,0,10);
  }
  links[1].onmouseover = function() {
    moveElement("preview",-200,0,10);
  }
  links[2].onmouseover = function() {
    moveElement("preview",-300,0,10);
  }
}
addLoadEvent(prepareSlideshow);
```

Now we need to make some changes to list.html. We can remove the markup with the "slideshow" div and the "preview" image. We also need to include one more set of <script> tags to reference the insertAfter.js file.

```
<!DOCTYPE html>
<html lang="en">
<head>
  <meta charset="utf-8" />
  <title>Web Design</title>
  <link rel="stylesheet" href="styles/layout.css" media="screen" />
</head>
<body>
  <h1>Web Design</h1>
  <p>These are the things you should know.</p>
  <ol id="linklist">
    <li>
      <a href="structure.html">Structure</a>
    </li>
    <li>
```

```
      <a href="presentation.html">Presentation</a>
    </li>
    <li>
      <a href="behavior.html">Behavior</a>
    </li>
  </ol>
  <script src="scripts/addLoadEvent.js"></script>
  <script src="scripts/insertAfter.js"></script>
  <script src="scripts/moveElement.js"></script>
  <script src="scripts/prepareSlideshow.js"></script>
</body>
</html>
```

Write the insertAfter function to a file called insertAfter.js and place it in the scripts folder:

```
function insertAfter(newElement,targetElement) {
  var parent = targetElement.parentNode;
  if (parent.lastChild == targetElement) {
    parent.appendChild(newElement);
  } else {
    parent.insertBefore(newElement,targetElement.nextSibling);
  }
}
```

The other file we need to update is the style sheet, layout.css. Remove this line from prepareSlideshow.js:

```
preview.style.position = "absolute";
```

Now place that declaration in the style sheet, where it belongs:

```
#slideshow {
  width: 100px;
  height: 100px;
  position: relative;
  overflow: hidden;
}
#preview {
  position: absolute;
}
```

Now refresh list.html in a web browser. You will see no difference in functionality. Everything is behaving just as before. The difference is that now there is better separation of structural, presentational, and behavioral elements. If you view the same page with JavaScript disabled, the slideshow image simply doesn't appear.

Functionally, the JavaScript slideshow is working very well. With JavaScript enabled, the slideshow adds some nice visual feedback, responding to the user's actions. With JavaScript disabled, the functionality degrades gracefully.

If you wanted to visually associate the list of links more closely with the slideshow, you could do that by editing layout.css. You could float the two elements side by side. You could also place a border around the slideshow if you wanted it to stand out more.

What's next?

This chapter began with a definition of animation: changing an element's position over time. Using a combination of CSS-DOM and JavaScript's setTimeout function, it's quite easy to create a simple animation.

The difficulty with animation isn't technical; it's practical. You can create a lot of cool effects with animation, but there aren't many situations where it's useful or helpful to the user to move elements around. The JavaScript slideshow example in this chapter is a notable exception. It took some work to get it to work smoothly and degrade gracefully, but the final result is worth it. You now have a reusable function that you can use whenever you want to create a slideshow or some other practical use of animation.

The next chapter focuses on the latest incarnation of HTML: HTML5. You'll learn how to take advantage of the new features it offers.

CHAPTER 11

■ ■ ■

HTML5

What this chapter covers:

- What HTML5 is

- How you can use it today

- A brief introduction to a number of new HTML5 features including canvas, audio, video and forms

I began this book with an over-the-shoulder look at the history of JavaScript and the emergence of a standardized Document Object Model. Today, the emergence of HTML5 is blurring the lines between the DOM, style, and behavior, so let's take a look at what's new and where things are headed in the future.

What is HTML5?

HTML5 is the now and the future of the HTML language. From specifications in HTML4 to XHTML to Web Apps 1.0 and back to HTML5, its path to inception has faced many hurdles and battles. The fighting and political struggles behind HTML5's creation—some of which are still going on—play out like an afternoon soap opera, but the end result is something good. Finally, we can all be excited as we're on the verge of a unification of multiple technologies to create the next evolution in the Web.

The most accurate way to approach web design is to view web pages in terms of three layers:

1. Structure

2. Style

3. Behavior

Each one of these layers requires a different technology. The respective technologies are

1. HyperText Markup Language

2. Cascading Style Sheets

3. JavaScript and the Document Object Model

Arguably you could add a fourth layer, which covers the browser's JavaScript APIs and includes things like cookies or window properties.

With the evolution of HTML5, structure, style, and behavior (together with additional JavaScript APIs) have been bundled into a nice little collection, but it's just that—a collection. HTML5 gives you a balanced set of technologies you can pick and choose from and call upon as needed.

For example, in the structure layer, HTML5 adds new markup elements such as `<section>`, `<article>`, `<header>`, and `<footer>`. I won't be discussing all the new tags here, so I suggest you check out the specification for the complete list (`http://www.w3.org/TR/html5/`). HTML5 also includes more interactive and media elements such as `<canvas>`, `<audio>`, and `<video>`. Forms have also been enhanced to include color pickers, date pickers, sliders, and progress bars. With all these additions, you'll notice that many of these elements such as `<video>` also come with their own JavaScript and DOM APIs.

In the behavior layer, HTML5 defines how each new element will interact in the DOM and what additional APIs will be available. Video elements allow you to customize the controls and influence playback methods. Form elements allow you to control progress. You can draw freeform graphics, images, and other objects into a `<canvas>` element.

Along with the markup and behavior, the presentation layer has also been improved. The CSS 3 modules include everything from advanced selectors to transitions, transformations, and animation. These modules begin to shift many traditional DOM scripting tasks, such as animation and locating elements, into their proper location in the presentation, where they should be in most cases. You'll still see a lot of DOM scripting used to influence advanced animations, but many simple interactions will no longer require timers or JavaScript.

Lastly, new JavaScript APIs include a host of other modules for everything from geolocation, storage, and drag-and-drop to sockets, multithreading, and in-browser SQL.

Regardless of which new features of HTML5 you intend to incorporate, remember that all the existing (X)HTML4 code you've worked so hard on is still perfectly fine. There's little that you'll need to change to conform to HTML5. "Upgrading" most of your documents is as simple as changing the doctype to `<!DOCTYPE html>`. That's it.

Of course if you want your pages to validate properly, you'll have to replace obsolete elements like `<acronym>` with `<abbr>`, but remember that validation is a tool to help you be a better programmer, not a religion. Also, newer elements like `<section>` or `<article>` won't always play nice with older browsers, but more on that later.

As you saw in Chapter 8, HTML, including HTML5, can be lax in its markup requirements compared to XHTML. HTML5 aims to be backward-compatible with both existing HTML and XHTML documents, so how you decide to mark up your document, and which rules you want to adhere to, are completely up to you. If you want to close all tags and have perfect form in your markup, that's great. If you're lazy and don't feel like closing all your tags, that's fine, too. In fact—hold onto your hats—this HTML5 document will validate perfectly well, despite some obvious missing pieces:

```
<!DOCTYPE html>
<meta charset=utf-8 />
<title>This is a valid HTML5 document</title>
<p>Try me at http://validator.w3.org/check</p>
```

Despite a successful validation, if you're going to be professional about your work I suggest you include basic structural elements such as `<html>`, `<head>`, and `<body>` even though a browser may add them for you.

So where does that leave us? Can we use these fancy new features today? The answer is yes, and I encourage you to do so as long as you keep a few things in mind. Detecting HTML5 support as a whole isn't possible—it's a collection, not a whole—but you can rely on trusty old feature detection and progressive enhancement just as you have throughout the book.

A little help from a friend

If you want to start using HTML5 today, then by all means go for it! When you take the plunge there's a tool that will help you out along the way: Modernizr.

Modernizr (`http://www.modernizr.com/`) is an open source JavaScript library that uses rich feature detection to give you better control of your HTML5 documents. Modernizr doesn't add missing functionality; you're not going to be able to use local storage in Internet Explorer 6, for example. What Modernizr does is help fill in the gaps by providing a number of different CSS hooks and feature-detection properties. It is an essential tool for using HTML5 today and will help in more ways than one.

When you embed Modernizr in your document it will perform a number of small miracles as the page loads.

First, it alters the class attribute of the <html> element by creating additional classes based on what HTML5 features are available. To begin your Modernizr document, you typically add a no-js class to the <html> element:

```
<html class="no-js">
```

You can use this to apply CSS styles in cases where JavaScript isn't supported:

```
.nojs selector {
  style properties
}
```

Modernizr then detects the various features that are supported by the browser and alters the class accordingly. If a feature is supported, it will indicate so by adding classes similar to these:

```
<html class="js canvas canvastext geolocation crosswindowmessaging websqldatabase indexeddb
hashchange historymanagement draganddrop websockets rgba hsla multiplebgs backgroundsize
borderimage borderradius boxshadow opacity cssanimations csscolumns cssgradients
cssreflections csstransforms csstransforms3d csstransitions video audio localstorage
sessionstorage webworkers applicationcache svg smil svgclippaths fontface">
```

If a feature is not supported, Modernizr will append a no- prefix to the same set of classes:

```
<html class="js no-canvas no-canvastext no-geolocation no-crosswindowmessaging no-
websqldatabase no-indexeddb no-hashchange no-historymanagement no-draganddrop no-websockets
no-rgba no-hsla no-multiplebgs no-backgroundsize no-borderimage no-borderradius no-boxshadow
no-opacity no-cssanimations no-csscolumns no-cssgradients no-cssreflections no-csstransforms
no-csstransforms3d no-csstransitions no-video no-audio no-localstorage no-sessionstorage no-
webworkers no-applicationcache no-svg no-smil no-svgclippaths no-fontface">
```

Depending on the browser's support of features, you'll get a mix-and-match list of the *feature* and *no-feature* classes.

You can now reliably use these classes in your CSS to detect support for each feature and progressively upgrade the user experience:

```
.multiplebgs article p {
  /* properties for browsers that
     support multiple backgrounds */
}
.no-multiplebgs article p {
  /* optional fallback properties
     for browsers that don't */
}
```

Likewise, the Modernizr library provides JavaScript feature detection that you can incorporate directly into your DOM scripts as well:

```
if ( !Modernizr.inputtypes.date ) {
  /* No native date support, use a custom date picker script */
  createDatepicker(document.getElementById('birthday'));
}
```

Modernizr will also help legacy browsers handle the new elements such as <section> and <article>. If you hadn't noticed in the past, in most browsers you could create your own elements like <foo> and apply whatever styles you like as long as you didn't care about validation. To an older browser, the new HTML5 elements such as <section> are no different. To use them, all you need to do is include some base styles so the browser can render the block elements properly:

```
article, aside, footer, header, hgroup, nav, section {
  display: block;
}
```

The only special case is Internet Explorer. To add new unknown elements in IE, you need to first create the element with the following JavaScript:

```
document.createElement('article');
```

Modernizr handles all this for us, but remember, that doesn't mean you can suddenly start embedding movies with the <video> element. It doesn't add the underlying JavaScript and DOM APIs or other technologies required for all the elements.

Embedding Modernizr is easy. Just download the library from http://www.modernizr.com/ and add a script to the <head> of your document:

```
<script src="modernizr-1.5.min.js"></script>
```

Be sure this script goes into the <head> of the document. Although that goes against what was suggested in Chapter 5, "Best Practices," this is a special case for a good reason. You want Modernizr to load *before* the remainder of the markup, so that the new HTML5 elements can be appropriately created in advance of the document-rendering process. If you added it at the end of the document, your browser would begin rendering the document and applying styles before Modernizer had a chance to apply its magic.

A few examples

To whet your appetite a little, let's look at canvas, video/audio, and forms as a few quick examples of what the new APIs offer in HTML5. To try these out you'll need one of the following browsers:

- Apple Safari 5+

- Google Chrome 6+

- Mozilla Firefox 3.6+

- Opera 10.6+

- Microsoft Internet Explorer 9+

Canvas

Every browser has the ability to display a static image. You can make the image animate with GIFs, and you can change a few styles with CSS or JavaScript, but that's about it. There's little or no possible interaction with these static images. The <canvas> element changes all that by allowing you to manipulate and create images and graphics on the fly.

Adding a canvas to your document is a breeze:

```
<canvas id="draw-in-me" width="120" height="40">
  <p>Powered By HTML5 canvas</p>
```

```
</canvas>
```

Drawing on the canvas is another story. You can check out the <canvas> element specification (http://www.whatwg.org/specs/web-apps/current-work/multipage/the-canvas-element.html) for all the details, but in essence <canvas> uses math and position concepts similar to those in any vector-based drawing application such as Adobe Illustrator or in vector-based coding languages.

■ **Note** If you use Illustrator, you can try to export your work directly to <canvas> using the Ai->Canvas plug-in (http://visitmix.com/labs/ai2canvas/), although as with any WYSIWYG editor you should check over the output and manually edit it for best results.

Using <canvas>, here's how you might draw a black box with rounded corners and a 2-pixel white stroke:

```
function draw() {
  var canvas = document.getElementById('draw-in-me');
  if (canvas.getContext) {
    var ctx = canvas.getContext('2d');
    ctx.beginPath();
    ctx.moveTo(120.0, 32.0);
    ctx.bezierCurveTo(120.0, 36.4, 116.4, 40.0, 112.0, 40.0);
    ctx.lineTo(8.0, 40.0);
    ctx.bezierCurveTo(3.6, 40.0, 0.0, 36.4, 0.0, 32.0);
    ctx.lineTo(0.0, 8.0);
    ctx.bezierCurveTo(0.0, 3.6, 3.6, 0.0, 8.0, 0.0);
    ctx.lineTo(112.0, 0.0);
    ctx.bezierCurveTo(116.4, 0.0, 120.0, 3.6, 120.0, 8.0);
    ctx.lineTo(120.0, 32.0);
    ctx.closePath();
    ctx.fill();
    ctx.lineWidth = 2.0;
    ctx.strokeStyle = "rgb(255, 255, 255)";
    ctx.stroke();
  }
}
window.onload = draw;
```

In this example, the ctx variable refers to the *context* of the canvas. The context is a flat two-dimensional drawing surface whose origin (0,0) is at the top-left corner of the <canvas> element, with the coordinate space having x values increasing when going right, and y values increasing when going down. You can then create various two-dimensional shapes or lines by specifying points in the context. You can also paint the lines with different fill and stroke styles.

The result is shown here in Chrome:

That's a very crude example. The <canvas> element uses an API similar to other 2D drawing libraries. You can create and paint paths from one point to another using several points and curves like the example just shown, but the canvas isn't limited to vector paths. You can display and manipulate bitmap images as well.

For example, let's use a <canvas> object to take a color image and automatically create a grayscale version in the browser. Then we can have the image switch from the grayscale canvas image to the original color image as the cursor hovers over it.

Create a simple HTML file called grayscale.html that links to an image on the same domain as the script. We'll include Modernizr as well for good measure:

```
<!DOCTYPE html>
<html lang="en">
<head>
<meta charset="utf-8" />
  <title>Grayscale Canvas Example</title>
  <script src="scripts/modernizr-1.6.min.js"></script>
</head>
<body>
<img src="images/avatar.png" id="avatar" title="Jeffrey Sambells" alt="My Avatar"/>
<script src="scripts/grayscale.js"></script>
</body>
</html>
```

Next create the grayscale.js file and add the following script:

```
function convertToGS(img) {

  // For good measure return if canvas isn't supported.
  if (!Modernizr.canvas) return;

  // Store the original color version.
  img.color = img.src;

  // Create a grayscale version.
  img.grayscale = createGSCanvas(img);

  // Swap the images on mouseover/out
  img.onmouseover = function() {
    this.src = this.color;
  }
  img.onmouseout = function() {
    this.src = this.grayscale;
  }

  img.onmouseout();

}

function createGSCanvas(img) {

  var canvas=document.createElement("canvas");
  canvas.width= img.width;
  canvas.height=img.height;

  var ctx=canvas.getContext("2d");
  ctx.drawImage(img,0,0);

  // Note: getImageData will only work for images
  // on the same domain as the script.
  var c = ctx.getImageData(0, 0, img.width, img.height);
  for (i=0; i<c.height; i++) {
    for (j=0; j<c.width; j++) {
     var x = (i*4) * c.width + (j*4);
      var r = c.data[x];
      var g = c.data[x+1];
      var b = c.data[x+2];
      c.data[x] = c.data[x+1] = c.data[x+2] = (r+g+b)/3;
    }
  }

  ctx.putImageData(c,0,0,0,0, c.width, c.height);

  return canvas.toDataURL();

}
```

```
// Add a load event.
// use addLoadEvent function if alongside other scripts.
window.onload = function() {
  convertToGS(document.getElementById('avatar'));
}
```

■ **Note** A word of caution: Different browsers have different security considerations when reading data from files such as images. For this example to work properly, you need to serve the image and document from the same web site. Also, it may not work if you're trying to load the page from your local hard drive using the file protocol. You could alter your browser's security settings; however, I recommend just uploading this example to a web server instead.

This script alters the avatar image when the page loads by applying mouseover and mouseout event handlers in the convertToGS function.

```
img.color = img.src;
img.grayscale = createGSCanvas(img);
img.onmouseover = function() {
  this.src=this.color;
}
img.onmouseout = function() {
  this.src=this.grayscale;
}
```

These event handlers change the src of the image between the original color version in the src of the image and a grayscale version created by the createGSCanvas function.

To convert the color image to grayscale in the createGSCanvas function, we create a new canvas element, and then draw the color image into its context:

```
var canvas=document.createElement("canvas");
canvas.width= img.width;
canvas.height=img.height;

var ctx=canvas.getContext("2d");
ctx.drawImage(img,0,0);
```

Now we can retrieve the raw image data and loop though every pixel to convert the color value to its grayscale equivalent by averaging the red, green, and blue color components:

```
var c = ctx.getImageData(0, 0, img.width, img.height);
for (i=0; i<c.height; i++) {
  for (j=0; j<c.width; j++) {
    var x = (i*4) * c.width + (j*4);
    var r = c.data[x];
    var g = c.data[x+1];
    var b = c.data[x+2];
    c.data[x] = c.data[x+1] = c.data[x+2] = (r+g+b)/3;
  }
}
```

Now all that's left to do is put the grayscale data back into the canvas's context and return the raw image data for the source of the new grayscale image.

```
ctx.putImageData(c, 0, 0, 0, 0, c.width, c.height);
return canvas.toDataURL();
```

Now the image can switch between the color image and a grayscale version of the original color image even though we only supplied the color source.

So why use <canvas> instead of images? The power of the canvas comes when you modify it based on the users' actions. Previously, the only way to provide a high level of rich interactivity was to rely on browser plug-ins such as Flash or Silverlight. Now with <canvas> you can draw whatever objects and pixels you like on the screen. You can use it to manipulate images or create visually rich user interface elements. But, like Flash, it shouldn't be used for the wrong purposes. Just because you could create an entire website completely contained in a canvas doesn't mean you should.

Also note that for screen readers and other assistive technologies, the canvas is just as inaccessible as Flash and comes with many of the same burdens. Always remember to choose your technologies wisely and progressively enhance as necessary.

Audio/Video

Perhaps the most discussed element in HTML5 is <video>, along with its sibling the <audio> element. These two elements finally bring native video and audio support to HTML, but they come with a few headaches.

Before HTML5, embedding video in a web page involved a tag soup of different repetitive <object> and <embed> elements, some of which were not even valid elements in HTML4. The object markup referenced the various movie player plug-ins such as QuickTime, RealPlayer, or Flash and used those plug-ins to present the movie in the browser. For example, to embed a Flash movie you've probably seen something like this:

```
<object classid="clsid:d27cdb6e-ae6d-11cf-96b8-
444553540000" width="100" height="100"
codebase="http://fpdownload.adobe.com/pub/shockwave/cabs/flash/swflash.cab#version=9,0,0,0">
<param name="movie" value="moviename.swf">
<param name="play" value="true">
<param name="loop" value="true">
<param name="quality" value="high">
<embed src="moviename.swf" width="100" height="100"
play="true" loop="true" quality="high"
pluginspage=" http://get.adobe.com/flashplayer" />
</object>
```

Besides the object code, third-party plug-ins come with their own issues and limitations. For the embedded code to work, the plug-in has to be available, and it has to be the right version. Plug-ins also run in a sealed container, limiting how you can alter and interact with the video content through your scripts. Unless the plug-in provides an API, it's basically a little walled garden in the middle of your document.

The new HTML5 <video> element finally defines a standard way to interact with and embed a movie into an HTML document. It also simplifies it down to one simple tag:

```
<video src="movie.mp4">
  <!-- Alternative content when video is not supported -->
  <a href="movie.mp4">Download movie.mp4</a>
</video>
```

213

Here I'm including a video using the mp4 file type and providing an alternate download link if the browser doesn't support the <video> element.

Likewise, <audio> works the same way:

```
<audio src="sound.ogg">
  <!-- Alternative content when audio is not supported -->
  <a href="sound.ogg">Download sound.ogg</a>
</audio>
```

Simple, elegant, and sexy—if only it were that easy...

The Return of Tag Soup

Unfortunately, there's still a bit of an issue with the HTML5 <video> and <audio> elements. The markup is simplified and has additional attributes to display controls or alter playback; however, it doesn't specify what video formats are supported.

To understand the implications of the video format you need to think about what a video actually is.

A video such as movie.mp4 is actually a container of several things. The mp4 extension indicates that this video is packaged using MPEG 4, based on Apple's QuickTime technologies. The container specifies where the various audio and video tracks are located in the file as well as other attributes required for playback. Other containers include m4v (another MPEG 4 extension), avi (Audio Video Interleave), flv (Flash Video), and others.

Within each movie container, audio and video tracks are encoded using various codecs. The codec specifies how the browser should decode the audio and video in order to play it back to you. The codec is really an algorithm that is used to compress and store the video to decrease the overall file size, with or without losing quality. There are many different video codecs, but the primary three that you'll see on the web are H.264, Theora, and VP8. Likewise, audio has its own set of codecs, and the common ones you'll see are mp3 (MPEG-1 Audio Layer 3), aac (Advanced Audio Coding), and ogg (Ogg Vorbis).

■ **Note** One non-technical issue with the H.264 codec is licensing. H.264 has an underlying licensing fee associated with its use in decoders and encoders. What you don't need to pay for is distribution of H.264 content that has already been licensed to encode and will need a license to decode. In other words, you won't have to pay a fee to show an H.264 movie on your website, but browser manufacturers who decode the movie and the software manufacturers who created the program to encode the movie are subject to the license. In an attempt to remove licensing issues surrounding video formats, Google released the underlying patents for the VP8 codec (in the WebM container) into the public domain under an irrevocable patent promise. Their hope was to offer a license-free solution in WebM/VP8/Vorbis that all browser manufacturers could implement, giving everyone a common format.

So where do all these different container formats and codecs leave us? Well, not every browser supports every container and codec, so you're back to offering multiple formats. Some versions of Firefox, Chrome, and Opera support Theora/Vorbis/Ogg. IE9, Safari, Chrome, Mobile Safari, and Android support H.264/ACC/MP4, while IE9, Firefox, Chrome, and Opera also support WebM (another container format for VP8 and Vorbis).

The result of this mess is that no one combination of formats is supported across all browsers. Let's hope that this situation will change in the future; otherwise, this whole HTML5 video endeavor seems a little less amazing. For now, to ensure that everyone has the opportunity to view your videos, you need to encode each video in multiple formats and include several sources in the video element:

```
<video id="movie" preload controls>
  <source src="movie.mp4" />
  <source src=" movie.webm"
    type='video/webm; codecs="vp8, vorbis"' />
  <source src="movie.ogv"
    type='video/ogg; codecs="theora, vorbis"' />
  <p>Download movie as
    <a href="movie.mp4">MP4</a>,
    <a href="movie.webm">WebM</a>,
    or <a href="movie.ogv">Ogg</a>.</p>
</video>
```

For maximum HTML5 compatibility, you need to include three versions:

- One that uses H.264 and AAC audio in an MP4

- One that uses WebM (VP8 + Vorbis)

- One that uses Theora video and Vorbis audio as an Ogg file

Not shown in the example is an alternate plug-in version. For ultimate backward compatibility with non-HTML5 browsers, you may also include alternate plug-in video players such as Flash or QuickTime. I've opted to show a direct download link to one of the available formats to subtly encourage users to use a more advanced browser.

■ **Note** There's an important gotcha is the order of the video formats. The MP4 is placed as the first source to allow iOS-based devices like the iPad, iPhone, and iPod Touch to read the video sources properly. Mobile Safari in pre-iOS 4 devices only recognizes one source in the <video> element, so the iOS-compatible format is listed first.

All in all, this ends up a lot messier and not so sexy anymore. Considering the time it takes to re-encode into the various formats and the storage requirements of three or more files, you may wonder why not stick with one Flash version, since you're going to include it anyway. Offering the newer <video> element as an option is more forward thinking and offers you greater control of the content from within your documents and scripts when HTML5 is available.

With HTML5 video you can (or will be able to) apply CSS properties to alter the video's appearance, size and shape, add subtext such as captions and lyrics, or overlay content by combining video and canvas. You can even go as far as processing the video to detect movement by injecting the video into a <canvas> object and then analyzing the image, as you saw earlier with the grayscale image.

To give you a simple example of the <video> element's API, let's see how we can customize video controls and create our own simple Play button.

Customizing Controls

When a <video> element is displayed in the browser it includes some standard browser styled playback controls. To customize a control's appearance or to add new controls you have a number of DOM properties to work with. These include the following, among others:

- currentTime returns the current playback position, expressed in seconds.

- duration returns the duration of the media, expressed in seconds or infinity for a stream.

- paused indicates whether the media is paused or not.

Also, there are a number of media-related events that you can use to trigger your own scripts. These include the following, among others:

- play occurs when the media begins playing.

- pause occurs when the media is paused.

- loadeddata occurs when the media is ready to start playing at the current playback position.

- ended occurs when the media has stopped because it reached the end of its duration.

Using these and other properties and events you can easily create your own video controls to do pretty much whatever you'd like the video to do. Everything from Pause and Play buttons to scrubber bars (progress indicators) is possible.

Whatever controls you decide to create, always remember to include the control property on the video element itself:

```
<video src="movie.ogv" control>
```

This presents a common video control interface as shown here in Chrome, and can be removed by your custom control DOM script as necessary.

Now, let's put our DOM scripting skills to work and create our own simple video control.

■ **Note** If you need sample files to work with, you can download them along with the source code for this book from `http://www.friendsofed.com`.

Start by creating a simple HTML page called movie.html that includes a <video> element with a movie in the appropriate formats we saw earlier. Also include a player.css stylesheet and a player.js script:

```
<!DOCTYPE html>
<html lang="en">
<head>
<meta charset="utf-8" />
  <title>My Video</title>
  <link rel="stylesheet" href="styles/player.css" />
</head>
<body>

<div class="video-wrapper">
 <video id="movie" controls>
    <source src="movie.mp4" />
    <source src=" movie.webm"
      type='video/webm; codecs="vp8, vorbis"' />
    <source src="movie.ogv"
      type='video/ogg; codecs="theora, vorbis"' />
    <p>Download movie as
      <a href="movie.mp4">MP4</a>,
      <a href="movie.webm">WebM</a>,
      or <a href="movie.ogv">Ogg</a>.</p>
  </video>
</div>

  <script src="scripts/player.js"></script>
</body>
</html>
```

In the player.js file we're going to alter any <video> elements on the page by removing the built-in controls and then adding our own Play button. Add the following complete functions to the player.js file:

```
function createVideoControls() {
  var vids = document.getElementsByTagName('video');
  for (var i = 0 ; i < vids.length ; i++) {
    addControls( vids[i] );
  }
}

function addControls( vid ) {

  vid.removeAttribute('controls');

  vid.height = vid.videoHeight;
  vid.width = vid.videoWidth;
  vid.parentNode.style.height = vid.videoHeight + 'px';
```

```
    vid.parentNode.style.width = vid.videoWidth + 'px';

    var controls = document.createElement('div');
    controls.setAttribute('class','controls');

    var play = document.createElement('button');
    play.setAttribute('title','Play');
    play.innerHTML = '&#x25BA;';

    controls.appendChild(play);

    vid.parentNode.insertBefore(controls, vid);

    play.onclick = function () {
      if (vid.ended) {
        vid.currentTime = 0;
      }
      if (vid.paused) {
        vid.play();
      } else {
        vid.pause();
      }
    };

    vid.addEventListener('play', function () {
      play.innerHTML = '&#x2590;&#x2590;';
      play.setAttribute('paused', true);
    }, false);

    vid.addEventListener('pause', function () {
      play.removeAttribute('paused');
      play.innerHTML = '&#x25BA;';
    }, false);

    vid.addEventListener('ended', function () {
      vid.pause();
    }, false);
}

window.onload = function() {
  createVideoControls();
}
```

The functions in the player.js file do a number of things. First, we locate all the video elements on the page and apply our addControls function:

```
function createVideoControls() {
  var videos = document.getElementsByTagName('video');
  for (var i = 0 ; i < videos.length ; i++) {
    addControls( videos[i] );
  }
}
```

In the `addControls` function we remove the existing `controls` property so that the built-in controls don't appear, and then we create a few DOM objects to act as the Play/Pause control by appending them as siblings to the video elements:

```
function addControls( vid ) {

  vid.removeAttribute('controls');

  vid.height = vid.videoHeight;
  vid.width = vid.videoWidth;
  vid.parentNode.style.height = vid.videoHeight + 'px';
  vid.parentNode.style.width = vid.videoWidth + 'px';

  var controls = document.createElement('div');
  controls.setAttribute('class','controls');

  var play = document.createElement('button');
  play.setAttribute('title','Play');
  play.innerHTML = '&#x25BA;';

  controls.appendChild(play);

  vid.parentNode.insertBefore(controls, vid);
```

Next, we attach a click event to the Play button so we can click it to start the movie:

```
play.onclick = function () {
  if (vid.ended) {
    vid.currentTime = 0;
  }
  if (vid.paused) {
    vid.play();
  } else {
    vid.pause();
  }
};
```

Finally, using the play, pause, and ended events, we alter the Play button's state to show a Pause button if the movie is not already paused:

```
vid.addEventListener('play', function () {
  play.innerHTML = '&#x2590;&#x2590;';
  play.setAttribute('paused', true);
}, false);

vid.addEventListener('pause', function () {
  play.removeAttribute('paused');
  play.innerHTML = '&#x25BA;';
}, false);

vid.addEventListener('ended', function () {
  vid.pause();
}, false);
```

> ■ **Note** You'll notice that I used the addEventListener method to attach the events to the video. addEventListener is the proper DOM method to use for attaching event handlers to objects. In earlier chapter we avoided addEventListener and used the HTML-DOM on prefixed properties such as onclick because Internet Explorer (up to version 8) used an alternate attachEvent method. Internet Explorer 9, which supports <video> and is required for this chapter, also supports the proper addEventListener method so it's safe to use in this example.

To style the controls, add the following to the player.css file. You can alter the appearance however you like using CSS:

```css
.video-wrapper {
  overflow: hidden;
}

.video-wrapper .controls {
  position: absolute;
  height:30px;
  width:30px;
  margin: auto;
  background: rgba(0,0,0,0.5);
}

.video-wrapper button {
  display: block;
  width: 100%;
  height: 100%;
  border: 0;
  cursor: pointer;
  font-size: 17px;
  color: #fff;
  background: transparent;
}

.video-wrapper button[paused] {
  font-size: 12px;
}
```

When the page finishes loading, the window.load event runs the createVideoControls function, and the result is a very crude video control interface that allows you to play and pause the video.

Obviously this simple example is a very minimal set of video controls. You'll probably want to add a scrubbing bar with a play position indicator, various time stamps, or other special controls using the video's other properties and events. The choice of controls to create is now up to you. I suggest you look at the rest of the video-related properties available in the HTML5 video specification (http://www.whatwg.org/specs/web-apps/current-work/multipage/video.html#video) and a working example at http://www.w3.org/2010/05/video/mediaevents.html. Also check out *The Definitive Guide to HTML5 Video*, by Silvia Pfeiffer (Apress, 2011) to learn more about the <video> element and see what else you can do with it.

Forms

The last of the HTML5 elements we'll experiment with is the form. Forms are a staple of every web page, but until the advent of HTML5, the selection of input types was a little sparse. Text, radio controls, and checkboxes were great for simple forms, but more often than not DOM scripting had to fill a void when more interaction was necessary. If you wanted something like a date input, it was up to you to create the necessary JavaScript and the appropriate interface. Thankfully, HTML5 introduces a number of new elements, input types, and attributes to fill these holes but, as usual, your DOM scripting talents aren't going to go to waste anytime soon.

The new input types are

- `email` for email address specific inputs

- `url` for URL-specific inputs

- `date` and `time` for calendar inputs

- `number` for numeric inputs

- `range` for sliders

- `search` for search boxes

- tel for telephone numbers
- color for color pickers

They offer a number of advantages over the stuffy old type="text". Because you're explicitly telling the browser the type of data you're expecting, the browser can offer better input control, such as altering the keyboard input on a mobile device. Here, we see that mobile Safari on the iPhone shows one keyboard for text and a modified keyboard targeted at email addresses:

Likewise, new attributes include these:

- autocomplete to incorporate a list of suggested completions for text
- autofocus to automatically focus an element of the form
- form to allow you to group form elements placed outside of the <form> tags
- min, max, and step for ranges and numbers
- pattern to define a regular expression that is used to validate the value of the input
- placeholder for temporary initial hints in a text field
- required to indicate the field is required

These attributes let the browser take over control of many tasks that were formerly the responsibility of DOM scripts, such as presenting autocomplete suggestions and form validation. In all cases, however, we need to account for situations where some browsers don't understand newer types and attributes.

You can jump right in today with new input types because they're backward-compatible—sort of. For an HTML5 input such as email:

```
<input type="email" />
```

an older browser will default the type back to text and present the standard text input we're all familiar with. That's great for email or maybe search types but not so great for a range slider. In this case the user interface would be a text box instead of the slider you want, as shown here with Safari and Internet Explorer.

To accommodate incompatible browsers, you need to fall back to another solution using feature detection.

The Modernizr library, presented earlier in the chapter, provides simple compatibility checks. To check whether an input type is supported, use the inputtypes.*type* property:

```
If ( !Modernizr.inputtypes.date ) {
  // Apply a date picker script
}
```

or, to check for support of specific attributes, you can use the input.*attribute* property:

```
if ( !Modernizr.input.placeholder ){
  // Apply a placeholder hint script
}
```

If you're not using Modernizr, you can use the following inputSupportsType function to check if a browser supports a specific input type:

```
function inputSupportsType(type) {
  if (!document.createElement) return false;
  var input = document.createElement('input');
  input.setAttribute('type',type);
  if (input.type == 'text' && type != 'text') {
    return false;
  } else {
    return true;
  }
}
```

To use the inputSupportsType function, apply the same logic as the Modernizr example:

```
If ( !inputSupportsType('date') ) {
  // Apply a date picker script
}
```

To check for specific attributes, you can use the following elementSupportsAttribute function:

```
function elementSupportsAttribute(elementName, attribute) {
  if (!document.createElement) return false;
  var temp = document.createElement(elementName);
  return ( attribute in test );
}
```

Again, apply similar logic to the elementSupportsAttribute function, giving it both the element name and the attribute that you want to test:

```
if ( !elementSupportsAttribute( 'input', 'placeholder' ) ){
  // Apply a placeholder hint script
}
```

With feature detection in hand, you can safely start experimenting with the new HTML5 form elements knowing that your trusty DOM scripts are there if no native alternative is available.

For example, let's say you want a placeholder message in a text input field. In HTML5 you can easily use the placeholder attribute, as shown here:

```
<input type="text" id="first-name" placeholder="Your First Name" />
```

The placeholder temporarily displays in the text input field when there is no value in a browser like Safari or Chrome:

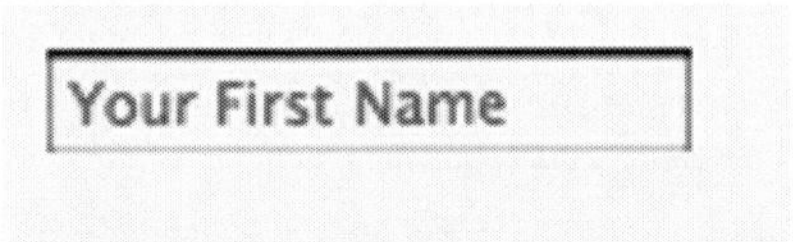

To achieve the same result in a browser that doesn't understand the placeholder attribute, you can use a simple DOM script to replicate the same functionality:

```
if ( !Modernizr.input.placeholder ) {
  var input = document.getElementById('first-name')
  input.onfocus = function () {
    var text = this.placeholder || this.getAttribute('placeholder');
    if ( this.value == text ) {
      // Reset the value to hide the temporary
      // placeholder value.
      this.value = '';
    }
  }
  input.onblur = function () {
    if ( this.value == '' ) {
      // Set the input value to the placeholder value.
      this.value = this.placeholder || this.getAttribute('placeholder');
    }
  }
  // Execute onblur to initially
  // add the placeholder text.
  input.onblur();
}
```

Of course, the only disadvantage with this alternate solution is that it requires JavaScript to achieve the functionality, so be sure to choose your inputs wisely for situations where JavaScript isn't available.

Replicating more advanced functionality, such as autocomplete and sliders, is going to require a lot more work. Your best bet is to use an existing library that has already done all the hard work. See this book's appendix for some examples of various libraries you may want to experiment with.

Is there anything else?

Yes! There's a lot more to HTML5 than just a few new tags and properties, but keep in mind that HTML5 is an evolving specification and things could still change before all the dust settles. It's a little early to use some of the new features, especially where there is very limited browser support, but that doesn't mean that we can't have some fun. The HTML JavaScript APIs include a number of new modules we've always wanted. For example, soon you'll have these capabilities:

- Much better client-side storage for large and complicated datasets, with the `localStorage` and `sessionStorage` features (`http://dev.w3.org/html5/webstorage/`)

- Open two-way communication with server-side scripts, with web sockets (`http://dev.w3.org/html5/websockets/`)

- Background processing in JavaScript, with web workers (`http://www.whatwg.org/specs/web-workers/current-work/`)

- Standardized drag-and-drop (`http://www.whatwg.org/specs/web-apps/current-work/multipage/dnd.html#dnd`)

- In-browser geolocation services (`http://www.w3.org/TR/geolocation-API/`)

These features aren't all DOM-related, but they're technologies that you're going to be seeing and using daily in the very near future, so it would be good to pay attention now.

For more reading and examples, here are some more resources to get you started:

- The W3C HTML5 Working Draft: `http://www.w3.org/TR/html5/`

- The WHATWG HTML5 (including next-generation additions still in development): `http://www.whatwg.org/specs/web-apps/current-work/`

- HTML5 interactive demos: `http://html5demos.com/`

- HTML5 Presentation / Code / Samples and Tutorials: `http://html5rocks.com`

- Dive into HTML5, by Mark Pilgrim: `http://diveintohtml5.org/`

What's Next

In this chapter, you were introduced to HTML5 and the importance of feature detection using tools such as Modernizr. You saw how feature detection could be used to offer fallback for newer HTML5 features such as these:

- The `<canvas>` element, which allows you to draw vector and bitmap images into your documents

- The `<audio>` and `<video>` elements, which allow you to embed video content directly into your web pages—without plug-ins

- New form types and attributes that give you a wider range of built-in input options

Until now, you've seen DOM scripting enhancements in isolation. In the next chapter, I'm going to apply all the concepts and techniques that you've been learning into one final project.

It's time to put it all together.

■ ■ ■

Putting It All Together

What this chapter covers:

- Content structure

- Style application

- JavaScript, DOM, and Ajax enhancements

You've seen a lot of examples of the DOM in action, but those theoretical examples have been in isolation. Now it's time to put them all together in a real-world situation. In this chapter, you're going to build a website from scratch, complete with JavaScript enhancements.

The brief

You are one lucky web designer. You have been chosen to design the website for what is quite possibly the coolest band on the planet: Jay Skript and the Domsters!

All right, so there's no such band. But play along with me here. For the purposes of this chapter, pretend not only that the band exists, but that you have indeed been asked to design the band's website.

The website, like the band, needs to look cool. If you can add some nifty interactive features, that will go down well. However, the site also needs to be accessible and search-engine-friendly.

The purpose of the site is to provide information about the band. Whatever design decisions you make, that must remain the top priority. Let's see what you have to work with.

Raw materials

The client has provided you with the building blocks for the website: introductory text about the band, a list of tour dates, and some pictures. This won't be a large website. It's basically a brochure site, which makes it even more important that it conveys the right feeling.

Site structure

Based on the content provided by the client, you can create a site map fairly easily. The structure isn't very complicated. You can store all the pages in one folder.

In preparation for building the site, create a folder called images to hold the image files you will use. Create another folder called styles to hold your CSS. Also create a folder called scripts to hold your JavaScript files.

Your directory structure now looks like this:

- /images

- /styles

- /scripts

You need one page to provide all the background information about the band. You can put the photos together in an image gallery on another page. The tour dates will also get their own page. You'll need to create a contact page where visitors can get in touch with the band. Finally, an introductory home page will set the scene and give a brief description of what awaits the visitor within the site. Here is your list of pages to work with:

- Home

- About

- Photos

- Live

- Contact

You will turn this list into the following files:

- index.html

- about.html

- photos.html

- live.html

- contact.html

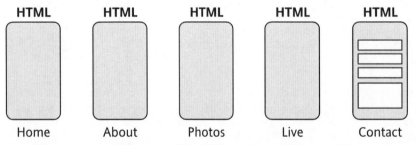

The content on each page will be different, but each page will use the same basic structure. It's time to create a template for these pages.

Page structure

Each page of the site will be divided into a number of sections.

- The header will contain the branding for the site. This is where the logo will go. You will use <header> for the header.

- The navigation will have a list of links to all the pages. You will use <nav> for the navigation.

- The content will contain the meat and bones of each page. You will use <article> for the content.

Since you're using HTML5 elements, you'll also include the Modernizr library (introduced in Chapter 11) in the <head> of these documents. You can download the latest version (Modernizr 1.6 at the time of writing) from http://modernizr.com and place it in the scripts folder.

You can create a template like this in fairly short order:

```
<!DOCTYPE html>
<html lang="en">
<head>
  <meta charset="utf-8" />
  <title>Jay Skript and the Domsters</title>
  <script src="scripts/modernizr-1.6.min.js"></script>
</head>
<body>
  <header>
    <nav>
      <ul>
        <li><a href="index.html">Home</a></li>
        <li><a href="about.html">About</a></li>
        <li><a href="photos.html">Photos</a></li>
        <li><a href="live.html">Live</a></li>
        <li><a href="contact.html">Contact</a></li>
      </ul>
    </nav>
  </header>
  <article>
  </article>
</body>
</html>
```

Save this as template.html.

Now that you have a structure in place, you can begin to insert the content on a page-by-page basis. But before doing that, let's take a peek at the final design if the site.

Design

You know what structural elements need to be included on every page of the site. Armed with this knowledge, and the raw materials provided by the client, you can get to work on the visual design. It's time to fire up Photoshop, Fireworks, or any other graphic design tool of your choice. Create any kind of design you like. In the words of the best celebrity chefs, "Here's one I made earlier."

With the visual design finalized, you can slice up your mock-up for graphical elements. Save a portion of the tiling background image as background.gif. The band name becomes logo.gif. A portion of the tiling gradient in the navigation bar becomes navbar.gif. Save the silhouetted figure as guitarist.gif. Put all these files in the images folder.

■ **Note** If you're not a design wizard, you can download the image files I used in this chapter from the book's page on the friends of ED website (http://www.friendsofed.com).

CSS

You have a basic HTML template. You know how you want the website to look. By applying CSS to the template, you can reproduce your design for the Web.

You could write all your CSS in one file, but that would make it much trickier to modify. You'll probably find it easier to make changes later if you split up your CSS now.

You can divide your CSS however you like. I recommend having one file for the overall layout, another that deals purely with color, and a third for handling typography:

- layout.css

- color.css

- typography.css

Each one of these files can be imported from a basic style sheet:

```
@import url(layout.css);
@import url(color.css);
@import url(typography.css);
```

Save this three-line file as basic.css in the styles folder. If you ever need to add a new style sheet or remove an existing one, you need to edit only basic.css.

You can call this basic style sheet from your template with a `<link>` tag in the head of the document. While you're at it, add an `<img>` tag inside the header, pointing to the logo. You can also add some dummy "lorem ipsum" text to the `<article>`:

```
<!DOCTYPE html>
<html lang="en">
<head>
  <meta charset="utf-8" />
  <title>Jay Skript and the Domsters</title>
  <script src="scripts/modernizr-1.6.min.js"></script>
  <link rel="stylesheet" media="screen" href="styles/basic.css" />
</head>
<body>
  <header>
    <img src="images/logo.gif" alt="Jay Skript and the Domsters" />
    <nav>
      <ul>
        <li><a href="index.html">Home</a></li>
        <li><a href="about.html">About</a></li>
        <li><a href="photos.html">Photos</a></li>
        <li><a href="live.html">Live</a></li>
        <li><a href="contact.html">Contact</a></li>
      </ul>
    </nav>
  </header>
  <article>
    <h1>Lorem Ipsum Dolor</h1>
    <p>Lorem ipsum dolor sit amet, consectetuer adipiscing elit.
Nullam iaculis vestibulum turpis. Pellentesque mattis rutrum
nibh. Quisque orci, euismod sit amet, sollicitudin et,
ullamcorper at, lorem.
Pellentesque habitant morbi tristique senectus et netus
et malesuada fames ac turpis egestas.
Ut lectus. Mauris eu sapien non enim dapibus imperdiet.
Sed eu mauris sed pede mollis commodo.
Fusce eget est. Sed ullamcorper enim nec est.
Cras dui felis, porta vitae, faucibus laoreet, sollicitudin eget,
enim. Nulla auctor. Fusce interdum diam ac eros.
Mauris egestas. Fusce in elit et sem aliquet pretium.
Donec nunc erat, sodales ac, facilisis a, molestie eu, massa.
Aenean nec justo eu neque malesuada aliquet.</p>
  </article>
</body>
</html>
```

You now have the basic template.

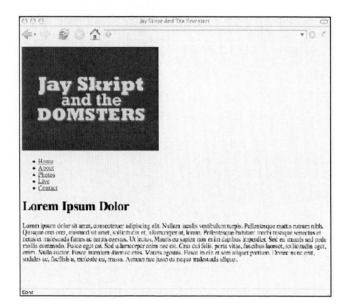

Color

The c|olor.css style sheet is the most straightforward. Make sure that wherever you apply color to an element, you also specify a background color. Otherwise, there's a danger that you might accidentally make some of your text invisible.

```
body {
  color: #fb5;
  background-color: #334;
}
a:link {
  color: #445;
  background-color: #eb6;
}
a:visited {
  color: #345;
  background-color: #eb6;
}
a:hover {
  color: #667;
  background-color: #fb5;
}
a:active {
  color: #778;
  background-color: #ec8;
}
header {
  color: #ec8;
  background-color: #334;
  border-color: #667;
```

```css
}
header nav {
  color: #455;
  background-color: #789;
  border-color: #667;
}
article {
  color: #223;
  background-color: #edc;
  border-color: #667;
}
header nav ul {
  border-color: #99a;
}
header nav a:link,header nav a:visited {
  color: #eef;
  background-color: transparent;
  border-color: #99a;
}
header nav a:hover {
  color: #445;
  background-color: #eb6;
}
header nav a:active {
  color: #667;
  background-color: #ec8;
}
article img {
  border-color: #ba9;
  outline-color: #dcb;
}
#imagegallery a {
  background-color: transparent;
}
```

Now the template looks more colorful.

Typography

It isn't always easy to decide where to put certain style declarations. Fonts and sizes clearly belong in the typography.css file. But what about margins and padding? It's hard to say whether they are part of the layout or should be considered typographical information. Here, the padding information is in layout.css, as shown in the previous section. Margins are applied in typography.css.

```css
body {
    font-size: 76%;
    font-family: "Helvetica","Arial",sans-serif;
}
body * {
    font-size: 1em;
}
a {
    font-weight: bold;
    text-decoration: none;
}
header nav {
    font-family: "Lucida Grande","Helvetica","Arial",sans-serif;
}
header nav a {
    text-decoration: none;
    font-weight: bold;
}
article {
```

```css
  line-height: 1.8em;
}
article p {
  margin: 1em 0;
}
h1 {
  font-family: "Georgia","Times New Roman",sans-serif;
  font: 2.4em normal;
}
h2 {
  font-family: "Georgia","Times New Roman",sans-serif;
  font: 1.8em normal;
  margin-top: 1em;
}
h3 {
  font-family: "Georgia","Times New Roman",sans-serif;
  font: 1.4em normal;
  margin-top: 1em;
}
#imagegallery li {
  list-style-type: none;
}
textarea {
  font-family: "Helvetica","Arial",sans-serif;
}
```

Now the template has color, layout, and typography styles applied.

Each of the CSS files—color.css, layout.css, and typography.css—resides in the styles folder along with the basic.css style sheet.

Markup

Your template looks good. Your style sheets are working well. Now you can start to build the pages of the site.

Begin with the home page, index.html. It contains a single introductory paragraph within the `<article>` element:

```
<p id="intro">
Welcome to the official website of Jay Skript and the Domsters.
Here, you can <a href="about.html" title="About">learn more about the band</a>,
view <a href="photos.html" title="Photos">photos of the band</a>,
find out about <a href="live.html" title="Tour Date">tour dates</a>
and <a href="contact.html" title="Contact">get in touch with the band</a>.
</p>
```

Here's the home page:

This paragraph has been marked up with an `id` of `"intro"`. You might use this to style the introduction in a special way. You can also use it as a hook for some DOM scripting.

JavaScript

Before you start adding enhancements with the DOM, you should think about how you are going to manage your JavaScript files. When your site requires a lot of long complicated scripts, it's generally a good idea to separate your files, as we've done elsewhere in the book. However, this site is fairly simple, and the JavaScript code is short. To reduce the number of requests, you'll put all your code into one file called global.js. This will also make it easier to minify when you're finished.

Start by creating global.js in your scripts folder. Now you'll add a few common functions you'll be using throughout the site.

You'll definitely be using the addLoadEvent function (from Chapter 6). You will need this whenever you write a function that should be executed when the document is fully loaded.

```
function addLoadEvent(func) {
  var oldonload = window.onload;
  if (typeof window.onload != 'function') {
    window.onload = func;
  } else {
    window.onload = function() {
      oldonload();
      func();
    }
  }
}
```

The insertAfter function (from Chapter 7) will also come in handy. It's a useful corollary to the insertBefore method.

```
function insertAfter(newElement,targetElement) {
  var parent = targetElement.parentNode;
  if (parent.lastChild == targetElement) {
    parent.appendChild(newElement);
  } else {
    parent.insertBefore(newElement,targetElement.nextSibling);
  }
}
```

You may also need the addClass function (from Chapter 9).

```
function addClass(element,value) {
  if (!element.className) {
    element.className = value;
  } else {
    newClassName = element.className;
    newClassName+= " ";
    newClassName+= value;
    element.className = newClassName;
  }
}
```

Call this file by adding a <script> tag to end of your template page as well as index.html, immediately before the closing </body> tag:

```
  </article>
  <script src="scripts/global.js"></script>
</body>
</html>
```

The global.js file will be included on every page of the site so all the functions can be shared among the pages.

There's one more function you'll want to add to the global.js file right away: highlightPage, which you'll write in the next section.

Page highlighting

When you are creating each page from your existing template, you will be inserting markup into the `<article>` element. In your site, this is the part of the document that changes from page to page.

Ideally, you should also be updating the list in the `<nav>` element as well. If the current page is index.html, then there's no reason for a link to index.html in the navigation list.

In practice, it isn't always possible to edit the navigation on a page-by-page basis. Quite often, the fragment of markup containing the navigation will be dropped into each page using a server-side include. Let's assume that that's the case with this website. There could be a server-side include containing this chunk of markup:

```
<header>
  <img src="images/logo.gif" alt="Jay Skript and the Domsters" />
  <nav>
    <ul>
      <li><a href="index.html">Home</a></li>
      <li><a href="about.html">About</a></li>
      <li><a href="photos.html">Photos</a></li>
      <li><a href="live.html">Live</a></li>
      <li><a href="contact.html">Contact</a></li>
    </ul>
  </nav>
</header>
```

This could be included using Apache Server Side Includes (SSIs), PHP, ASP, or a number of other server-side languages.

The advantage of this technique is that reusable chunks of markup are centralized. If you ever need to update the header or the navigation, you can do so in one file. The disadvantage is that it becomes harder to customize these chunks for each page.

At the very least, the current page should be highlighted in some way. The visitor should have some kind of "you are here" message.

Update the color.css file to include styles for a class called here:

```
header nav a.here:link,
header nav a.here:visited,
header nav a.here:hover,
header nav a.here:active {
  color: #eef;
  background-color: #799;
}
```

To apply those colors, add the here class to the navigation link pointing to the current page, like this:

```
<a href="index.html" class="here">Home</a></li>
```

If you're using a server-side include, this might not be so easy. Ideally, the server-side technology will be robust enough to create the correct markup for each page. This isn't always the case, though.

JavaScript rides to the rescue.

In this case, JavaScript is a last resort. It would be much better if the here class were added directly in the markup. Use the JavaScript solution only when the markup is beyond your control.

First, remove any class attributes you may have added to the navigation. Then write a function called highlightPage to do the following:

1. Get all the links in the navigation list.

2. Loop through these links.

3. If you find a link that matches the current URL, add the here class.

As usual, begin the function with a test for the DOM methods you will be using. You should also test that the various elements exist.

```
function highlightPage() {
  if (!document.getElementsByTagName) return false;
  if (!document.getElementById) return false;
  var headers = document.getElementsByTagName('header');
  if (headers.length == 0) return false;
  var navs = headers[0].getElementsByTagName('nav');
  if (navs.length == 0) return false;
```

Grab all the navigation links and loop through them:

```
var links = navs[0].getElementsByTagName("a");
var linkurl;
for (var i=0; i<links.length; i++) {
```

Next, you're going to compare the URL of the link with the URL of the current page. You can get the URL of the link using getAttribute("href"). You can get the URL of the current page using window.location.href.

```
linkurl = links[i].getAttribute("href");
```

JavaScript provides a number of methods for comparing strings. The indexOf method finds the position of a substring within a string:

```
string.indexOf(substring)
```

This method returns the first occurrence of the substring. In this case, you simply want to find out if one string is within another—is the link URL within the current URL?

```
currenturl.indexOf(linkurl)
```

If a match is not found, the indexOf method will return a value of -1. A return of any other value means there was a match. If the indexOf method does not return a value of -1, you want to proceed with the final step of the function:

```
if (window.location.href.indexOf(linkurl) != -1) {
```

This link must be a link to the current page. Add the here class to the link:

```
links[i].className = "here";
```

All that remains is to close the if statement, close the for loop, and close the function. Do this with closing curly braces. Then call highlightPage using the addLoadEvent function.

```
function highlightPage() {
  if (!document.getElementsByTagName) return false;
  if (!document.getElementById) return false;
  var headers = document.getElementsByTagName('header');
  if (headers.length == 0) return false;
  var navs = headers[0].getElementsByTagName('nav');
  if (navs.length == 0) return false;
  var links = navs[0].getElementsByTagName("a");
```

```
  for (var i=0; i<links.length; i++) {
  var linkurl;
  for (var i=0; i<links.length; i++) {
    linkurl = links[i].getAttribute("href");
    if (window.location.href.indexOf(linkurl) != -1) {
      links[i].className = "here";
    }
  }
}
addLoadEvent(highlightPage);
```

Save this function in global.js. If you reload index.html, you will see that the **Home** link is now highlighted.

You can expand the highlightPage function to kill two birds with one stone.

By giving a unique id attribute to the body element of each page, you will be able to add styles specifically for that page. You can add a unique id to each page by grabbing the text from the current link—the one that now has the class here. Convert this string to lowercase using JavaScript's toLowerCase method:

```
var linktext = links[i].lastChild.nodeValue.toLowerCase();
```

This takes the value of the last child of the current link, which is the link text, and converts it to lowercase. If the text within the link is "Home," then the linktext variable will be "home". Apply this variable as the id attribute of the body element:

```
document.body.setAttribute("id",linktext);
```

This is the equivalent of writing id="home" in the <body> tag.

The highlightPage function now looks like this:

```
function highlightPage( href ) {
if (!document.getElementsByTagName) return false;
  if (!document.getElementById) return false;
```

242

```
var headers = document.getElementsByTagName('header');
if (headers.length == 0) return false;
var navs = headers[0].getElementsByTagName('nav');
if (navs.length == 0) return false;
var links = navs[0].getElementsByTagName("a");
for (var i=0; i<links.length; i++) {
var linkurl;
for (var i=0; i<links.length; i++) {
  linkurl = links[i].getAttribute("href");
  if (window.location.href.indexOf(linkurl) != -1) {
    links[i].className = "here";
    var linktext = links[i].lastChild.nodeValue.toLowerCase();
    document.body.setAttribute("id",linktext);
  }
 }
}
addLoadEvent(highlightPage);
```

The index.html file now has an id of "home" on the body element; the about.html file has an id of "about"; the photos.html file has an id of "photos"; and so on.

These newly inserted identifiers can act as hooks in your CSS. You can specify a different background image for the header of each individual page.

Create an image for each page, 250 pixels by 250 pixels. You can use the ones I made earlier: lineup.gif, basshead.gif, bassist.gif, and drummer.gif. Put these files in the images folder.

You can now update the layout.css file with background-image declarations:

```
#about header {
  background-image: url(../images/lineup.gif);
}
#photos header {
  background-image: url(../images/basshead.gif);
}
#live header {
  background-image: url(../images/bassist.gif);
}
#contact header {
  background-image: url(../images/drummer.gif);
}
```

Now each page will show its own unique image in the header.

JavaScript slideshow

The home page needs something special. It's the first page that most visitors to the site will see, so it's the ideal place to add some sizzle. The JavaScript slideshow that you built in Chapter 10 is perfect for this.

The "intro" paragraph has links to all the other pages on the site. When visitors hover over one of those links, it would be good to give them a glimpse of what awaits them. You could show smaller versions of the images from the headers of each page.

Shrink all the header images down to 150 by 150 pixels and combine them into one 750-pixel-long image called slideshow.gif. Place this image in the images folder.

The montage image looks like this:

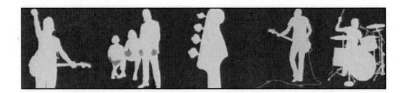

For the slideshow to work, you'll need to add to your global.js file. Copy the moveElement function that you wrote in Chapter 10:

```
function moveElement(elementID,final_x,final_y,interval) {
  if (!document.getElementById) return false;
  if (!document.getElementById(elementID)) return false;
  var elem = document.getElementById(elementID);
  if (elem.movement) {
    clearTimeout(elem.movement);
  }
  if (!elem.style.left) {
    elem.style.left = "0px";
  }
  if (!elem.style.top) {
    elem.style.top = "0px";
  }
  var xpos = parseInt(elem.style.left);
  var ypos = parseInt(elem.style.top);
  if (xpos == final_x && ypos == final_y) {
    return true;
  }
  if (xpos < final_x) {
    var dist = Math.ceil((final_x - xpos)/10);
    xpos = xpos + dist;
  }
  if (xpos > final_x) {
    var dist = Math.ceil((xpos - final_x)/10);
    xpos = xpos - dist;
  }
  if (ypos < final_y) {
    var dist = Math.ceil((final_y - ypos)/10);
    ypos = ypos + dist;
  }
  if (ypos > final_y) {
    var dist = Math.ceil((ypos - final_y)/10);
    ypos = ypos - dist;
  }
  elem.style.left = xpos + "px";
  elem.style.top = ypos + "px";
  var repeat = "moveElement('"+elementID+"',"+final_x+","+final_y+","+interval+")";
  elem.movement = setTimeout(repeat,interval);
}
```

Now you need to create the slideshow elements and prepare the links. In this case, the slideshow will be placed directly after the "intro" paragraph if it's found in the document.

```
function prepareSlideshow() {
```

```
if (!document.getElementsByTagName) return false;
if (!document.getElementById) return false;
if (!document.getElementById("intro")) return false;
var intro = document.getElementById("intro");
var slideshow = document.createElement("div");
slideshow.setAttribute("id","slideshow");
var preview = document.createElement("img");
preview.setAttribute("src","images/slideshow.gif");
preview.setAttribute("alt","a glimpse of what awaits you");
preview.setAttribute("id","preview");
slideshow.appendChild(preview);
insertAfter(slideshow,intro);
```

Now loop through all the links in the "intro" paragraph. Move the preview element based on which link is being moused over. For instance, if the href value of the link contains the string "about.html", move the preview element to –150 pixels; if the href value contains the string "photos.html", move the preview element to –300 pixels; and so on.

To make the animation snappy, pass the moveElement function an interval value of just five milliseconds:

```
var links = intro.getElementsByTagName("a");
var destination;
for (var i=0; i<links.length; i++) {
  links[i].onmouseover = function() {
    destination = this.getAttribute("href");
    if (destination.indexOf("index.html") != -1) {
      moveElement("preview",0,0,5);
    }
    if (destination.indexOf("about.html") != -1) {
      moveElement("preview",-150,0,5);
    }
    if (destination.indexOf("photos.html") != -1) {
      moveElement("preview",-300,0,5);
    }
    if (destination.indexOf("live.html") != -1) {
      moveElement("preview",-450,0,5);
    }
    if (destination.indexOf("contact.html") != -1) {
      moveElement("preview",-600,0,5);
    }
  }
}
```

Call the function using addLoadEvent:

```
addLoadEvent(prepareSlideshow);
```

Save all this in global.js.

You'll also need to update your styles. Add these lines to layout.css:

```
#slideshow {
  width: 150px;
  height: 150px;
  position: relative;
  overflow: hidden;
```

```
}
#preview {
  position: absolute;
  border-width: 0;
  outline-width: 0;
}
```

Refresh index.html in a web browser to see the slideshow in action.

It looks pretty good. You can make it look even better by placing the animation in a window frame.

Create an image, 150 by 150 pixels, that is mostly transparent, but with some rounded corners the same color as the background of the content div. Call it frame.gif and put it in the images folder.

Add the following lines to the prepareSlideshow function in home.js. Put them right after the creation of the slideshow element:

```
var frame = document.createElement("img");
frame.setAttribute("src","images/frame.gif");
frame.setAttribute("alt","");
frame.setAttribute("id","frame");
slideshow.appendChild(frame);
```

To make sure that this container appears above the animation, add these lines to layout.css:

```
#frame {
  position: absolute;
  top: 0;
  left: 0;
  z-index: 99;
}
```

Refresh index.html to see the slideshow, complete with window frame.

Right now, the slideshow animates whenever a visitor hovers over a link in the "intro" paragraph. If you want, the animation could also happen when a link in the navigation div is moused over.

Change this line:

```
var links = intro.getElementsByTagName("a");
```

to this:

```
var links = document.getElementsByTagName("a");
```

The finished prepareSlideshow function now looks like this:

```
function prepareSlideshow() {
  if (!document.getElementsByTagName) return false;
  if (!document.getElementById) return false;
  if (!document.getElementById("intro")) return false;
  var intro = document.getElementById("intro");
  var slideshow = document.createElement("div");
  slideshow.setAttribute("id","slideshow");
  var frame = document.createElement("img");
  frame.setAttribute("src","images/frame.gif");
  frame.setAttribute("alt","");
  frame.setAttribute("id","frame");
  slideshow.appendChild(frame);
  var preview = document.createElement("img");
  preview.setAttribute("src","images/slideshow.gif");
  preview.setAttribute("alt","a glimpse of what awaits you");
```

```
preview.setAttribute("id","preview");
slideshow.appendChild(preview);
insertAfter(slideshow,intro);
var links = document.getElementsByTagName("a");
var destination;
for (var i=0; i<links.length; i++) {
  links[i].onmouseover = function() {
    destination = this.getAttribute("href");
    if (destination.indexOf("index.html") != -1) {
      moveElement("preview",0,0,5);
    }
    if (destination.indexOf("about.html") != -1) {
      moveElement("preview",-150,0,5);
    }
    if (destination.indexOf("photos.html") != -1) {
      moveElement("preview",-300,0,5);
    }
    if (destination.indexOf("live.html") != -1) {
      moveElement("preview",-450,0,5);
    }
    if (destination.indexOf("contact.html") != -1) {
      moveElement("preview",-600,0,5);
    }
  }
}
}
addLoadEvent(prepareSlideshow);
```

Now if you hover over any of the links in the navigation list, the slideshow animation will be triggered.

Internal navigation

The next page in the site is the About page. Add this markup in the `<article>` element of about.html:

```
<h1>About the band</h1>
<nav>
  <ul>
    <li><a href="#jay">Jay Skript</a></li>
    <li><a href="#domsters">The Domsters</a></li>
  </ul>
</nav>
<section id="jay">
  <h2>Jay Skript</h2>
    <p>Jay Skript is going to rock your world!</p>
    <p>Together with his compatriots the Domsters,
  Jay is set for world domination. Just you wait and see.</p>
    <p>Jay Skript has been on the scene since the mid 1990s.
  His talent hasn't always been recognized or fully appreciated.
  In the early days, he was often unfavorably compared to bigger,
  similarly named artists. That's all in the past now.</p>
</section>
<section id="domsters">
  <h2>The Domsters</h2>
    <p>The Domsters have been around, in one form or another,
  for almost as long. It's only in the past few years that the Domsters
  have settled down to their current, stable lineup.
  Now they're a rock-solid bunch: methodical and dependable.</p>
</section>
```

The About page now looks like this:

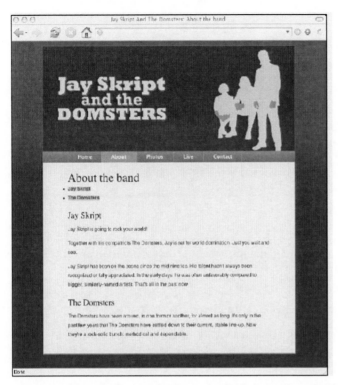

The page looks and works fine. It's a little long, though. That's why there are internal links inside the article's <nav> element. Each of these links leads to a <section> with a specific id attribute.

Using JavaScript and the DOM, you can selectively show and hide these sections so that only one is visible at any one time. Here's a function you can add to global.js that will show a <section> with a specified id, while hiding all the other sections:

```
function showSection(id) {
  var sections = document.getElementsByTagName("section");
  for (var i=0; i<sections.length; i++ ) {
    if (sections[i].getAttribute("id") != id) {
      sections[i].style.display = "none";
    } else {
      sections[i].style.display = "block";
    }
  }
}
```

The showSection function updates the display style property of each section. The display property is set to "none" on all the sections, except for the one with the specified id. The id is passed as an argument to the function. The display property for the div with this id is set to "block".

The showSection function needs to be executed whenever someone clicks a link in the <nav> list in the <article> element.

Create a function called `prepareInternalnav`. Start looping through all the links in the article's navigation list:

```
function prepareInternalnav() {
  if (!document.getElementsByTagName) return false;
  if (!document.getElementById) return false;
  var articles = document.getElementsByTagName("article");
  if (articles.length == 0) return false;
  var navs = articles[0].getElementsByTagName("nav");
  if (navs.length == 0) return false;
  var nav = navs[0];
  var links = nav.getElementsByTagName("a");
  for (var i=0; i<links.length; i++ ) {
```

The `href` value of each link is the `id` of a `section`, but with the "#" symbol at the start to indicate that the link is internal. You can extract the `id` of the `section` by using the `split` method. This is a handy way of splitting a string into two or more parts based on a dividing character:

array = *string*.split(*character*)

In this case, you want everything after the "#" character. Split the `href` value on this character. The resulting array contains two elements: the first is everything before the "#" character (in this case, an empty string), and the second is everything afterward. Remember that the first element in an array has an index of 0. You're interested in the second element of the array, which has an index of 1:

```
var sectionId = links[i].getAttribute("href").split("#")[1];
```

This will extract everything after the first "#" character and assign the result to the variable `sectionId`.

Add a short test to make sure that an element with this `id` actually exists. If it doesn't, carry on to the next iteration of the loop.

```
if (!document.getElementById(sectionId)) continue;
```

When the page loads, you'll want to hide all the sections by default. Do that by adding this line:

```
document.getElementById(sectionId).style.display = "none";
```

Now you can add the `onclick` event handler for the link. When the link is clicked, you want to pass the variable `sectionId` to the `showSection` function. There's a problem of scope, however. The variable `sectionId` is a local variable. It exists only while the `prepareInternalnav` function is being executed. It won't exist within the event handler function.

You can get around this problem by creating your own custom property for each link. Call the property `destination` and assign it the value of `sectionId`:

```
links[i].destination = sectionId;
```

That property has a persistent scope. You can query that property from the event handler function:

```
links[i].onclick = function() {
  showSection(this.destination);
  return false;
}
```

Close the `prepareInternalnav` function with some closing curly braces. Call the function with `addLoadEvent`:

```
addLoadEvent(prepareInternalnav);
```

Here's what the final the prepareInternalnav function looks like in global.js:

```
function prepareInternalnav() {
  if (!document.getElementsByTagName) return false;
  if (!document.getElementById) return false;
  var articles = document.getElementsByTagName("article");
  if (articles.length == 0) return false;
  var navs = articles[0].getElementsByTagName("nav");
  if (navs.length == 0) return false;
  var nav = navs[0];
  var links = nav.getElementsByTagName("a");
  for (var i=0; i<links.length; i++ ) {
    var sectionId = links[i].getAttribute("href").split("#")[1];
    if (!document.getElementById(sectionId)) continue;
    document.getElementById(sectionId).style.display = "none";
    links[i].destination = sectionId;
    links[i].onclick = function() {
      showSection(this.destination);
      return false;
    }
  }
}
```

```
addLoadEvent(prepareInternalnav);
```

Load about.html in a web browser and test the functionality. Clicking one of the internal links shows the relevant section only. The example here shows the About page with only part of the content displayed.

This function could be very useful on much longer pages. If you had a page of frequently asked questions, for example, each question could be an internal link. Clicking a question would reveal the answer to that question while keeping all the other answers hidden.

JavaScript image gallery

The next page you'll make is photos.html. This is the ideal place for the JavaScript image gallery that you've been perfecting in this book.

The client has provided you with four 400-by-300-pixel photos of Jay Skript and the Domsters in action:

- concert.jpg
- bassist.jpg
- guitarist.jpg
- crowd.jpg

Create a new folder called photos in the images folder. Put these four images in the photos folder. Make 100-by-100-pixel thumbnails of each image:

- thumbnail_concert.jpg
- thumbnail_bassist.jpg
- thumbnail_guitarist.jpg
- thumbnail_crowd.jpg

Place these in the photos folder, too.

Create a list of links pointing to the full-sized images. Give this list the id "imagegallery". Put an `<img>` tag in each link. The `src` of each image is a thumbnail image.

```
<h1>Photos of the band</h1>
<ul id="imagegallery">
  <li>
    <a href="images/photos/concert.jpg" title="The crowd goes wild">
      <img src="images/photos/thumbnail_concert.jpg" alt="the band in concert" />
    </a>
  </li>
  <li>
    <a href="images/photos/bassist.jpg" title="An atmospheric moment">
      <img src="images/photos/thumbnail_bassist.jpg" alt="the bassist" />
    </a>
  </li>
  <li>
    <a href="images/photos/guitarist.jpg" title="Rocking out">
      <img src="images/photos/thumbnail_guitarist.jpg" alt="the guitarist" />
    </a>
  </li>
  <li>
    <a href="images/photos/crowd.jpg" title="Encore! Encore!">
      <img src="images/photos/thumbnail_crowd.jpg" alt="the audience" />
    </a>
  </li>
</ul>
```

Put this list within the `<article>` element of photos.html.

Update the layout.css file so that the thumbnails appear horizontally rather than vertically:

```
#imagegallery li {
  display: inline;
}
```

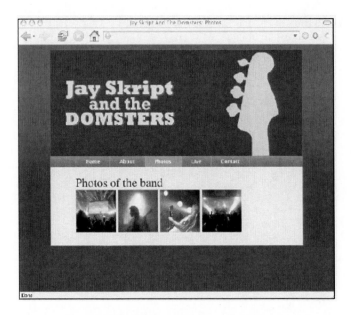

You need one more image for the image gallery script to work. Make a placeholder image. Call it placeholder.gif and put it in the images folder.

Now you can take your image gallery scripts from Chapters 6 and 7 and add them to your global.js file in the scripts folder.

```
function showPic(whichpic) {
  if (!document.getElementById("placeholder")) return true;
  var source = whichpic.getAttribute("href");
  var placeholder = document.getElementById("placeholder");
  placeholder.setAttribute("src",source);
  if (!document.getElementById("description")) return false;
  if (whichpic.getAttribute("title")) {
    var text = whichpic.getAttribute("title");
  } else {
    var text = "";
  }
  var description = document.getElementById("description");
  if (description.firstChild.nodeType == 3) {
    description.firstChild.nodeValue = text;
  }
  return false;
}

function preparePlaceholder() {
  if (!document.createElement) return false;
  if (!document.createTextNode) return false;
  if (!document.getElementById) return false;
  if (!document.getElementById("imagegallery")) return false;
  var placeholder = document.createElement("img");
  placeholder.setAttribute("id","placeholder");
```

```
    placeholder.setAttribute("src","images/placeholder.gif");
    placeholder.setAttribute("alt","my image gallery");
    var description = document.createElement("p");
    description.setAttribute("id","description");
    var desctext = document.createTextNode("Choose an image");
    description.appendChild(desctext);
    var gallery = document.getElementById("imagegallery");
    insertAfter(description,gallery);
    insertAfter(placeholder,description);
}

function prepareGallery() {
    if (!document.getElementsByTagName) return false;
    if (!document.getElementById) return false;
    if (!document.getElementById("imagegallery")) return false;
    var gallery = document.getElementById("imagegallery");
    var links = gallery.getElementsByTagName("a");
    for ( var i=0; i < links.length; i++) {
        links[i].onclick = function() {
            return showPic(this);
        }
    }
}

addLoadEvent(preparePlaceholder);
addLoadEvent(prepareGallery);
```

There's just one small change: the description text has been placed above the placeholder image. Load photos.html in a web browser to see the image gallery in action.

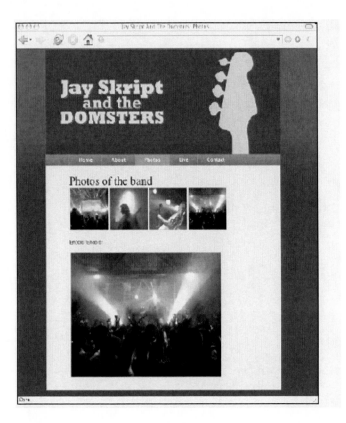

Table enhancements

You've been given a list of tour dates for Jay Skript and the Domsters. For each concert, there is a date, a city, and a venue. This is tabular data, so the Live page will consist of a `<table>` of concert dates.

```
<h1>Tour dates</h1>
<table summary="when and where you can see the band">
  <thead>
  <tr>
    <th>Date</th>
    <th>City</th>
    <th>Venue</th>
  </tr>
  </thead>
  <tbody>
  <tr>
    <td>June 9th</td>
    <td>Portland, <abbr title="Oregon">OR</abbr></td>
    <td>Crystal Ballroom</td>
  </tr>
  <tr>
    <td>June 10th</td>
```

```
      <td>Seattle, <abbr title="Washington">WA</abbr></td>
      <td>Crocodile Cafe</td>
    </tr>
    <tr>
      <td>June 12th</td>
      <td>Sacramento, <abbr title="California">CA</abbr></td>
      <td>Torch Club</td>
    </tr>
    <tr>
      <td>June 17th</td>
      <td>Austin, <abbr title="Texas">TX</abbr></td>
      <td>Speakeasy</td>
    </tr>
    </tbody>
</table>
```

Put this <table> within the <article> element of live.html.
You can add some table cell styling to layout.css as well:

```
td {
  padding: .5em 3em;
}
```

Update color.css with declarations for table headers and rows:

```
th {
  color: #edc;
  background-color: #455;
}
tr td {
  color: #223;
  background-color: #eb6;
}
```

If you load live.html in a web browser, you will see a perfectly normal, somewhat nondescript table.

This is the perfect opportunity to use the table styling functions from Chapter 9: stripeTables and highlightRows. You can also add the displayAbbreviations function from Chapter 8.

Add them all to your global.js file and call them with addLoadEvent:

```
function stripeTables() {
  if (!document.getElementsByTagName) return false;
  var tables = document.getElementsByTagName("table");
  for (var i=0; i<tables.length; i++) {
    var odd = false;
    var rows = tables[i].getElementsByTagName("tr");
    for (var j=0; j<rows.length; j++) {
      if (odd == true) {
        addClass(rows[j],"odd");
        odd = false;
      } else {
        odd = true;
      }
    }
  }
}

function highlightRows() {
  if(!document.getElementsByTagName) return false;
  var rows = document.getElementsByTagName("tr");
  for (var i=0; i<rows.length; i++) {
    rows[i].oldClassName = rows[i].className
    rows[i].onmouseover = function() {
      addClass(this,"highlight");
    }
    rows[i].onmouseout = function() {
```

```
      this.className = this.oldClassName
    }
  }
}

function displayAbbreviations() {
  if (!document.getElementsByTagName || !document.createElement
➥ || !document.createTextNode) return false;

  var abbreviations = document.getElementsByTagName("abbr");
  if (abbreviations.length < 1) return false;
  var defs = new Array();
  for (var i=0; i<abbreviations.length; i++) {
    var current_abbr = abbreviations[i];
    if (current_abbr.childNodes.length < 1) continue;
    var definition = current_abbr.getAttribute("title");
    var key = current_abbr.lastChild.nodeValue;
    defs[key] = definition;
  }
  var dlist = document.createElement("dl");
  for (key in defs) {
    var definition = defs[key];
    var dtitle = document.createElement("dt");
    var dtitle_text = document.createTextNode(key);
    dtitle.appendChild(dtitle_text);
    var ddesc = document.createElement("dd");
    var ddesc_text = document.createTextNode(definition);
    ddesc.appendChild(ddesc_text);
    dlist.appendChild(dtitle);
    dlist.appendChild(ddesc);
  }
  if (dlist.childNodes.length < 1) return false;
  var header = document.createElement("h3");
  var header_text = document.createTextNode("Abbreviations");
  header.appendChild(header_text);
  var articles = document.getElementsByTagName("article");
  if (articles.length == 0) return false;
  var container = articles[0];
  container.appendChild(header);
  container.appendChild(dlist);
}

addLoadEvent(stripeTables);
addLoadEvent(highlightRows);
addLoadEvent(displayAbbreviations);
```

The highlightRows and displayAbbreviations functions have been updated slightly:

- In highlightRows, instead of applying a style property directly, it uses the addClass function to apply the highlight class. This class is applied when the user hovers over a row. Before that, the function takes a snapshot of the old className property and stores it as a custom property called oldClassName. When the user moves off the table row, the className property is reset to the value of oldClassName.

259

- In displayAbbreviations, the last few lines have been modified to find the article element, instead of the div with an id of content as it was in Chapter 8.

These two changes point our further improvements you could make to these functions. For example, displayAbbreviations may be more portable if you add an argument to identify to which element the new list should be appended.

Add some styles for the definition list to layout.css:

```
dl {
  overflow: hidden;
}
dt {
  float: left;
}
dd {
  float: left;
}
```

Update typography.css as well:

```
dt {
  margin-right: 1em;
}
dd {
  margin-right: 3em;
}
```

Finally, add the color information for the odd and highlight classes to color.css:

```
tr.odd td {
  color: #223;
  background-color: #ec8;
}
tr.highlight td {
  color: #223;
  background-color: #cba;
}
```

Load live.html in a web browser to see the enhanced <table>. Every second row has been given a class of odd.

Form enhancements

There's just one more page of the site to build. It's an important page. There needs to be some way for visitors to get in touch with the band.

Just about every website lists some kind of contact information, even if it's just an email address. For this website, you're going to build a contact form.

Contact forms, or any other form, will always require some kind of server-side technology to further validate and store the data in your underlying database or system. This can be done with Perl, PHP, ASP, or just about any other server-side programming language. For this example, however, we're not going to create a server-side script. Instead, we'll create a regular-old HTML page to act as a stand-in "thank-you" page. For now, the data in isn't going anywhere (it's a fictional band, remember). If this were a real site, you would want to do some real processing in the server-side script, and store the information in a database or email it to the appropriate people, before displaying a thank-you message.

Make a file called contact.html. It should have the same structure as template.html, but with this <form> inside the <article>:

```
<h1>Contact the band</h1>
<form method="post" action="submit.html">
<fieldset>
    <p>
     <label for="name">Name:</label>
     <input type="text" id="name" name="name"
➥ placeholder="Your name" required="required" />
    </p>
    <p>
     <label for="email">Email:</label>
     <input type="email" id="email" name="email"
➥ placeholder="Your email address" required="required" />
```

261

```
    </p>
    <p>
     <label for="message">Message:</label>
     <textarea cols="45" rows="7" id="message"
➡ name="message" required="required"
➡ placeholder="Write your message here."></textarea>
    </p>
    <input type="submit" value="Send" />
   </fieldset>
</form>
```

Update the layout.css file:

```
label {
  display: block;
}
fieldset {
  border: 0;
}
```

You now have a contact form.

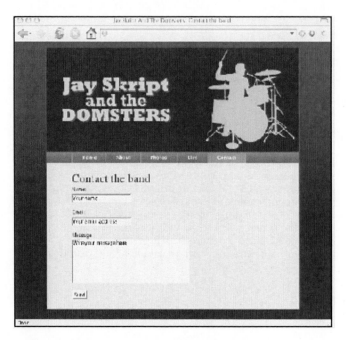

Next, make a file called submit.html. Again, it should have the same structure as template.html, but with a thank-you message inside the <article>.

```
<h1>Thanks!</h1>
<p>Thanks for contacting us. We'll get back to you as soon as we can.</p>
```

The submit.html thank-you page doesn't actually do anything with the form contents, but you get the idea.

Labels

There are three form fields, name, email, and message. Each field has a corresponding <label> tag.

The label element is a useful aid to accessibility. Using the for attribute, it specifically associates a piece of text with a form field. This can be of tremendous value to screen-reading software.

The label element can be equally valuable to visitors without any visual impairments. Many browsers create a default behavior for label elements: if the text within a label is clicked, the associated form field is brought into focus. This is a really nice little usability enhancement. Unfortunately, not all browsers implement this behavior.

The behavior might not be implemented by default, but there's no reason why you can't add it yourself. All you need is a few lines of JavaScript.

1. Get all the label elements in the document.

2. If the label has a for attribute, attach an event handler.

3. When the label is clicked, extract the value of the for attribute. This value is the id of a form element.

4. Make sure the form element exists.

5. Bring that form element into focus.

Call the function focusLabels in global.js and execute the function when the page loads using addLoadEvent.

```
function focusLabels() {
  if (!document.getElementsByTagName) return false;
  var labels = document.getElementsByTagName("label");
  for (var i=0; i<labels.length; i++) {
    if (!labels[i].getAttribute("for")) continue;
    labels[i].onclick = function() {
      var id = this.getAttribute("for");
      if (!document.getElementById(id)) return false;
      var element = document.getElementById(id);
      element.focus();
    }
  }
}
addLoadEvent(focusLabels);
```

Load contact.html in a web browser. Clicking the text in a label brings the associated form field into focus. Depending on the browser you're using, this may have always been the case. However, you've leveled the playing field. All browsers will execute this behavior now.

Placeholder values

Each field in the contact form has some placeholder text in an HTML5 placeholder attribute. The name field has "your name", the email field has "your email", and so on.

■ **Note** Placeholder values are also useful from an accessibility viewpoint. Checkpoint 10.4 of the Web Accessibility Initiative guidelines states, "Until user agents handle empty controls correctly, include default, place-holding characters in edit boxes and text areas. [Priority 3]." For more on the Web Accessibility Initiative, see http://www.w3.org/WAI/.

Historically, some browsers have had problems recognizing empty form fields. This made keyboard navigation particularly difficult. Visitors were not able to tab to empty fields.

Much like using <label> tags, this accessibility enhancement turns out to be useful for everyone. Even if users are not navigating by keyboard, it's still very handy for them to be able to see what they should be writing in each form field.

There's one drawback to having placeholder values in the HTML5 placeholder attribute. When the user comes along with an older browser, the field will be blank (without a placeholder).

You can ensure a placeholder appears by using JavaScript. This time, though, you won't be using methods and properties of the DOM Core. Instead, you'll be using one of the most useful objects in the HTML-DOM: the Form object.

THE FORM OBJECT

As you know, every element in a document is an object. Each element has DOM properties like `nodeName`, `nodeType`, and so on.

Some elements have even more properties than those provided by the DOM Core. Every form element in a document is an object of the type `Form`. Each `Form` object has a property called `elements.length`. This value returns the number of form elements contained by a form:

```
form.elements.length
```

This is different from `childNodes.length`, which returns the total number of nodes contained by an element. The `elements.length` property of a `Form` object returns only those elements that are form elements, such as `input` elements, `textarea` elements, and so on.

Collectively, all of these form fields are the `elements` property of a `Form` object. This is an array that contains all the form elements:

```
form.elements
```

Again, this differs from the `childNodes` property, which is also an array. The `childNodes` array will return every node. The `elements` array will return only `input`, `select`, `textarea`, and other form fields.

Each form element in the `elements` array comes with its own set of properties. The `value` property, for instance, gives you the current value of a form element:

```
element.value
```

This is equivalent to the following:

```
element.getAttribute("value")
```

Every form field in contact.html has an initial `placeholder` attribute. You can grab these placeholders and temporarily insert them as the `value` for the form field. Then you can automatically remove the placeholder from the `value` whenever the field is brought into focus. Likewise, if the user moves on without entering a value in the field, you can reapply the placeholder value. This is similar to the placeholder example in Chapter 11.

You'll write a function called `resetFields` that takes a `Form` object as its single argument. It will do the following:

1. Check if the browser supports the `placeholder` attribute. If it does not, continue.

2. Loop through all the elements in the form.

3. If the element is a submit button, move on to the next iteration of the loop.

4. Add an event handler for when the element is brought into focus. If the value is equal to the placeholder, set the value of the element to empty.

5. Add another event handler for when the element no longer has focus. If the value of the element is empty, change it back to its placeholder value.

6. To allow for styling, also add a placeholder class to the input when the placeholder value is displayed.

Here's the function:

```
function resetFields(whichform) {
  if (Modernizr.input.placeholder) return;
  for (var i=0; i<whichform.elements.length; i++) {
    var element = whichform.elements[i];
    if (element.type == "submit") continue;
    var check = element.placeholder || element.getAttribute('placeholder');
    if (!check) continue;
    element.onfocus = function() {
      var text = this.placeholder || this.getAttribute('placeholder');
      if (this.value == text) {
        this.className = '';
        this.value = "";
      }
    }
    element.onblur = function() {
      if (this.value == "") {
        this.className = 'placeholder';
        this.value = this.placeholder || this.getAttribute('placeholder');
      }
    }
    element.onblur();
  }
}
```

The function is using two event handlers. The onfocus event is triggered when the user tabs to or clicks an element. The onblur event is triggered when the user moves out of the form element. For good measure, onblur is called immediately after it is created to apply the placeholder value if necessary.

■ **Note** You need to use both the HTML-DOM placeholder attribute and the DOM getAttribute('placeholder') method due to the different implementations of unknown attributes across different browsers.

Add the resetFields function to your global.js file. You need to activate the function by passing it a Form object. Write another function called prepareForms that loops through each Form object in the document and passes each one to the resetFields function.

```
function prepareForms() {
  for (var i=0; i<document.forms.length; i++) {
    var thisform = document.forms[i];
    resetFields(thisform);
  }
}
```

Call the prepareForms function using addLoadEvent:

```
addLoadEvent(prepareForms);
```

To make the placeholder stand out, modify the color of the fields with the `placeholder` class in your color.css file:

```
input.placeholder {
  color: grey;
}
```

Reload contact.html in a browser that doesn't support HTML5 to see the effects of the `resetFields` function. You'll find that your `resetFields` function produces the same effect as the HTML5 `placeholder` attribute does in an HTML5-enabled browser.

Click any form field, or any label for that matter. The default value will disappear. If you move on to another field without entering anything, the default value reappears. If you insert something, the default value does not reappear.

Form validation

The next task that you're going to perform on the contact form involves one of the oldest uses of JavaScript.

Client-side form validation has been around almost as long as JavaScript. The theory is simple. When a user submits a form, run some tests on the values provided. If required fields have not been filled in, the user is told with an alert box which fields need to be fixed.

HTML5-enabled browsers have finally started to implement some native form validation for different types of fields. For example, in Opera 10, email input types are automatically validated:

When you try to submit a form using an email input field, Opera automatically verifies it using RFC-compliant email validation, even if JavaScript isn't available. HTML5 also includes other types of validation, such as URLs entered into URL input fields. In these cases, you don't need to add any additional markup to the form; the browser will just validate it based on the input type.

HTML5 also includes a `required` attribute that indicates that the value for the field is required and can't be left blank. Opera 10 also supports this feature without any additional scripting:

That's all good for browsers that support HTML5, but for your client's band site, you must be a little more flexible and include some JavaScript form validation as well.

Adding JavaScript form validation sounds straightforward, and it usually is. But if JavaScript form validation is implemented badly, it can cause more harm than good. If the code has been written sloppily, the user may end up never being able to submit the form.

There are three things to remember when you are writing JavaScript form-validation functions:

- Bad form validation can be worse than no validation at all.

- Never rely solely on JavaScript. It's not a substitute for server-side validation. Just because you validate a form with JavaScript doesn't mean you shouldn't check the values again when they are sent to the server.

- Client-side validation is about helping users properly fill out the form and not waste their time with an incomplete submission. Server-side validation is about protecting the database and underlying systems.

It's best to keep form validation as simple as possible. To begin, you can just check whether the user has provided any value at all. The following function, isFilled, takes an element from a form as its single argument.

```
function isFilled(field) {
  if (field.value.replace(' ','').length == 0) return false;
  var placeholder = field.placeholder || field.getAttribute('placeholder');
  return (field.value != placeholder);
}
```

By checking the length of the value property after removing the spaces, you can see if the value has more than zero characters (and it's not all spaces). If it does not contain characters, the function returns a value of false. Otherwise, it continues on to the next comparison.

By comparing the value property to the placeholder property, you can find out if the user has simply left the placeholder text in the field. If the two values are the same, the function returns a value of false. If both tests are passed, the field has been filled in, and the isFilled function returns a value of true.

Next is a similar function called isEmail. It does a very crude test to check if the value of a form field looks like an email address.

```
function isEmail(field) {
  return (field.value.indexOf("@") != -1 && field.value.indexOf(".") != -1);
}
```

This function runs two tests using the indexOf method. This method finds the first occurrence of a string within another string. If the search string is found, it returns the position. If the search string isn't found, it returns a value of -1. The first test looks for the @ character in the value property of the form field. This character must be present in an email address. If the @ isn't found, the isEmail function returns a value of false. The second test works exactly the same way, except this time the test is looking for the dot (.) character. If this character can't be found in the value property of the field, the function returns false. If both tests are passed, the isEmail function returns true.

The isEmail function isn't foolproof. It's still entirely possible to enter fake email addresses or even strings that could never be email addresses. Still, it's not worth getting too clever. The more complicated a test becomes, the greater the likelihood of false positives. As an example, many email validators incorrectly assume there is a three-character limit for any domain extension. This error makes the form impassable by anyone with an .info, a .name, or a similar email address.

You now have two validation functions, isFilled and isEmail. You don't want to run these functions on every form field. You need some way of indicating which fields need to be filled in and which fields should be email addresses.

In your markup, you're using the HTML5 required attribute:

```
<input type="text" id="name" name="name" value="Your name" required="required" />
...
<input type="email" id="email" name="email" value="Your email address"
➥ required="required" />
```

■ **Note** In the markup shown here, I've used required="required", instead of just a required attribute without any value. In HTML5, either is valid due to the flexible syntax. However, I prefer to stick to the more strict XHTML syntax, which implies values for all attributes and a closing / on single tags.

You can also use these attributes in your CSS files. For example, you could style required fields with a thicker border or a different background color.

And you can use the attributes in your JavaScript. Write a function called validateForm. This function will take a Form object as its single argument and do the following:

1. Loop through the elements array of the form.

2. If the required attribute is found, pass the element to the isFilled function.

3. If the isFilled function returns a value of false, display an alert message and have the validateForm function return a value of false.

4. If the email type is found, pass the element to the isEmail function.

5. If the isEmail function returns a value of false, display an alert message and have the validateForm function return a value of false.

6. Otherwise, the validateForm function returns a value of true.

Here's the finished validateForm function:

```
function validateForm(whichform) {
  for (var i=0; i<whichform.elements.length; i++) {
    var element = whichform.elements[i];
    if (element.required == 'required') {
      if (!isFilled(element)) {
        alert("Please fill in the "+element.name+" field.");
        return false;
      }
    }
  }
```

```
      if (element.type == 'email') {
        if (!isEmail(element)) {
          alert("The "+element.name+" field must be a valid email address.");
          return false;
        }
      }
    }
  }
  return true;
}
```

Now you just need to run your forms through the validateForm function when they are submitted. You can add the behavior for the onsubmit event handler in the prepareForms function:

```
function prepareForms() {
  for (var i=0; i<document.forms.length; i++) {
    var thisform = document.forms[i];
    resetFields(thisform);
    thisform.onsubmit = function() {
      return validateForm(this);
    }
  }
}
```

Whenever a form is submitted, the submit event is triggered, which is intercepted by the onsubmit event handler. When this happens, the form is passed to the validateForm function. If validateForm returns true, the form is submitted to the server. If validateForm returns false, the submission is canceled.

Save all of the form validation functions in global.js.

Refresh contact.html in a web browser. Try submitting the contact form with empty or default values. You will be greeted with a terse alert message telling you the first thing that needs to be fixed.

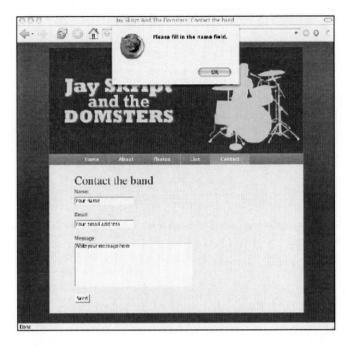

Form submission

The last task that you're going to perform on the contact form adds a little Ajax fun to the page. Remember that submit.html page you created earlier? If you submit the form right now, the form loads submit.html to display the thank-you message. But it would be a more pleasant experience if the form was sent through an Ajax request and the thank-you message appeared inline where the form originally was. Instead of loading a new page, you're going to Hijax the submit request and display the result yourself. (Hijax was introduced in Chapter 7.)

Start by adding the getHTTPObject function from Chapter 7 to your global.js file:

```
function getHTTPObject() {
  if (typeof XMLHttpRequest == "undefined")
    XMLHttpRequest = function () {
      try { return new ActiveXObject("Msxml2.XMLHTTP.6.0"); }
        catch (e) {}
      try { return new ActiveXObject("Msxml2.XMLHTTP.3.0"); }
        catch (e) {}
      try { return new ActiveXObject("Msxml2.XMLHTTP"); }
        catch (e) {}
      return false;
  }
  return new XMLHttpRequest();
}
```

Next, you need to create a loading image and append it to the document when the Ajax request starts. If you don't have an animated loading GIF handy, head over to http://ajaxload.info and create your own. Call the animated GIF loading.gif, and put it in the images folder.

Now, add the following displayAjaxLoading function to global.js. This function takes a DOM element as its argument and then removes any children from that element. Once children are removed, it appends an image with the loading.gif as the source.

```
function displayAjaxLoading(element) {
  while (element.hasChildNodes()) {
    element.removeChild(element.lastChild);
  }
  var content = document.createElement("img");
  content.setAttribute("src","images/loading.gif");
  content.setAttribute("alt","Loading...");
  element.appendChild(content);
}
```

Now comes the fun part. Write a new function called submitFormWithAjax. This function will take a Form object as the first argument and a target object as the second argument.

1. Call the displayAjaxLoading function to remove the children from the target element and add the loading.gif image.

2. Assemble the form values into a URL-encoded string to send in the Ajax request.

3. Create an Ajax request using POST and send the form values to submit.html.

4. If the request is successful, parse the response and display it in the target element.

5. If the request fails, display an error message.

Start off the submitFormWithAjax function by checking to see if you have a valid XMLHttpRequest object before altering the DOM to display the loading image.

```
function submitFormWithAjax( whichform, thetarget ) {
  var request = getHTTPObject();
  if (!request) { return false; }
 displayAjaxLoading(thetarget);
```

Next, create a URL-encoded data string to send to the server as the body of the POST request. The string uses the familiar format you see in URL variables:

name=value&name2=value2&name3=value3

Each of the values from the form needs to be escaped in the data string. For example, if the form contains a message such as **Why does 2+2=4?**, your string could look something like this:

message=Why does 2+2=4?&name=me&email=me@example.com

The plus (+), equal (=), and question mark (?) characters now pose problems in the string:

- Does = mean that there is a field with the name 2 and a value of 4?

- Is the + an encoded space, or does it mean a plus sign?

- Does the ? start an argument list?

To alleviate these problems, you can use the encodeURIComponent JavaScript function to encode the values to a URL-safe string. This function converts ambiguous characters into their ASCII equivalents:

message=Why%20does%202%2B2%3D4%3F%26&name=Me&email=me%40example.com

To do this for your form elements, loop though the fields the same way you did when validating the form, but instead of the check, collect the name and encoded value for each field in an array:

```
var dataParts = [];
var element;
for (var i=0; i<whichform.elements.length; i++) {
  element = whichform.elements[i];
  dataParts[i] = element.name + '=' + encodeURIComponent(element.value);
}
```

Once you have all the parts, join them together with an ampersand (&):

```
var data = dataParts.join('&');
```

Next, start your POST request using the original form's action:

```
request.open('POST', whichform.getAttribute("action"), true);
```

and the application/x-www-form-urlencoded header to the request:

```
request.setRequestHeader("Content-type", "application/x-www-form-urlencoded");
```

This header is required for POST requests and indicates that the request contains an URL-encoded form.

Now your request is ready. But before you send it off, you need to create your onreadystatechange event handler to deal with the response.

The response you're going to get back from the server is the submit.html page. This page is just like all the other pages in the Domsters site. It contains a header, navigation, and content. Since you're loading the result back into the existing page, you don't need the header and navigation. All you're really interested in is the content within the <article> element. The rest of the markup is there for when Ajax is not available and submit.html loads as a regular page.

If this were a server-side script in your favorite flavor of programming language, you could alter the response to output only the desired bits. For now, let's assume that you don't want to alter any server-side scripts. You just want to improve the user experience with a little Ajax.

To extract the <article> from the response, you're going to use something called a *regular expression*. In simple terms, a regular expression is a pattern that you can use to match various parts of a string.

Here's the regular expression you'll be using to extract the <article> element's content:

```
/<article>([\s\S]+)<\/article>/
```

In JavaScript, a regular expression pattern begins and ends with a /, which denotes the start and end of a pattern. If the pattern itself contains a /, then it must be escaped with a \, as done for the closing </article> tag in this pattern.

To match characters in a regular expression pattern, you simply enter the characters you're looking for. You want to begin with <article> and end with </article>, so you start and end your pattern the same way.

■ **Note** Regular expressions use some special characters such as brackets and symbols. If you want to match them directly, they will need to be escaped, just like /. For example, if you want to include an asterisk (*) in your pattern, you need to use *, because * is a quantifier used to indicate repetition. For a list of special characters, see http://en.wikipedia.org/wiki/Regular_expression.

```
        if (submitFormWithAjax(this, article)) return false;
        return true;
      }
    }
  }
}
```

Now submit your form, and you'll see your thank-you message appear without the entire page reloading. You can check this by looking at the browser's address bar. After the form submits, notice you're still on the contact.html page, not the submit.html page, as you were before.

The contact page is finished, and with it, the website.

Minification

Your website is now working as expected, but there's one last thing you can do to improve its overall performance. At the moment, the global.js file is about 13KB. That is not too big, but you can make it smaller by minifying it. As discussed in Chapter 5, several different minification tools are available. Here, let's use Google's Closure Compiler. It has a nice web form that will let you paste your JavaScript into it and get back a minified result.

Open http://closure-compiler.appspot.com/home in a web browser and copy and paste your global.js into the text area under the // **ADD YOUR CODE HERE** line, as shown here.

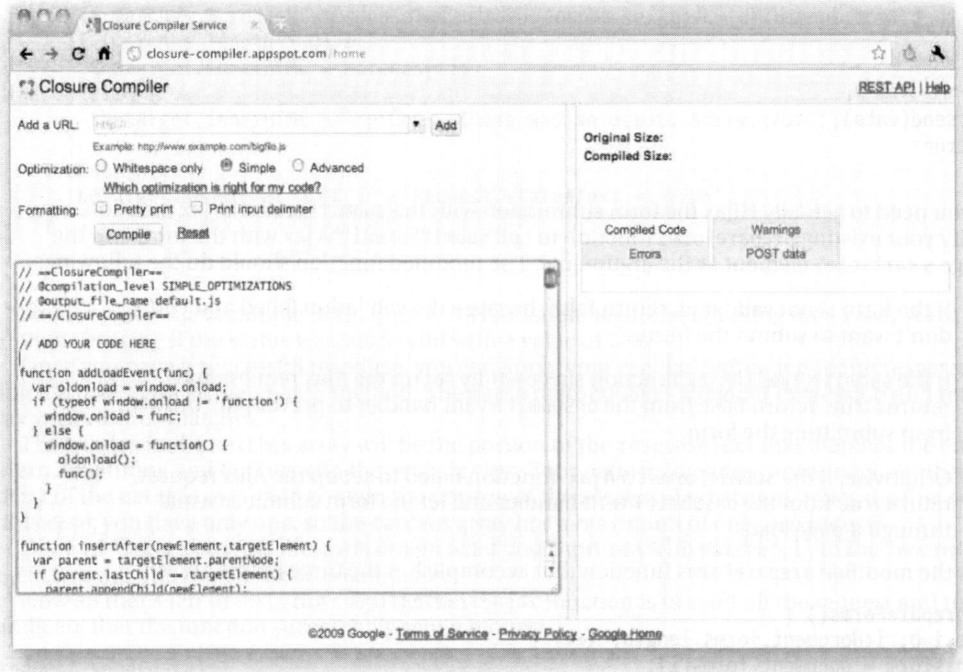

Click the Compile button, and you'll be presented with a compiled version of your code, along with before and after statistics. For my working global.js file, I got these results:

- An original size of 12.43KB (3.12KB gzipped)

- A compiled size of 8.62KB (2.36KB gzipped)

- Saved 30.64% off the original size (24.22% off the gzipped size)

Depending on the number of comments and other code you've added, your results will vary.

Copy and paste the minified version into a global.min.js file in your scripts folder, and update all the `<script>` tags in your files to use this new minified version.

What's next?

The website for Jay Skript and the Domsters is ready to be unleashed on the Web. You've created a stylish online presence for the band. You wrapped the content in valid, semantically meaningful HTML5. You implemented the design with external style sheets. Finally, you added some extra behavioral pizzazz and usability enhancements using the power of JavaScript and the DOM.

If you removed any or all of those enhancements, the site would still look and work perfectly fine. The DOM scripts are not essential, but together, they make visiting the site more pleasurable. It almost seems a shame that the band is completely fictional!

So, what's next? In one sense, you're done! Not only have you learned the theory behind DOM scripting, you have applied it in building an entire website. You can create practical and powerful functions using the methods and properties that you've learned about in this book.

In another sense, you're just beginning. I've shown you just some of things that you can do with just a few DOM methods. There are many more uses for those methods. There are other methods that I haven't mentioned.

DOM scripting is a powerful technology. I hope that this book has given you a taste of what can be accomplished with JavaScript and the DOM. I also hope that you will employ DOM scripting in a responsible, usable way. It's all too easy to get bogged down in the minutiae of using a particular tool to the detriment of the final product. I find it helpful to step back occasionally and take a look at the bigger picture. The grand vision of the World Wide Web is the same today as when it was invented by Tim Berners Lee:

> *The power of the Web is in its universality. Access by everyone regardless of disability is an essential aspect.*

Hypertext documents on the Web are inherently accessible. They become restricted only when we choose to make them that way. Using a combination of web standards and best practices, we can ensure that the Web remains an open, accessible place:

- Use meaningful markup to structure your content.

- Keep presentational information separate using CSS.

- Apply behavioral changes responsibly using unobtrusive JavaScript that degrades gracefully.

We are at a crossroads in the development of the Web. The boundary between desktop software and web applications is becoming more blurred every day with the emergence of methodologies like Ajax and the advancements in HTML5. Together, we will face many challenges as we strive to move the Web forward while remaining true to its original purpose as a universal medium.

What happens next is up to you. This is an exciting time to be a web designer.

APPENDIX

∎∎∎

DOM Scripting Libraries

Throughout the book you've focused on learning the basics of the DOM. You used the standard set of DOM methods to perform common tasks and learned how best to apply those methods in your scripts. You may have noticed that sometimes your code was a little verbose and repetitive. Restricting yourself to only DOM methods such as `document.getElementById` can get tiring, especially when libraries provide almost magical functions like $ that do even more.

Libraries are packages of reusable code that offer a number of advantages.

- Their code has been tested and proven by a large user base.

- They can easily fit into your existing development frameworks.

- They provide quick, elegant solutions for most of your mundane day-to-day DOM scripting tasks, reducing multiple lines of code down to a single function.

- They provide cross-browser solutions so you don't have to worry about every different browser.

Libraries free you to work on the good stuff in your applications, vastly increasing your productivity. They are wonderful, but using a library is not the bandage for every problem.

- Libraries are created by others, not you. That means you might not understand what's going on inside and dealing with bugs or problems may be more difficult.

- To use a library, you need to include that library along with your scripts. This adds another request to your page load and may use up valuable bandwidth.

- Mixing and matching libraries can lead to conflicts or a lot of redundant features.

Libraries can also become a crutch if you never venture beyond them. Before diving in, be sure to take the time to actually learn both JavaScript and the DOM as you have in this book. Since Chapter 1, I've emphasized the necessity of learning how things work and not simply what they do. There are many wonderful libraries out there, some of which I'll point out here, but having no understanding of what's going on behind the scenes will be detrimental to both you and your web application. Without that deeper understanding, you'll be lost in the small details that a library often assumes you already know.

Just to be clear, I'm not personally affiliated with any of these libraries, so I have no personal bias towards one or the other. I'm also not saying these libraries are ultimately the best for every situation nor are they the only ones available. These examples simply provide some of the cleanest alternative solutions for tasks you've already worked through in the book.

We're going to revisit some of the topics you've already seen, including these:

- Syntax

- Selecting elements

- Manipulating the DOM document
- Handling events
- Animation
- Ajax

You'll see how libraries can handle these tasks—often with much less code for you—leaving more time to focus on business logic instead of repetitive boring scripting.

■ **Note** Each library can accomplish pretty much every task in one way or another, so I'll point out one or two methods that I consider the best or most useful for each area—I won't be covering every aspect of each library, so be sure to check the documentation for each to find out what else is available.

Before you begin to work with libraries, it's important to choose the right one. Let's look at a few things that might help you decide.

Choosing a library

When you decide it's time to investigate a library, the biggest problem is choosing among the hundreds that are available. There are several criteria you should consider in your decision:

- **Does it have all the features you're looking for?** Mixing and matching libraries can be problematic. Common methods such as $() or get() often use the same syntax but handle things differently. Additionally, if you use more than one library at the same time, you'll usually end up with a lot of duplicated features and redundant code.

- **Does it have more features than you need?** Having too few features is one problem, but a bulky library with way too many is also a problem. When a library has more features than you need, or you're not taking advantage of them all, you may want to consider a lighter version that won't take as long to download. This is especially important in mobile environments.

- **Is it modular?** Libraries with abundant features often work around file size by modularizing features into different files. This lets you minimize file size by loading only the files and features you need. Most of the time, you'll have to be sure to include all the necessary files, but a few libraries may offer a dynamic loading mechanism where you only need to include one file and that file will fetch others as necessary. Just be careful about the number of requests you anticipate. Often one large request is better than several smaller ones.

- **Is it well supported?** Lack of an active developer community means no bug fixes or feature improvements. Also, having many eyes looking at and sharing the same library means fewer bugs and more reliable results. A good community behind the library brings not only fixes and features but also a lot of support when you run into a problem and need more help.

- **Does it have documentation?** Without documentation, you'll be lost. Sure, you might come across some example that others have hacked together, but a lack of official documentation usually indicates a lack of enthusiasm by developers and thus a project that may be going nowhere.

- **Does it have the right license?** Just because you can view the source online doesn't mean it's free for the taking. Before using a library, verify that its license covers what you intended to do with it and that you've met any special requirements.

Once you've chosen an appropriate library and you're producing great things, don't forget to try to contribute back to the community! These libraries are all built by dedicated developers who are often working with what little spare time they have to improve the tools you use daily. If you can't help with development efforts or bug testing, you could always provide examples and tutorials or simply help build the documentation—any effort is helpful and will make the library even better.

A few libraries

For this Appendix I've selected a few examples based on the preceding criteria as well as general popularity and a bit of personal preference. Most examples use jQuery but there are several other libraries with similar features. Each has its own pros and cons as outlined here.

- **jQuery** (`http://jquery.com`) describes itself as "a fast and concise JavaScript Library that simplifies HTML document traversing, event handling, animating, and Ajax interactions for rapid web development. jQuery is designed to change the way that you write JavaScript." jQuery's extremely powerful selection method, chaining syntax, and simplified Ajax and event methods will make your code compact and easy to follow. There is also a very large community behind jQuery with a number of different plug-in developers who've added features beyond the library basics.

- **Prototype** (`http://prototypejs.org`) describes itself as "a JavaScript Framework that aims to ease development of dynamic web applications." Prototype has a number of great DOM-manipulation functions as well as one of the more popular Ajax objects. It was one of the first popular JavaScript libraries and was the library that originated the $() selector function.

- **The Yahoo! User Interface (YUI) Library** (`http://developer.yahoo.com/yui`) describes itself as "a set of utilities and controls, written in JavaScript, for building richly interactive web applications using techniques such as DOM scripting, DHTML, and AJAX. The YUI Library also includes several core CSS resources." YUI has a great developer community and tons of documentation. The libraries are filled with every feature you can think of from simple DOM manipulation to advanced effects and fully featured widgets. As a whole, the library is nicely divided into small files and namespaces but it sometimes becomes overwhelming trying to determine what you need and where to find it—you know it's big when just the cheat sheet is over 20 pages.

- **Dojo Toolkit** (`http://www.dojotoolkit.org/`) says that it "saves you time, delivers powerful performance, and scales with your development process. It's the toolkit experienced developers turn to for building great web experiences." Dojo is a full-featured JavaScript toolkit used by a number of large companies. It has a large developer community, good documentation, and several books devoted to it.

- **MooTools** (http://mootools.net/) describes itself as "a compact, modular, Object-Oriented JavaScript framework designed for the intermediate to advanced JavaScript developer. It allows you to write powerful, flexible, and cross-browser code with its elegant, well documented, and coherent API." MooTools is extensively documented and has a large user community. It not only includes a number of great DOM enhancements but also integrates the Moo.fx effects library for simple and complex animations.

■ **Note** Some libraries, such as Prototype and jQuery, share the same $() function syntax. If you decide to use a library in your production environment, be sure to read the documentation for your chosen library to see how it may differ from what I'm presenting here or how it may conflict with other libraries.

Content delivery networks

Whenever possible you want to reduce the overall size of your documents and allow the browser to cache files as much as possible. In addition, you want to serve those files up as fast as possible. In the case of libraries, if a number of different sites use the same library, it would make sense to host that library in a common location that all sites could access and share. This way, if users go from site to site they don't need to download the same file over and over again.

A content delivery network (CDN) solves the problem of shared library distribution. The CDN is a network of servers whose sole responsibility is delivering common content. These servers each contain copies of the library and are placed at various geographical locations to maximize bandwidth and speed. Browsers will access a library at a common URL while the underlying structure of the CDN allows the closest and speediest server to serve the file, avoiding bottlenecks in the overall system.

Google provides a free CDN for a number of libraries, including

- Dojo

- jQuery

- MooTools

- Prototype

- Yahoo! User Interface Library (YUI)

For a full list of the most recent versions and the specific details of each library, see http://code.google.com/apis/libraries/devguide.html.

To use a CDN, you simply include the library like any other JavaScript file. For example, as of this writing the most recent Google CDN jQuery URL is https://ajax.googleapis.com/ajax/libs/jquery/1.4.3/jquery.min.js, so you can add the following <script> to your documents:

```
<script src="https://ajax.googleapis.com/ajax/libs/jquery/
➥ 1.4.3/jquery.min.js"></script>
```

If you're hesitant to rely solely on Google or another service as your distribution network, it's a good idea to provide a failsafe fallback to a local file on your server in case the CDN becomes unavailable. You can simply check to see if the appropriate objects are loaded and then include a local library if necessary:

```
<script src="https://ajax.googleapis.com/ajax/libs/jquery/
➥ 1.4.3/jquery.min.js"></script>
<script>!window.jQuery && document.write(unescape('%3C
➥ script src="scripts/jquery-1.4.3.min.js"%3E%3C/script%3E'))</script>
```

> ■ **Note** This method uses `document.write` to add a `<script>` tag to the document if the jQuery library didn't create the global window.jQuery object. The $ function used elsewhere in the Appendix is the short form for the proper `jQuery` object name.

With this code in place, if the server goes down it won't take your site with it.

Syntax

Before presenting some examples I should point out a few syntax options that many libraries rely on.

> ■ **Note** A number of libraries, such as jQuery, Prototype, MooTools and others, offer the dollar sign $() function as a shortcut to their selector method. I use this throughout the Appendix so that the code is more generic. Just remember that though the syntax of the function calls may appear similar, the underlying objects they create are drastically different. Make sure you read the documentation for your selected library to see how its $ function works.

Most libraries offer the ability to "chain" methods together using dot notation—a period joins the method calls—similar to the way you've already seen when using methods such as getElemenById:

```
document.getElementById('example').nodeName;
```

This is a fundamental aspect of libraries such as jQuery, in which methods are created specifically to allow you to write complicated scripts in very short chains. It's not uncommon to see one-line scripts that do a lot of work. For example, to remove and then add a class name to every paragraph in a document using jQuery, you can do this:

```
$('p').removeClass('classFoo').addClass('classBar');
```

That's a lot cleaner than the add class function you created in Chapter 9. We'll get more into that $('p') selector in a moment.

One additional thing I will mention is iteration. Libraries offer looping structures for manipulating lists of elements, and the chaining syntax often provides a very clean way of doing this.

For example, using jQuery again, you can replicate this loop from Chapter 3:

```
var items = document.getElementsByTagName("li");
for (var i=0; i < items.length; i++) {
  alert(typeof items[i]);
```

```
}
```

with the jQuery each method:

```
$('li').each(function(i){
  alert( typeof this );
});
```

The jQuery each method, as well as other looping methods, uses a callback applied to each element in the list. The callback receives only the element's index in the list as an argument and the method executes in the context of the node, so this in the example refers to the li element itself.

With these things in mind, let's see how you can use libraries to make element selection a lot more powerful.

Selecting elements

So far you've seen how you can select elements by ID, by tag, and by class name using the built-in DOM methods getElementById, getElementsByTagName, and getElementsByClassName, respectively.

Selecting elements by ID is great, but selecting elements using the full range of CSS selectors is even better. Many libraries incorporate advanced selector methods such as the $ function in jQuery. With this method you can select:

- By ID with the pound sign $('#elementid')

- By class with a dot $('.element-class')

- By tag with a tag name $('tag')

That's not really anything too special, but you can also use a variety of CSS selectors (http://www.w3.org/TR/css3-selectors/#selectors) to select specific elements.

▪ **Note** When an ID such as #elementid is used as the selector in the $ function, that function still returns a list of objects, but the list will have only one element instead of multiple. This allows you to use each and other jQuery methods on single elements.

CSS selectors

Beyond an ID's class and tags, here are a few examples of the advanced selectors you can use in most libraries:

- $('*') selects all elements.

- $('tag') selects all *tag* elements for each of the available HTML tags.

- $('tagA tagB') selects all *tagB* elements that are descendants of *tagA* elements.

- $('tagA,tagB,tagC') selects all *tagA* elements, *tagB* elements, and *tagC* elements.

- $('#id') and $('tag#id') are ID selectors for any ID or a specific tag-ID combination.

- $('.className') and $('tag.className') are selectors that can be used for any class or *tag* class combination.

You can also combine selectors such as $('#myList li') or $('ul li a.selectMe') to select any mix of descendant selectors separated by a space.

jQuery also includes the following CSS 2.1 attribute selectors:

- $('tag[attr]') selects all *tag* elements that have attribute *attr*.

- $('tag[attr=value]') selects all *tag* elements where *value* is exactly equal to the *attr* attribute value.

- $('tag[attr*=value]') selects all *tag* elements where *value* is contained in the *attr* attribute value.

- $('tag[attr~=value]') selects all *tag* elements where *value* is a word contained in the *attr* attribute value (separated by spaces).

- $('tag[attr^=value]') selects all *tag* elements where *value* matches the beginning of the *attr* attribute value.

- $('tag[attr$=value]') selects all *tag* elements where *value* matches the end of the *attr* attribute value.

- $('tag[attr|=value]') selects all *tag* elements where *value* matches the first part of a hyphenated *attr* attribute value.

- $('tag[attr!=value]') selects all *tag* elements where *value* is not equal to *attr*.

You can also use a number of different child and sibling selectors, as follows:

- $('tagA > tagB') selects all *tagB* elements that are direct child descendants of *tagA* elements.

- $('tagA + tagB') selects all *tagB* sibling elements that immediately follow *tagA* elements.

- $('tagA ~ tagB') selects all elements with a preceding sibling *tagB* element.

Also, you can use several pseudo-class and pseudo-element selectors including these:

- $('tag:root') selects the *tag* element that is the root of the document.

- $('tag:nth-child(n)') selects all *tag* elements that are the *n*th children of their parents, counting from the first one.

- $('tag:nth-last-child(n)') selects all *tag* elements that are the *n*th child of their parents, counting from the last one.

- $('tag:nth-of-type(n)') selects all *tag* elements that are the *n*th sibling of their type, counting from the first one.

- $('tag:nth-last-of-type(n)') selects all *tag* elements that are the *n*th sibling of their type, counting from the last one.

- $('tag:first-child') selects any *tag* element that is the first child of its parents.

- $('tag:last-child') selects any *tag* element that is the last child of its parent.

- $('*tag*:first-of-type') selects any *tag* element that is the first sibling of its type.

- $('*tag*:last-of-type') selects any *tag* element that is the last sibling of its type.

- $('*tag*:only-child') selects any *tag* element that is an only child of its parent.

- $('*tag*:only-of-type') selects any *tag* element that is the only sibling of its type.

- $('*tag*:empty') selects all *tag* elements that have no children.

- $('*tag*:enabled') selects all user interface *tag* elements that are enabled.

- $('*tag*:disabled') selects all user interface *tag* elements that are disabled.

- $('*tag*:checked') selects all user interface *tag* elements that are checked, such as check boxes and radio buttons.

- $('*tag*:not(s)') selects all tag elements that don't match the selectors.

Different libraries have varying support for each selector type, so check the documentation for your chosen library.

With these selectors, you can quickly access very specific elements in your documents based on their position rather than class or ID. This will help you keep your markup free of script-specific IDs and classes as well as reduce your element selection code. For example, you can take this code that uses DOM methods to select all the links within nav elements within articles:

```
var links = [];
var articles = document.getElementsByTagName("article");
for (var a = 0; a < articles.length; a++ ) {
  var navs = articles[a].getElementsByTagName("nav");
  for (var n = 0; n < navs.length; n++ ) {
    var links = nav[n].getElementsByTagName("a");
    for (var l = 0; l < links.length; l++ ) {
      links[links.lengh] = links[l];
    }
  }
}
// Do something with links.
```

and reduce it to just a few characters:

```
var links = $('article nav a');
// Do something with links.
```

Now your code is much cleaner and much more readable.

Library-specific selectors

Some libraries also support their own set of selectors. For example, jQuery supports $('*tag*:even') and $('*tag*:odd') selectors for even and odd elements, and to replicate the table stripe table function from Chapter 12:

```
function stripeTables() {
  if (!document.getElementsByTagName) return false;
  var tables = document.getElementsByTagName("table");
  for (var i=0; i<tables.length; i++) {
```

```
      var odd = false;
      var rows = tables[i].getElementsByTagName("tr");
      for (var j=0; j<rows.length; j++) {
        if (odd == true) {
          addClass(rows[j],"odd");
          odd = false;
        } else {
          odd = true;
        }
      }
    }
  }
}
```

you can simply select every odd table row and apply CSS properties in one line of jQuery:

```
$("tr:odd").addClass("odd");
```

As you can see, it's much more elegant.

Other custom selectors in jQuery include these:

- $('*tag*:even') selects even-numbered elements from the matched element set—great for highlighting table rows!

- $('*tag*:odd') selects odd-numbered elements from the matched element set.

- $('*tag*:eq(0)') and $('*tag*:nth(0)') select the *n*th element from the matched element set, such as the first paragraph on the page.

- $('*tag*:gt(n)') selects all matched elements whose index is greater than *n*.

- $('*tag*:lt(n)') selects all matched elements whose index is less than *n*.

- $('*tag*:first') is equivalent to :eq(0).

- $('*tag*:last') selects the last matched element.

- $('*tag*:parent') selects all elements that have child elements (including text).

- $('*tag*:contains('test')') selects all elements that contain the specified text.

- $('*tag*:visible') selects all visible elements (this includes items that have a display property using block or inline or a visibility property using visible, and that aren't form elements of type hidden).

- $('*tag*:hidden') selects all hidden elements (this includes items that have a display property using none, or a visibility property using hidden, or are form elements of type hidden).

These allow you to quickly modify elements, such as the font weight of the first paragraph on the page:

```
$("p:first").css("font-weight","bold");
```

Or you can quickly show all hidden <div> elements:

```
$("div:hidden").show();
```

You could even hide all the div elements that contain the word "scared":

```
$("div:contains('scared')").hide();
```

287

Finally, jQuery also includes a number of form-specific expressions you can use to access form elements:

- `:input` selects all form elements (`input`, `select`, `textarea`, `button`).

- `:text` selects all text fields (`type="text"`).

- `:password` selects all password fields (`type="password"`).

- `:radio` selects all radio fields (`type="radio"`).

- `:checkbox` selects all checkbox fields (`type="checkbox"`).

- `:submit` selects all submit buttons (`type="submit"`).

- `:image` selects all form images (`type="image"`).

- `:reset` selects all reset buttons (`type="reset"`).

- `:button` selects all other buttons (`type="button"`).

Filtering with a callback

When advanced expressions still can't provide what you need or a library doesn't support one, you can always walk the DOM with a callback function and run whatever code you like against each element. In all the following examples, returning true from the callback will include the element and returning false will exclude the element from the resulting list.

Callbacks can be especially useful when you want to create a reverse selector. All CSS selectors identify the rightmost element in the selector, so there's no way to select "All anchor tags that have a single image as a child." You can, however, accomplish this fairly easily with a callback. Let's use the following list as an example:

```
<ul>
    <li>
        <a name="example1"><img src="example.gif" alt="example"/></a>
    </li>
    <li>
        <a name="example2">No Images Here</a>
    </li>
    <li>
        <a name="example3">
            Two here!
            <img src="example2.gif" alt="example"/>
            <img src="example3.gif" alt="example"/>
        </a>
    </li>
</ul>
```

Using the YUI `YAHOO.util.Dom.getElementBy` method, you can simply use the existing DOM element properties you've seen earlier in the book to filter your list:

```
var singleImageAnchors = YAHOO.util.Dom.getElementsBy(function(e) {
    // Look for <A> nodes with one child image
    return (e.nodeName == 'A' && e.getElementsByTagName('img').length == 1);
});
```

The `singleImageAnchors` variable will contain a list with a reference to `<a name="example1">`, as it's the only anchor with one image as a child in the example list.

Prototype and jQuery provide `findAll` and `filter` methods, respectively. You use these last two in the chaining context to filter out elements returned from the expression.

First, here's how it looks in Prototype (using the $$ selector function):

```
// Prototype library callback filter
var singleImageAnchors = $$('a').findAll(function(e) {
  return (e.descendants().findAll(function(e) {
    return (e.nodeName == 'IMG');
  }).length == 1);
});
```

Here's the same method in jQuery:

```
// jQuery library callback filter
var singleImageAnchors = $('a').filter(function() {
  return ($('img',this).length == 1)
});
```

In most cases the Prototype and jQuery expression selectors should be enough to filter the list of elements, but in cases where you need more in-depth analysis of the elements, callbacks can be very powerful.

Manipulating the DOM document

Libraries are chock-full of different DOM-manipulation methods, as that's pretty much the point of the library in the first place. I'll just point out a few and let you explore the documentation for each library to find the rest.

Creating content

Using jQuery to create new DOM elements is very easy. You can define HTML as the input to the $ function to create nodes. For example here we'll append a new div to the body of a document. The div will have an `id` of `example` and the content of `Hello`:

```
$('<div id="example">Hello</div>').appendTo(document.body);
```

Or you can use the jQuery template plug-in (`http://api.jquery.com/category/plugins/templates/`).

▥ **Note** You can use the Microsoft CDN to include the template plug-in in your document. The download URL at the time of writing is `http://ajax.microsoft.com/ajax/jquery.templates/beta1/jquery.tmpl.min.js`.

The jQuery template plug-in allows you to specify strings of HTML with special variables such as `${term}`, which is then replaced using an array of data or other templates.

For example, you could take the `displayAbbreviations` function from Chapter 8:

```
function displayAbbreviations() {
 if (!document.getElementsByTagName || !document.createElement
```

```
⇒|| !document.createTextNode) return false;
  var abbreviations = document.getElementsByTagName("abbr");
  if (abbreviations.length < 1) return false;
  var defs = new Array();
  for (var i=0; i<abbreviations.length; i++) {
    var current_abbr = abbreviations[i];
    var definition = current_abbr.getAttribute("title");
    var key = current_abbr.lastChild.nodeValue;
    defs[key] = definition;
  }
  var dlist = document.createElement("dl");
  for (key in defs) {
    var definition = defs[key];
    var dtitle = document.createElement("dt");
    var dtitle_text = document.createTextNode(key);
    dtitle.appendChild(dtitle_text);
    var ddesc = document.createElement("dd");
    var ddesc_text = document.createTextNode(definition);
    ddesc.appendChild(ddesc_text);
    dlist.appendChild(dtitle);
    dlist.appendChild(ddesc);
  }
  var header = document.createElement("h2");
  var header_text = document.createTextNode("Abbreviations");
  header.appendChild(header_text);
  document.body.appendChild(header);
  document.body.appendChild(dlist);
}
```

and rewrite it using jQuery and the jQuery template plug-in:

```
function displayAbbreviations() {
  // Create an array of the abbreviations.
  var data = $('abbr').map(function(){
    return {
      desc:$(this).attr('title'),
      term:$(this).text()
    };
  }).toArray();
  // Append to the document and apply a template.
  $('<h2>Abbreviations</h2>').appendTo(document.body).after(
    $.tmpl( "<dt>${term}</dt><dd>${desc}</dd>", data )
      .wrapAll("<dl/>")
  );
}
```

This could be taken a step further by removing the template from the function itself and defining the abbreviations template on a page-by-page basis. See the template documentation at http://api.jquery.com/tmpl/ for more specifics about template abstraction using <script> elements.

Manipulating content

To simply manipulate your existing document and move things around you can use methods such as jQuery's appendTo or insertAfter. These let you locate large sets of elements and move them all to become children of another element.

For example, you can relocate all the elements of one list to another:

```
$('ul#list1 li').appendTo("ul#list2");
```

This works because each element has only one reference in a document. By telling an element to be the child of another, you're automatically removing it from its original parent. If you want to copy the element instead, you could use the jQuery clone method:

```
$('ul#list1 li').clone().appendTo("ul#list2");
```

DOM manipulation is well ingrained in almost every library, and they each have a number of other handy shortcuts to remove, insert, append, prepend, and more.

Handling events

As you've seen throughout the book, events are the lifeblood of user interaction. Without events, you couldn't interact with the page.

You already have some basic event methods in your arsenal. If you've chosen to use a library, many have their own event management built in. Also, they offer the ability to register and invoke custom events that aren't part of the built-in browser events or the W3C events.

Load events

You already have an event registration method for page load events in your addLoadEvent:

```
function addLoadEvent(func) {
  var oldonload = window.onload;
  if (typeof window.onload != 'function') {
    window.onload = func;
  } else {
    window.onload = function() {
      oldonload();
      func();
    }
  }
}
```

You've used this function to execute other functions when the page loads:

```
function myFucntion() {
  // Do something after the page loads.
}
addLoadEvent(myFunction);
```

This could also have been written as

```
addLoadEvent(function() {
  // Do something after the page loads.
});
```

The various libraries have similar methods, but each may take a different approach to applying them. For example, jQuery approaches the task of using the chaining syntax by supplying a special method for each event type (http://api.jquery.com/category/events/).

In the case of your addLoadEvent, jQuery supplies a ready method that works in a similar way:

```
$(document).ready(handler);
$(handler);
```

The second method assumes that the document object is the target of the ready method. The ready method is given an anonymous function to use as the event handler when the document is ready:

```
$(document).ready(function() {
  // Do something after the page loads.
});
```

If ready is called after the DOM has already been initialized, the new callback will be executed immediately.

To use the jQuery methods the same way as your addLoadEvent function, just replace addLoadEvent with $:

```
function myFucntion() {
  // Do something after the page loads.
}
$(myFunction);
```

or just

```
$(function() {
  // Do something after the page loads.
});
```

Other events

Along with load events, libraries such as jQuery include a number of element-specific events, such as blur, focus, click, dblclick, mouseover, mouseout, and submit, to name a few.

Using these methods, you can register event handlers for each element in groups of DOM elements, such as a click event for every link on the page:

```
$('a').click( function(event) {
    // Open the new window using the existing href value;
    window.open(this.getAttribute('href'));
    // Prevent default action of the link
    return false;
});
```

A very nice side effect of these methods is that you can invoke the event listener on the elements if you call the appropriate method without any input:

```
$('a:first').click();
```

For example, you could replicate the resetFields and prepareForms functions from Chapter 12:

```
function resetFields(whichform) {
  for (var i=0; i<whichform.elements.length; i++) {
    var element = whichform.elements[i];
    if (element.type == "submit") continue;
    var hasPlaceholder = element.placeholder || element.getAttribute('placeholder');
```

```
    if (!hasPlaceholder) continue;
    element.onfocus = function() {
    var text = element.placeholder || element.getAttribute('placeholder');
    if (this.value == text) {
      this.className = '';
      this.value = "";
     }
    }
    element.onblur = function() {
      if (this.value == "") {
        this.className = 'placeholder';
        this.value = element.placeholder || element.getAttribute('placeholder');;
      }
    }
    element.onblur();
  }
}
function prepareForms() {
  for (var i=0; i<document.forms.length; i++) {
    var thisform = document.forms[i];
    resetFields(thisform);
    }
  }
}
addLoadEvent(prepareForms)
```

Using jQuery selectors and event methods, all that form preparation can be reduced down to this:

```
$(function() {
  $('form input[placeholder]').focus(function(){
    var input = $(this);
    if (input.val() == input.attr('placeholder')) {
      input.val('').removeClass('placeholder').;
    }
  }).blur(function(){
    var input = $(this);
    if (input.val() == '') {
      input.val(input.attr('placeholder')).addClass('placeholder');
    }
  }).blur();
});
```

Ajax

Since the explosion of Ajax, JavaScript libraries have become more and more popular. The first object in many libraries was the Ajax object, or at least, it was the object that made the library popular.

Ajax with Prototype

The Prototype library, originally part of the Ruby on Rails project, gained popularity because of its Ajax object. Prototype offers a few different flavors of Ajax methods:

- `Ajax.Request(url, options)` performs a basic `XMLHttpRequest` request.

- `Ajax.Updater(element, url, options)` is a wrapper for a request that automatically appends the content of the request to a given DOM node.

- `Ajax.PeriodicalUpdater(element, url, options)` automatically appends the content of the request to a given DOM node on a regular interval.

The options for each method include several properties:

- `contentType` is the Content Type header for your request. The default value is `application/x-www-form-urlencoded`.

- `method` is the HTTP method for your request. Prototype treats many other request types, such as `put` and `delete`, by overriding them with `post` and including the original request method in a `_method` parameter in the request. The default value is `post`.

- `parameters` are the parameters to send along with the request. You can define this using a URL-encoded string like you'd include on a get request, or you can use any hash-compatible object, such as an array or object with property names representing the parameter names.

- `postBody`, which defaults to null, is the content you'd like to include in the body of a `post` request. If empty, the body will include the contents of the parameters option.

- `requestHeaders` is an object or array representing the additional headers you'd like to include in the request. In object form, the property name and value will represent the request header name and value, respectively. Arrays are a little tricky, as the even indexed items—starting with 0—represent the header names while odd indexes—starting at 1—represent the previous header's value. By default, Prototype will include a few headers if not overridden in this property:

  - `X-Requested-With`, by default, is set to `XMLHttpRequest` and can be used server-side to identify Ajax requests. If you want you could set this to whatever you like.

  - `X-Prototype-Version` is set to Prototype's current version number.

  - `Accept`, by default, is set to `text/javascript`, `text/html`, `application/xml`, `text/xml`, and `*/*`.

  - `Content-type` is built based on the `contentType` value and encoding options.

Along with these properties, there are also a number of callback methods you can use to run code at various stages of the request or based on the response from the server. Each of the following callback methods will be invoked with two arguments including the `XMLHttpRequest` object and the JavaScript object in the response if and only if the response contains an X-JSON header. If the X-JSON header is missing, the second argument will be null. The only exception to this is the `onException` callback, which will receive the `Ajax.Request` instance as the first argument and the exception object as the second. The callbacks are listed here in the order they will be invoked in the request:

- `onException(ajax.request,exception)` will be invoked when an error arises in the request/response and can occur mixed in at any point with the callbacks below.

- onUninitialized(*XHRrequest,json*) may be invoked when the request object is created, but it may not always be invoked, so avoid using it.

- onLoading(*XHRrequest,json*) may be invoked when the request object is set up and its connection is opened, but again, it may not always be invoked, so avoid using it.

- onLoaded(*XHRrequest,json*) may be invoked when the request object has finished setting up and the connection is open and ready to send the request—but again, it may not always be invoked, so avoid using it.

- onInteractive(*XHRrequest,json*) may be invoked when the request object has received part of the response and is waiting for the remainder of the request. As you can guess, it may not always be invoked, so avoid using it.

- on###(*XHRrequest,json*) will be invoked provided the appropriate response code is set. ### represents the HTTP status code for the response. The callback will be invoked once the request is complete but before the onComplete callback. It will also prevent the execution of onSuccess and onFailure callbacks.

- onFailure(*XHRrequest,json*) will be invoked in the event a request completes but its status code is defined and not between 200 and 299.

- onSuccess(*XHRrequest,json*) will be invoked when the request completes and its status code is undefined or is between 200 and 299.

- onComplete(*XHRrequest,json*), will be invoked at the end of the request as the last possible callback in the chain.

Prototype also includes a global Ajax.Responders method for controlling and accessing all the Ajax requests coming into and out of the various Ajax.Request methods. For more on the Ajax.Responders method, see the Prototype online documentation at http://www.prototypejs.org/api/ajax/responders.

Here are a few examples of Prototype Ajax requests:

```
// Prototype Ajax.Request
// Create a new one-time request and alert its success
new Ajax.Request(
  'some-server-side-script.php',
  {
    method:'get',
    onSuccess: function (transport) {
      var response = transport.responseText || "no response text";
        alert('Ajax.Request was successful: ' + response);
    },
    onFailure: function (){
      alert('Ajax.Request failed');
    }
  }
);

// Prototype Ajax.Updater
// Create a one-time request that populates the #ajax-updater-target
// element with the content of the responseText
new Ajax.Updater(
  $('ajax-updater-target'),
  'some-server-side-script.php',
```

```
    {
        method: 'get',
        // Append it to the top of the target element
        insertion: Insertion.Top
    }
);

// Prototype Ajax.periodicalUpdater
// Create a periodic request that will automatically populate
// the #ajax-target-element every 10 seconds
new Ajax.PeriodicalUpdater(
    $('ajax-periodic-target'),
    'some-server-side-script.php ',
    {
        method: 'GET',
        // Append it to the top of the existing content
        insertion: Insertion.Top,
        // Run every 10 seconds
        frequency: 10
    }
);
```

Another very simple, yet very good, use of the `Ajax.Request` object is for intermittently saving the information in a form. This is especially useful in a blogging situation, where you may be sitting on the page for some time without any means of really saving what you're doing. The `Ajax.Request()` object, along with Prototype's Form serialization methods, could retrieve the current information in the form and save it to the server every few minutes, ensuring that you don't lose all your hard work:

```
// autosave using Prototype
// Save the content of the #autosave-form every 30 seconds
// and update the #autosave-status to indicate the save
setTimeout(function() {
    new Ajax.Updater(
        $('autosave-status'),
        ' some-server-side-autosave-script.php ',
        {
            method:'post',
            parameters : $('autosave-form').serialize(true)
        }
    );
},30000);
```

Ajax with jQuery

For a comparison with a different syntax, jQuery also includes a low-level `$.ajax` method that you can use to specify all sorts of properties, but let's look at a few quick and easy methods you can use with minimal effort:

- `$.post(url, params, callback)` retrieves data through a POST request.

- `$.get(url, params, callback)` retrieves data through a GET request.

- `$.getJSON(url, params, callback)` retrieves a JSON object.

- $.getScript(*url*, *callback*) retrieves and execute a JavaScript file.

These methods are all wrappers for the $.ajax() method, and their callback methods in all cases are invoked as the $.ajax() success callback. Each receives two arguments that define the request's responseText and the status of the request, respectively:

```
$.get('some-server-side-script.php',
  { key: 'value' },
  function(responseText, status){
      // Your Code
  }
);
```

The status will be one of these:

- success

- error

- notmodified

In the cases of both the getJSON and getScript methods, the response will be evaluated, so the argument for getJSON will be a JavaScript object.

Again, you can see some of these methods in action here:

```
// $.get() for quick Ajax calls
// Create a one-time request and alert its success
$.get('some-server-side-script.php',
  { key: 'value' },
  function(responseText,status){
      alert('successful: ' + responseText);
  }
);
```

```
// $.getJSON() to load a JSON object
// Create a one-time request to load a JSON file and alert its success
$.getJSON('some-server-side-script.php', function(json){
  alert('successful: ' + json.type);
});
```

jQuery also includes an additional load() method:

- $(*expression*).load(*url*, *params*, *callback*) loads the result of the URL into the DOM element.

This method will automatically populate the element or elements with the result:

```
// $(...).load() to automatically populate an element
// Create a one-time request that populates the #ajax-updater-target
// element with the content of the responseText
$("#ajax-updater-target").load(
  'some-server-side-script.php',
  { key: 'value' },
    function(responseText,status) {
      alert('successful: ' + responseText);
  }
);
```

The Prototype `Ajax.updater()` method acts in the same way.

The $() method can be used equally well for the periodic saving mechanism:

```
// Autosave using jQuery
// Save the content of the #autosave-form every 30 seconds
// and update the #autosave-status to indicate the save
setTimeout(function() {
  $('autosave-status').load(
      'some-server-side-script.php',
      $.param({
          title:$('#autosave-form input[@name=title]').val(),
          story:$('#autosave-form textarea[@name=story]').val()
      })
  );
},30000);
```

jQuery also has a number of plug-ins available, such as Mike Alsup's Ajax Form plug-in (`http://plugins.jquery.com/`), which make dealing with forms and Ajax even easier. Need to submit a comment form via Ajax as you did in Chapter 12? It's as simple as this:

```
$('#commentForm').ajaxForm(function() {
  alert("Thank you for your comment!");
});
```

This method serializes the contents of the form and sends the result to whatever script is referenced in the form's action attribute.

Animation and effects

So far you've seen how libraries can help you solve a lot of your DOM manipulations and scripting tasks. Now let's look at visual aesthetics and interactivity.

Some libraries, such as jQuery, have effect properties built in, while others rely on add-ons for their effect methods. If your library doesn't have effects, two you might want to consider are `Moo.fx` and `Script.aculo.us`:

- **Moof.fx** (`http://moofx.mad4milk.net/`) describes itself as "a superlightweight, ultratiny, megasmall JavaScript effects library, to be used with prototype.js or the mootools framework." Overall, Moo.fx is very easy to use and takes a low-level approach allowing you to identify an element and specify which CSS properties to modify over a given duration. These modifications will apply to the specific element only, not its children (unless the children inherit the CSS property through the cascade as usual). These low-level features allow you to create just about any effect you want with minimal effort.

- **Script.aculo.us** (`http://script.aculo.us`) "provides you with easy-to-use, cross-browser user interface JavaScript libraries to make your web sites and web applications fly." Script.aculo.us takes a high-level approach and specifies several core effects and combinations thereof. With these high-level effects, all children of the given element may also be affected. When you invoke an effect such as `Effect.Scale` on a paragraph, the font size will be scaled along with the physical width and height of the bounding element and any child elements within the paragraph. These high-level groupings make it simple to apply large, complicated effects, as it's all done for you.

Both of these libraries are built on top of Prototype, but in the case of Moo.fx, it's also available as part of the MooTools JavaScript library (http://mootools.net).

▥ **Note** Moo.fx relies on the $() and $$() methods to retrieve elements so again, if you're using these, be careful when mixing and matching libraries and be sure to check the documentation for the best ways to avoid conflicts.

CSS property-based animations

The most basic animation tasks involve changing the CSS properties of an object over time, as you saw in the moveElement function in Chapter 10:

```
function moveElement(elementID,final_x,final_y,interval) {
  if (!document.getElementById) return false;
  if (!document.getElementById(elementID)) return false;
  var elem = document.getElementById(elementID);
  if (elem.movement) {
    clearTimeout(elem.movement);
  }
  if (!elem.style.left) {
    elem.style.left = "0px";
  }
  if (!elem.style.top) {
    elem.style.top = "0px";
  }
  var xpos = parseInt(elem.style.left);
  var ypos = parseInt(elem.style.top);
  var dist = 0;
  if (xpos == final_x && ypos == final_y) {
    return true;
  }
  if (xpos < final_x) {
    dist = Math.ceil((final_x - xpos)/10);
    xpos = xpos + dist;
  }
  if (xpos > final_x) {
    dist = Math.ceil((xpos - final_x)/10);
    xpos = xpos - dist;
  }
  if (ypos < final_y) {
    dist = Math.ceil((final_y - ypos)/10);
    ypos = ypos + dist;
  }
  if (ypos > final_y) {
    dist = Math.ceil((ypos - final_y)/10);
    ypos = ypos - dist;
  }
  elem.style.left = xpos + "px";
  elem.style.top = ypos + "px";
  var repeat = "moveElement('"+elementID+"',"+final_x+","+final_y+","+interval+")";
```

```
      elem.movement = setTimeout(repeat,interval);
}
```

The problem with using timers and math is that the code quickly gets very long and complicated. Thankfully, libraries such as jQuery can be a big help here.

Your `moveElement` function was called with mouse events on links like this:

```
var links = list.getElementsByTagName("a");
// Attach the animation behavior to the mouseover event
links[0].onmouseover = function() {
  moveElement("preview",-100,0,10);
}
links[1].onmouseover = function() {
  moveElement("preview",-200,0,10);
}
links[2].onmouseover = function() {
  moveElement("preview",-300,0,10);
}
```

We can combine all the `moveElement` logic and assignment with jQuery and apply a simple animation to position the `preview` using the `animate` method. This method takes a list of CSS properties and their final values and alters those values from their current value over a specified duration:

```
$('a').each(function(i) {
  var preview = $('#preview');
  var final_x = i * -100;
  $(this).mouseover(function(){
    preview.animate({left:final_x}, 10);
  });
});
```

That's much easier that what you had in Chapter 10. jQuery uses only a few lines of code with no complicated math or timers to worry about.

You can go even further and tweak the motion applied to the animation. The jQuery animation method takes an additional argument to allow you to do this:

`$(expression).animate( properties, duration, easing )`

The *easing* argument lets you specify a function to calculate the speed of the animation at a specific period of time. These functions can get into very complex math, but they let you alter the speed to create ease-in/out or bouncing effects. The only easing functions in the jQuery library are the default, called `swing`, and one called `linear`, which progresses at a constant pace.

If you want more easing functions, you can find them in the jQuery UI suite (`http://jqueryui.com`) or the jQuery easing plug-in (`http://gsgd.co.uk/sandbox/jquery/easing/`).

Packaged animations

Libraries also come with a number of packaged animations that you can use right away with minimal effort. For example, without additional plug-ins, jQuery includes methods to

- `fadeIn` and `fadeOut`

- `fadeTo` by adjusting the opacity of the matched elements to a specific value

- `slideToggle`, `slideDown`, and `slideUp` hide and reveal matched elements with a sliding motion

Other libraries, such as Script.aculo.us, include more advanced animations, such as these:

- `Effect.Appear, Effect.Fade`
- `Effect.Puff`
- `Effect.DropOut`
- `Effect.Shake`
- `Effect.SwitchOff`
- `Effect.BlindDown` and `Effect.BlindUp`
- `Effect.SlideDown` and `Effect.SlideUp`
- `Effect.Pulsate`
- `Effect.Squish`
- `Effect.Fold`
- `Effect.Grow`
- `Effect.Shrink`

Remember accessibility

Used properly, subtle effects can provide visual cues to changes that would otherwise go unnoticed. They can call attention to certain aspects of the interface and guide interaction in the right direction, or they can simply impress and delight the viewer—adding a little bit of life to your otherwise boring old HTML.

When implementing effects, remember to keep accessibility in mind. Your site may look great when things are flashy and fun but if the effect limits the ability to access the desired information, you have a problem.

Summary

In this Appendix, I've touched on how libraries can help you accomplish your daily scripting tasks. This was by no means a complete description of every library or a complete list of their features. I highly suggest that you browse the documentation for each library to see what else each of them has and pick the one that's best for you.

When evaluating which library is right for you, be sure to take a good look at each one you're considering. Check for things like how they deal with library conflicts, too little or too many features, a strong community, and good support. Once you've chosen one, make sure to take advantage of all it has to offer but at the same time, take the time to learn how and why the libraries work the way they do. Relying on a library is fine as long as you're not taking it for granted.

Index

■ E

objects, in JavaScript, 27–29
  host objects, 29
  native objects, 28–29
odd class, 172, 260
odd variable, 166
oldClassName property, 259
oldonload variable, 81
on-the-fly markup creation, 95–122
  DOM methods for, 100–107
    appendChild method, 102
    createElement method, 101–102
    createTextNode method, 103–104
    examples of, 105–107
    insertAfter method, 110–112
    insertBefore method, 109
  using Ajax, 116–121
    and Hijax, 121
    progressive enhancement with, 121
    XMLHttpRequest object, 116–120
  using document.write method, 95–97
  using innerHTML property, 97–100
onblur event, 266
onclick attribute, 62
onclick event handler, 49–50, 62, 79, 86–87, 250
onclick method, 79
onComplete(XHRrequest,json) function, 295
onException(ajax.request,exception) function, 294
onFailure function, 295
onFailure(XHRrequest,json) function, 295
onfocus event, 266
onInteractive(XHRrequest,json) function, 295
onkeypress event handler, 86–88
onload event, 66, 80–82
onLoaded(XHRrequest,json) function, 295
onLoading(XHRrequest,json) function, 295
onmouseover event handler, 49, 189, 192
onreadystatechange event handler, 273
onreadystatechange function, 274
onreadystatechange property, 118–120
onsubmit event handler, 270, 275
onSuccess function, 295
onSuccess(XHRrequest,json) function, 295

onUninitialized(XHRrequest,json) function, 295
on###(XHRrequest,json) function, 295
open( ) method, 61
operations, in JavaScript, 17–19
operators, in JavaScript
  arithmetic, 17–19
  comparison, 20–21
  logical, 21–22
OR operator, 22, 68
origins, of JavaScript, 1–2
overflow property, 190

■ P

p element, 33–34, 42–43, 64, 96–98, 141
</p> tag, 96–97, 125
page element, 187
para element, 153–154
para variable, 105–106, 152–153, 158
paragraph element, 108
parameters property, 294
parent variable, 110
parentNode property, 109–110
parseFloat function, 179
parseInt function, 179
pattern attribute, 222
Pause button, 216, 219
pause event, 216, 219
paused property, 216
performance considerations, of JavaScript, 69–71
  minification of scripts, 70–71
  minimizing DOM access, 69
  reducing script requests, 70
Pfeiffer, Silvia, 221
photos folder, images folder, 252
photos.html file, 243, 252–253, 255
placeholder attribute, 222, 224, 264–267
placeholder class, 266–267
placeholder element, 92, 95, 109
placeholder values, for forms, 264–267
placeholder variable, 48, 82
placeholder.gif file, 254
Play button, 216–217, 219

XMLHttpRequest object, 116
XMLHttpRequest request, 119
xpos variable, 3, 179–180, 182–183, 197–198

■ Y, Z

Yahoo! User Interface (YUI), 281–282
YAHOO.util.Dom.getElementBy method, 288
ypos variable, 179–180, 182–183, 198
YUI (Yahoo! User Interface), 281–282